CW01216717

The Geometry of Genocide

STUDIES IN PURE SOCIOLOGY
Donald Black, Editor

THE GEOMETRY OF GENOCIDE

A STUDY IN PURE SOCIOLOGY

BRADLEY CAMPBELL

University of Virginia Press • Charlottesville and London

University of Virginia Press
© 2015 by the Rector and Visitors of the University of Virginia
All rights reserved
Printed in the United States of America on acid-free paper

First published 2015

9 8 7 6 5 4 3 2 1

Library of Congress Cataloging-in-Publication Data
Campbell, Bradley Keith.
　The geometry of genocide : a study in pure sociology / Bradley Campbell.
　　pages　cm. — (Studies in pure sociology)
　Includes bibliographical references and index.
　ISBN 978-0-8139-3741-0 (cloth : alk. paper) — ISBN 978-0-8139-3742-7 (e-book)
　1. Genocide. 2. Social control. I. Title.
　HV6322.7.C336 2015
　304.6'63—dc23
　　　　　　　　　　　　　　　　　　　　　　　　　　　2015019372

IN MEMORY OF MY FATHER,
AND FOR MY MOTHER

CONTENTS

	Preface	ix
1	Genocide as Social Control	1
2	Genocide as Predation	29
3	Indians and Whites in California	49
4	Muslims and Hindus in India	72
5	Muslims and Serbs in Bosnia	97
6	Tutsis and Hutus in Rwanda	125
7	Jews and Gentiles in Europe	150
	Conclusion	183
	Notes	205
	References	223
	Index	245

PREFACE

The American Civil War general William T. Sherman rightly said that war is hell. But if war is hell, what is genocide? War and genocide have similar horrors—"blood, guts, and gore" (Snyder 2014)—but for most of us genocide seems worse. We might appreciate the virtues of the loyal soldier fighting for his country, even in an unjust war, but what of those whose enemies are children and civilians rather than other armed fighters? What of those who shoot unarmed people in the backs of their heads as they lie helplessly in ditches and then pile more victims on top of them? What of the gas chambers?

We see in genocide an evil so stark—beyond even the hellishness of warfare—that we may want to look away. As political scientist and genocide scholar Adam Jones notes, those of us who study genocide will often hear, after telling someone about our work, some version of "Why would you want to study *that?*" (2006:xviii). I have heard it, and I can sympathize. Why try to understand something like genocide? Why disturb one's mind with those images? But since you, the reader, have now opened up a book on genocide, maybe you find as I do that you do not wish to look away—or cannot. Maybe you believe that good will result from better knowledge of genocide. Maybe you sense that otherwise you would fail to understand something significant about reality.

So we try to explain genocide, but how? In the traditional formulation, evil comes from "the world, the flesh, and the Devil." The theologian might study the Devil and the psychologist the flesh, but as a sociologist I study "the world"—human society. Examining genocide sociologically means identifying its social influences and the social context in which it occurs. Sociologists have various ways of doing this, though, and many are interested in the interactions between the social and psychological levels of reality. For example, they might examine how society shapes individuals. They might thus identify how culture, early childhood socialization, or some other societal feature motivates people to plan or participate in genocide. Another tack is to examine how individuals shape society. One way of doing this is to look at human behavior as resulting from individuals making the choices that most benefit themselves. Sociologists might thus show how the decision to engage in genocide benefits political actors in specific circumstances. We may learn a great deal from these and other approaches, but notice that each one focuses on some things and puts others to the side. Any coherent theory must do this, as does my own. The approach I use, called pure sociology, focuses exclusively on the social, leaving psychological and other individualistic factors out entirely.

I say more about pure sociology in chapter 1, but for now I simply ask you to keep an open mind. It might seem weird or even crazy to try to explain any behavior—much less extreme evil like genocide—without reference to the character or minds of those engaging in it. But I invite you to consider, even if you believe we must be losing something important by stripping away all but the social factors, that doing so might also reveal things about genocide that other approaches obscure.

Another thing that might seem weird or crazy is that I do not deal here with the morality of genocide. Genocide concerns us—it concerns me—precisely because of our moral reaction to it. We want to better understand these events that shock our consciences and leave us so confused. Yet our judgments of genocide do little to help us explain it scientifically, so the evil of genocide is another aspect of it that I put to the side. I shall discuss the reasons for this in more detail, but for now consider that most of those planning and carrying out genocide have not set out to do evil. On the contrary, they see themselves as meting out justice, protecting their communities from danger, or otherwise engaging in morally upright behavior. For them genocide is "a way which seemeth right" (Proverbs 14:12). This is an idea we might resist. If people can in good conscience engage in great evil, how can we be confident we are not similarly mistaken about our own beliefs and behaviors? But we must face such matters squarely if we are to make progress in understanding them.

I am grateful to those of you, the readers, who are willing to look more closely with me at this difficult subject, and to look at it in an unfamiliar way. I am also grateful to all who have helped with this book, directly by reading drafts and giving advice and indirectly by shaping my intellectual development. My first exposure to sociology was as an undergraduate at Lee University, in an introductory course taught by Karen Mundy in the spring of 1993, when I was just seventeen years old. Sociologists were interested in the things I was interested in, it seemed, and a year later I changed my major from accounting to sociology, though I had little idea of what I might end up doing. Eventually I went to Clemson University for a master's, and I am grateful to William Wentworth, James Hawdon, and John Ryan—the members of my thesis committee there—for supporting me in various ways, including by prodding me to go to a Ph.D. program. Their help, along with that of Brenda Vander Mey, who employed me as a research assistant, was generous and efficacious.

I began my work on genocide in the sociology department at the University of Virginia, and I thank the members of my doctoral dissertation committee—Donald Black, Jeffrey Olick, Milton Vickerman, and outside readers Elizabeth Arkush and Roberta Senechal de la Roche—for all of their help. I especially thank Donald Black, my dissertation advisor, who has done more to shape this book than anyone else. I knew little of his work until the first day of his Sociology of Law seminar in the fall of 2000, my first semester at the University of Virginia. He began that day by writing on the board, "Law varies directly with relational distance," and I was amazed to find out that this formulation applies cross-culturally and cross-historically—that it can explain facts as seemingly unconnected as the absence of law in hunter-gather societies and the variability in the application of the death penalty in the modern United States. I have been hooked on pure sociology ever since. Since then he has helped me in countless ways throughout my career and on this project, including by giving detailed feedback first on my dissertation and later on two earlier drafts of this book.

Elsewhere I have encouraged sociologists to think more about their vocation and to treat their work with moral seriousness (Campbell 2014a:451; 2014b:7). I know of no sociologist who does so more than Donald Black. He is an exemplar of vocational integrity—an idealist fearlessly and joyfully pursuing the scientific study of social life. And it is infectious. After nearly every conversation with him, I come away resolved to be a better sociologist.

I also thank University of Virginia professors Rae Blumberg, Stephan Fuchs, Paul Kingston, Krishan Kumar, and Murray Milner for the influence their courses have had on me, and I thank Laura Holian, Jason Manning, and Justin Snyder, once my fellow graduate students and still my fellow conspirators, for their friendship and conversation. Jason Manning and Justin Snyder also read drafts of this book, as did Mark Cooney, whose encouragement has been reassuring and whose consistently superb scholarship has been inspiring. Steven Gordon, my former department chair in the sociology department at California State University, Los Angeles, has been supportive, and his erudition and curiosity have made for enlightening discussions about genocide and other subjects. University of Virginia Press's History and Social Sciences editor, Richard Holway, gave helpful suggestions for improving the manuscript in its final stages, as did the anonymous reviewers. A number of others gave comments on my work on genocide at its earliest stages, including many whose names I have mentioned as well as Dirk Moses and the late Kurt Jonassohn.

Parts of those previous works appear in a modified form here. Specifically, much of chapter 1 draws from "Genocide as Social Control," published in 2009 in the journal *Sociological Theory*. "Contradictory Behavior during Genocides," published in 2010 in *Sociological Forum*, appears in a modified form as the first half of the concluding chapter, and part of chapter 1 and parts of chapters 6 and 7 draw from "Genocide as a Matter of Degree," published in 2011 in the *British Journal of Sociology*. "Genocide and Social Time," published in 2013 in *Dilemas: Revista de Estudos de Conflito e Controle Social,* appears in a modified form as part of chapter 1 and as the second half of the concluding chapter. I thank these journals and their various publishers for permission to use this material.

Finally, I am forever indebted to my parents, Sandra Campbell

McCall and the late Rodger Campbell. My father's support and encouragement lasted right up until his death in 2006, and my mother's continues. In one of the many disturbing incidents described in this book, a father hides and watches as attackers murder his four children. I am grieved to think of those children suffering while their father clings to his own life nearby. Yet even as it grieves me, it leads me to think of my own parents, in contrast, and of their continual and unhesitant selflessness toward my brother, my sister, and me. Though I have not deserved it, they have made my life possible, and I dedicate this book to them.

The Geometry of Genocide

1 GENOCIDE AS SOCIAL CONTROL

Genocide might appear incomprehensible. It seems unconnected to ordinary human experience, and we wonder how people could engage in such a shocking degree of violence toward their fellow human beings. Some scholars focus on "desk killers" who orchestrate evil from afar. Political theorist Hannah Arendt (1963), for example, famously spoke of the "banality of evil" in reference to Adolf Eichmann, one of the architects of the Holocaust, whose choices seemed driven by ordinary and careerist motives. Eichmann's personality was that of a bureaucrat, and he facilitated the destruction of European Jews just as he would have any other organizational goal. But what about the thousands of people physically carrying out the killing? They were not little Eichmanns pushing papers; their actions were not banal.

According to some scholars, though, these killers were still detached in some way from the killing they participated in. To take one example, sociologist Zygmunt Bauman (1989) argues that industrialized killing, where people focus on specialized tasks, allows the perpetrators to psychologically distance themselves from what they are doing. This might be true, but it does not really tell us much about the Holocaust, much less about other genocides. It might be plausible as an explanation of the Holocaust if we think only of the gas chambers, but actually Jews were as likely to be shot as gassed (Snyder 2010:xiv). And consider what such shooting was like. In the summer of 1942 the men of Police Battalion 101, a unit of Germany's Order Police, killed 1,500 Jews in Józefów, Poland. When they first began killing, the men sometimes aimed too high and caused their victims' skulls to explode. One of the killers described the result: "As a consequence, brains and bones flew everywhere. Thus, we were instructed to place the bayonet point on the neck" (quoted in Browning 1998:64). But this did not completely solve the problem, as another man's testimony illustrates: "Through the point-blank shot that was required, the bullet struck the head of the victim at such a trajectory that often the entire skull or at least the entire rear skullcap was torn off, and blood, bone splinters, and brains sprayed everywhere and besmirched the shooters" (quoted in Browning 1998:64). We do not see psychological distancing here. As Holocaust historian Christopher Browning points out, "Such a luxury . . . was not enjoyed by the men of Reserve Police Battalion 101, who were quite literally saturated in the blood of victims shot at point-blank range" (1998:162).

Nor was the treatment of Jews elsewhere particularly antiseptic. At one labor camp in Poland, German guards beat the Jewish prisoners with "whips into which small iron balls had been wrought" (Goldhagen 2009:436). Sometimes they beat them on a "whipping table"; other times they had them run the gauntlet. They also locked them in bunkers, gave them electric shocks, and forced them to stand barefoot in the snow (Goldhagen 2009:437). And consider also the various "death marches" of the final days of the war, when a Nazi defeat was certain. Rather than abandon Jewish prisoners who remained alive, Germans led them on forced marches away from the allied troops. A U.S. Army officer describes a group of women who had survived one of the marches: "In addition to their clothes being dirty, worn out, ill fitting, tattered and torn they were covered for the most part with human stool which was spread for the most part all over the floor. . . . They were too weak to walk to evacuate their bowels" (quoted in Goldhagen 1996:331). During their march these women were so hungry they tried to eat grass and, at one point, a rotting pile of animal fodder. Yet their guards even prevented them from eating food offered to them by German civilians. They beat prisoners who tried to accept food, and one guard took the food and fed it to chickens (Goldhagen 1996:347–48).

If we look closely at the killing in other genocides, what we see is similar. In 1994 Rwanda we see Hutus kill their Tutsi victims with low-tech weapons such as machetes and clubs studded with nails. They chop off arms, legs, and breasts. They throw children down wells (Diamond 2005:316). They impale people like kebabs (Hatzfeld 2005a:81). They cut the Achilles tendons of those they cannot kill right away to keep them from running (Alvarez 2001:109; Taylor 2002:164). Japanese soldiers in 1937 Nanjing bury their Chinese victims up to their necks and then run over their heads with tanks. Others they nail to wooden boards or set on fire (Chang 1997:87). They rape young girls before slashing them in half with a sword. They rape a Chinese woman and then kill her by lighting a firecracker they have shoved into her vagina (Chang 1997:91, 94–95). In 1860s California four white men kill every member of a group of thirty Yahi Indians, including infants and small children. One of the killers switches from a rifle to a revolver during the massacre because, as he puts it, the rifle "tore them up so bad" (quoted in Kroeber 1961:85). In 1915 Turkey, Turkish gendarmes play the so-called game of swords, which involves tossing Armenian women from horses and impaling them on swords sticking up from the ground (Balakian 2003:315). In 2002 India we see mutilated and charred bodies in the aftermath of Hindu attacks on Muslims: "None of the bodies were covered. They were all burnt and shrunken. There were a few bodies of women where 'lola dandas' [iron rods] were shoved up their vagina" (quoted in Ghassem-Fachandi 2006:135).

In these glimpses of genocide, we do not see bureaucratic efficiency, people just following orders. Instead we see the killers behaving with a disregard for the victims, if not outright zeal in humiliating and hurting them. As we approach the subject of genocide, we would do well to keep in mind what genocide looks like up close.

GENOCIDE AS A SUBJECT MATTER

The most extreme and well-known genocide, the Holocaust, resulted in the deaths of nearly 6 million Jews, about two-thirds of Europe's Jewish population. Other victims of genocide include 1 million Armenians in Turkey in 1915 and 1916; 800,000 Tutsis in Rwanda in 1994; 400,000 Africans in Sudan between 2002 and 2010; 200,000 Muslims in Bosnia in the early 1990s; 200,000 Gypsies in Nazi-controlled Europe between 1939 and 1945; 200,000 Chinese in Nanjing in 1937 and 1938; 100,000 Hutus in Burundi in 1972; 50,000 Kurds in Iraq in 1988, 20,000 Aborigines in Australia during the nineteenth century; 20,000 Hereros in South-West Africa (now Namibia) between 1904 and 1907; 10,000 Haitians in the Dominican Republic in 1937; thousands of California Indians in the 1850s; and 2,000 Muslims in Gujarat, India in early 2002.

All of these are cases of genocide, or, as I define it here, one-sided, ethnically based mass killing. Since genocide is one-sided rather than reciprocal, warfare is not genocide.[1] Since it involves killing on the basis of ethnicity, killings on the basis of class or political identity are not genocides.[2] And since genocide is mass killing, the suppression of a language or religion, the forcible transfer of children, and the nonlethal deportation of ethnic groups are not genocide.[3] This definition is narrower than some, broader than others.[4] It captures what most people mean by genocide, though, and it is easy to apply to actual cases.[5]

THE SIGNIFICANCE OF GENOCIDE

It should be clear that genocide is a phenomenon of vast human significance. It is an extreme form of behavior seemingly defying understanding. The number of victims can be shocking, all the more so when we look to see what the killers actually do. Genocide is a social backdrop for all sorts of other dramatic behaviors too. It involves a break from ordinary social reality, and unusual behaviors flourish—not just cruelty, but extreme cowardice and selfishness on the one hand and courage and self-sacrifice on the other, as victims and bystanders decide what to do in the midst of genocide.

Some simply try to protect themselves. In Rwanda a Hutu man orders his pregnant Tutsi wife to leave their home. "I don't want to die," he says. "If you die, it is your problem" (quoted in Nowrojee 1996). Others face moral dilemmas as they decide whom to save and how much to cooperate with the killers. Hutu attackers tell another Rwandan Hutu married to a Tutsi that he can save his wife and children if he will turn over his wife's parents and sister to be killed. He agrees (Gibbs et al. 1994). In Turkey some Armenians are told they will be spared if they convert to Islam. Most refuse and die along with their Christian neighbors (Miller and Miller 1993:71). In Eastern Europe Nazis seek the cooperation of Jewish leaders of the ghettos. Mordechai Chaim Rumkowski, leader of the Lodz ghetto, cooperates fully, at one point even begging the ghetto residents to turn over children, the sick, and the elderly to the Nazis: "Fathers and mothers, give me your children! . . . Give me the sick. In their place, we can save the healthy" (quoted in Midlarsky 2005:289). In explaining his actions, he says, "If I can save a hundred Jews in the ghetto, everything will have been worthwhile" (quoted in Midlarsky 2005:290).

During genocides we see acts of collective resistance by the victims, even when the odds of success are hopeless. In 1850s California a band of Yuki Indians gathers in an obvious place, as if to invite attack by a white militia, and when the attack begins they "let fly a volley of arrows" (quoted in Miller 1979:72). But they are only able to wound some of the whites, while the whites kill or wound nearly all of the Indians. And in the Warsaw ghetto in 1943 Poland, Jewish residents launch an armed rebellion despite having no chance of success (Einwohner 2003).

We see extreme acts of altruism, situations where people sacrifice and put their own lives at risk to rescue members of the targeted group. During the Holocaust, for example, Irene Gut, a young Polish woman working as the housekeeper for an elderly Nazi officer, saves twelve Jews by hiding them in the basement of the officer's house. After the officer discovers two of the Jews, Irene agrees to begin a sexual relationship with him, which he insists on as the price for his silence (Opdyke and Armstrong 1999).

Genocide is significant for another reason as well: it may transform entire societies. This was clearly the case with the Holocaust. While losing the broader war, the Nazis mostly achieved their goal of eliminating European Jewry. Even those who survived—less than 10 percent of the Jewish population in places like Poland and Lithuania—often emigrated after the war, and Jewish communities that had been in Eastern Europe for centuries and had developed their own traditions and language are now simply gone. The Armenian genocide (along with an expulsion of Greeks later on) allowed Turkey to develop as a fairly homogenous state, with only the Kurds (who are Muslims, unlike the Armenians and Greeks) left as a significant minority. And genocide in the Americas and Australia allowed white settlers to establish new societies on the natives' land. Even the Rwandan genocide drastically transformed the country, though the Hutu aggressors did not achieve their objective of preventing an invading Tutsi force from taking control. Most Tutsis now in Rwanda came there after the genocide, and according to political scientist Manus Midlarsky, "only with some effort can one find a Tutsi who was living in Rwanda in 1994" (2005:9).

Unsurprising given its significance, genocide is the focus of much cultural and scholarly activity. Major films deal with genocide, including recent films such as *The Pianist* (Polanski 2002), *Hotel Rwanda* (George 2004), and *The Reader* (Daldry 2008). So do novels such as *The Farming of Bones* (Danticat 1999), *The Book Thief* (Zusak 2007), and *The Bastard of Istanbul* (Shafak 2008). Philosophers and theologians also address the subject, often arguing that the Holocaust and other genocides raise issues about right and wrong, the nature of humanity, or the nature of God (see Abed 2006; Berkovits 1973; Davis 2005; Lee 2005; Moltmann 1974:277–78; Sontag 2005; Volf 2006:138–39; Wringe 2006). And many social scientists—political scientists, historians, psychologists, and sociologists—try to describe or explain some variable aspect of genocide. This book takes a scientific approach. It offers an explanation of genocide.

GENOCIDE AND MORALITY

A scientific approach to genocide differs from most others in that it does not deal with morality. This has not stopped social scientists from highlighting their condemnations of genocide, so prominent books on the topic have titles like *Becoming Evil* (Waller 2002), *Extraordinary Evil* (Coloroso 2007), *Facing Evil* (Woodruff and Wilmer 2001), and *The Roots of Evil* (Staub 1989).[6] But whether genocide is right or wrong, moral or immoral, good or evil, is a matter to be addressed by filmmakers, novelists, theologians, and philosophers—not social scientists. A moral judgment about genocide is at best a distraction from the task of explanation.[7] Worse, conceiving of genocide as a type of evil to be explained along with other evil acts may completely obscure what may be the most important fact about genocide: its perpetrators typically define their victims as evil.[8] In sociological terms, genocide is not just a deviant behavior (something condemned as immoral); it is also social control (a reaction to deviant behavior). Recognize this and genocide immediately becomes less mysterious. Though you and I see the targets of genocide as innocent victims and find the violence against them incomprehensible, to the killers the targets are not victims at all; they are offenders, wicked people who deserve their punishment.

But we still need to answer two questions: Why do the killers have grievances against the targets, and why do they handle their grievances with genocide? As I demonstrate here, we can answer these questions by drawing from sociologist Donald Black's theories of conflict and social control. The result is a new theory of genocide that explains not only why genocides occur, but also why some are more severe than others and why some people but not others participate in them. In these first two chapters, I discuss this theory and point to the many things about genocide it can explain. Then I examine genocide in five very specific locations. In these case studies we see the theory in action. We see that it can make sense of exactly what happens during genocides, such as who exactly kills whom. What distinguishes this theory from others—and what, I argue, makes it so successful—is its use of a novel theoretical strategy called pure sociology. Let us look briefly, then, at the main features of this strategy.

PURE SOCIOLOGY

The aim here is to understand genocide scientifically, and I have discussed why a scientific approach to genocide does not mix well with an ethical one. But those using a scientific approach might still explain genocide in a number of different ways. They might explain genocide with specific historical events (Melson 1992), broad cultural and historical trends (Bauman 1989; Freeman 1995a; Hinton 2002), the goals and opportunities of political elites (Valentino 2004), the characteristics of societies (Fein 1979; Goldhagen 1996, Kuper 1981), the characteristics of state regimes (Horowitz 2002; Rummel 1995), or the characteristics of individuals (Adorno et al. 1950; Kelman 1973). These various theories can be valuable, and I draw from many of them throughout the book. But all involve some kind of simplification. Every theory simplifies reality, leaving out some things while—if the theory is successful—revealing things we would not have seen otherwise.

Pure sociology is no different. Pure sociology gives us a way of homing in just on the social. In doing so it broadens the scope of the analysis in some ways—by including new kinds of sociological variables—and it narrows it in others—by excluding psychology, for example. The least we might expect from such an approach is that it would give us a new way of looking at genocide to complement the others. That alone would be valuable, but it does more than this. Pure sociology, we shall see, makes possible a powerful new theory of genocide. This theory cannot explain everything about genocide, and it is by no means the final word on the subject, but it can explain a great deal, and it can explain things that other theories cannot.

Pure sociology explains human behavior with its social geometry: its location and direction in social space and social time. These concepts will be unfamiliar to many readers, and they may seem very strange. But they just refer to the various ways people relate to one another (social space) and to the ways those relationships change (social time). For example, people might be intimates or strangers—close or distant in social space. Or one person might be higher in status than another, such as by having more wealth or authority—an elevated position in social space. And any social position might change; social space might fluctuate. Strangers might become intimates, or someone might lose wealth or authority. These social changes are movements of social time.

SOCIAL SPACE

Black introduced pure sociology in *The Behavior of Law* (1976), which explained law—or governmental social control—according to the position of a conflict in social space. Social control, remember, refers to any way of handling deviant behavior. It is a response to conflict, a situation where one person has a grievance against another. Law is one possible response, but not everyone who may use law does so. Someone who is assaulted or raped, for example, may call the police or not. And even when someone calls the police, the amount of law that follows is not always the same. So more law enters a conflict when a call to the police results in an arrest than when it does not, and more law enters when an arrest results in a conviction. What Black showed was that a conflict's position in social space predicts the amount of law it attracts. Within a society, conflicts with more distant adversaries attract more law, for example. One thing this predicts is that killings of intimates, such as family members or friends, should be treated less severely than killings of strangers. And they are (see, for instance, Lundsgaarde 1977:16).

SOCIAL TIME

Subsequent to the appearance of *The Behavior of Law,* Black and others applied pure sociology to the explanation of social control generally and of a number of specific forms of social control.[9] All used the same strategy: they explained the handling of conflict with the conflict's position in social space. Recently, though, Black has advanced pure sociology so that it is now possible to explain not just the handling of conflicts, but also the conflicts themselves. In *Moral Time* (2011) Black proposes that movements of social time cause conflict. A movement of social time, again, is a social change, such as an increase or decrease in intimacy. This new theory, then, explains why rape is deviant—why it causes conflict. It does so in part because it increases intimacy. And since the greatest and fastest social changes cause the most conflict, stranger rapes are more deviant—treated more severely—than acquaintance rapes. They involve a greater increase in intimacy.

By combining the two strategies, the pure sociology of conflict and social control explains the origin and intensity of a conflict, and it also explains how the conflict is handled. In the remainder of the chapter, we shall see that genocide has a particular social geometry—a location and direction in social space and time. Prior to any genocide, movements of social time cause conflict—they lead the future killers to form grievances against their targets. But the presence of grievances does not itself explain genocide, and even intense ethnic conflicts can be handled in multiple ways. Whether conflicts result in genocide depends also on their position in social space—on the social characteristics of the aggressors and targets. Let us now discuss each of these issues: the conflicts that lead to genocide and the handling of these conflicts.

GENOCIDE AND SOCIAL TIME

Every genocide begins with a conflict. And every conflict begins with a movement of social time—a social change. As noted above, movements of social time cause conflict, and the faster and greater the movements, the more conflict they cause.

Every deviant behavior is a movement of social time. Just as rape causes conflict because it increases intimacy, divorce causes conflict because it decreases intimacy. Likewise, heresy causes conflict because it alters culture by increasing diversity, and theft causes conflict because it alters stratification by shifting resources from one person to another. The same is true of cross-dressing, blasphemy, intolerance, insanity, bad manners, drunkenness, homicide, trespassing, promiscuity, adultery, lying, voyeurism, public nudity, and arrogance: all are movements of social time (Black 2011:3–9).

Not all movements of social time are deviant behaviors though. People sometimes praise those who form new relationships or achieve new successes, and many illnesses, injuries, and deaths have no human cause. But such movements of social time may cause conflict even when they are not themselves defined as deviant. They may cause or intensify conflicts about other things, as when former friends or lovers begin finding fault with each another as they grow more distant. Movements of social time may also lead to false accusations of wrongdoing. In many societies, for example, someone who is downwardly mobile, such as a wealthy person who suddenly becomes poor due to illness, may falsely accuse someone of witchcraft, while someone who is upwardly mobile, such as a poor person who suddenly becomes very wealthy, may be the target of false accusations (Black 2011:10–11, 15–16, 61–63, 83–84). Not all conflicts are as they seem, but all conflicts have the same kinds of causes: increases or decreases in diversity (in Black's terminology, overdiversity or underdiversity), increases or decreases in intimacy (overintimacy or underintimacy), or increases or decreases in stratification (overstratification or understratification) (Black 2011:5–6).

THE CAUSES OF GENOCIDE

The fundamental cause of genocide is overdiversity. Whenever two previously separated ethnic groups come into contact, conflict results. And wherever two ethnic groups live alongside one another, conflict is present. The latter situation may not seem to involve an increase in cultural diversity, and at the societal level it may not. But in any multicultural society people are constantly encountering those who are different, increasing the diversity in their lives. Diversity is thus an unstable property of social life, and as Black puts it, "who says diversity says conflict" (2011:102). This applies to all types of diversity, including political, religious, and ethnic diversity. All lead to cultural clashes.

Cultural clashes have a tendency to intensify. In most cases if I offend you, our conflict will remain between the two of us. But if my political beliefs offend you, so do the beliefs of all those who share them—Democrats if I am a Democrat, Republicans if I am a Republican. The same is true of religion: a conflict with me over religion is also a conflict with my coreligionists. In cultural conflicts, then, the stakes are high. All cultural conflicts are prone to collectivization. This is all the more true of ethnic conflicts, since ethnic groups, whatever the reality, are normally thought of as extended kinship groups, and ethnic identity is relatively unchangeable. One thing this means is that our family members, those who are closest to us, usually share our ethnicity. In any ethnic conflict, those we care about the most are likely all on the same side, and we join in their grievances and fight in their battles. Ethnic conflict is especially polarizing, and ethnicity is a dangerous cultural distinction.

An increase in ethnic diversity alone may lead to genocide or similar behavior, such as when certain tribal groups kill all outsiders they encounter (Black 2011:103). Usually, though, something else must happen: an inferior group rises (or threatens to rise) or a superior group falls (or is in danger of falling). These social changes are understratification, reductions in stratification. Genocide normally involves superior ethnic groups attacking inferior ones, but prior to the genocide, the stratification between these groups decreases, and this causes the conflict that leads to genocide. Note that even though this involves a change in inequality rather than culture, all conflicts that occur across cultural boundaries—such as across ethnic boundaries—are in danger of becoming cultural conflicts. When murders or thefts cross ethnic boundaries, they are no longer just murders or thefts of individuals, but offenses by one group against another. Even if the original conflict has nothing to do with ethnicity, interethnic conflict has the potential to become collective, with each side mobilizing its own ethnic supporters.[10]

SCENARIOS OF GENOCIDE

Colonialism is one situation that may involve large and sudden increases in diversity. In the 1850s, for example, white ranchers began moving into the Round Valley of northern California, the home of the Yuki Indians. Ethnic conflict began immediately as the white settlers made use of the valley without much regard to the prior inhabitants. They depleted wild game and other natural resources, fenced off areas of land used by the Indians, and kidnapped and enslaved Indian women and children, sometimes for their own use and sometimes to sell to others. The Indians then began killing stock belonging to the ranchers, and it was this offense, the Indians' theft, that led to genocide—in this case a series of unconnected genocidal expeditions. Whenever cows, horses, or hogs were missing or found dead, the aggrieved ranchers would gather together a group of men to go out and kill nearby Indians—perhaps 50 at a time (Carranco and Beard 1981; Miller 1979). As Black (2011:87) notes, theft is always a reduction of wealth, and when as in these cases someone of lower status steals from someone of higher status, theft decreases stratification, if only slightly.

The Round Valley genocide was similar to the killings of other California Indians and to the killings of Aborigines in Australia (Kroeber 1961; Reynolds 2006). In these cases the natives sometimes killed white settlers in addition to stealing from them, and in other colonial genocides even greater threats to stratification might occur. In South-West Africa, for instance, an organized rebellion against German imperialism led to genocide of the Hereros in the early 1900s (Drechsler 1980; Madley 2004). What we see in all these cases is a massive increase in diversity, when two previously separated ethnic groups come into contact, followed by a decrease in stratification—sometimes very small, but sometimes much larger—when the natives offend the settlers.

Many other cases of genocidal conflict, though, do not begin with sudden increases in diversity. In Rwanda Tutsis and Hutus had lived alongside one another for centuries prior to the 1994 genocide. The degree of overdiversity was low, the result of fluctuations of cultural diversity in daily life rather than the drastic increases that arise when previously separated groups come into contact. The degree of understratification, on the other hand, was much greater. The minority Tutsis had been politically subordinate to Hutus for decades when in 1990 the Rwandan Patriotic Front (RPF)—consisting mostly of Tutsi exiles from Rwanda—launched an invasion from Uganda. Prior to this, Rwanda's ruling party had faced an internal political challenge, and the president, Juvénal Habyarimana, had allowed rival political parties to form. After the invasion he began peace talks with the RPF and eventually agreed to what were known as the Arusha Accords, a power sharing agreement very favorable to the RPF.

The Arusha Accords would have excluded a major anti-Tutsi political party from the government, and they would have mandated that 50 percent of Rwanda's army officers and 40 percent of its troops come from the RPF. The president's party, though, and later President Habyarimana himself, opposed the agreement and sought to block its implementation. Others too began to see the RPF invasion and the Arusha Accords as a threat to the gains Hutus had made in the 1959 revolution, when the previously subordinate but majority Hutu population had gained political power. Each of the opposition parties split into two factions: a Hutu Power faction, which aligned with the regime to oppose the Arusha Accords, and a moderate faction, which continued to support the power-sharing agreement. The anti-Arusha Hutu Power forces gained further support with the October 21, 1993, assassination of the Hutu president of neighboring Burundi by Tutsi army officers and the anti-Hutu massacres that followed (Fujii 2009; Mamdani 2001; Prunier 1995).

The invasion by Tutsi exiles, the Arusha agreement, and the assassination of Burundi's president were all movements of social time, and they led to a resurgence of ethnic grievances in Rwanda. Extremists within the government and their allies portrayed the civil war in ethnic terms. Tutsis had oppressed Hutus in the past and now sought to do so again. All Tutsis were enemies, whether they were members of the Burundian military, members of the Uganda-based RPF, or ordinary Rwandan citizens. But another fateful event occurred on April 6, 1994, when President Habyarimana's plane was shot down. The Hutu

Power forces immediately blamed the Tutsis—the RPF and their "accomplices." The extremist forces began eliminating opposition leaders and formed an interim government composed only of the ruling party and the Hutu Power factions of the opposition parties. The RPF resumed its invasion, and the Hutu Power forces in Rwanda began killing Tutsi civilians—eventually about 800,000 of them.

In the Rwandan case, as with the colonial genocides, overdiversity and understratification together caused the genocide. Where the cultural changes are greatest, as in the colonial genocides, the immediate provocation to genocide might be small threats to ethnic stratification, such as thefts or isolated killings. But in a context of longstanding diversity, as in the Rwandan case, it takes something major, such as a rebellion or invasion. In Rwanda the RPF invasion and the events surrounding it threatened to end—or even to reverse—the political dominance of Hutus over Tutsis.

FALSE ACCUSATIONS

In the colonial genocides and in the Rwandan genocide, the movements of social time were largely identical to the aggressors' grievances against their targets. The grievances accurately describe the targets' behavior—the cause of the genocide. But the aggressors in genocides might also make false accusations. Indeed, most genocidal conflicts involve a mixture of true and false accusations. In Rwanda, for example, the RPF had certainly invaded Rwanda, but they probably did not assassinate President Habyarimana (Reuters 2012). Hutus also falsely accused many Tutsis of conspiring with or aiding the rebels.[11]

In other genocides the major accusations are completely false, perhaps delusional. This was the case during the Holocaust, where, according to political scientist Daniel Jonah Goldhagen, the Nazis' "proneness to wild, 'magical thinking' . . . and their incapacity for 'reality testing' generally distinguishes them from the perpetrators of other mass slaughters" (1996:412). One false accusation was of Jewish treachery—a "stab in the back" that led to Germany's defeat in World War I (Friedländer 1997:73–74; Staub 1989:100). But the idea of Jews as organized conspirators went much further. For example, the Nazis believed that all their apparent enemies were simply Jewish puppets. The Nazis' form of socialism—National Socialism—differed from both capitalism and communism, and they believed that international Jewry was the real source behind both of those competing economic systems. This belief was later confirmed, they thought, by the alliance of capitalist and communist nations—the United States, Britain, and the Soviet Union—against Germany (Snyder 2010:217). More broadly, the Nazis believed that the Jews sought to dominate all of humanity and that they were thus behind all sorts of other evils. Nazi propagandist Joseph Goebbels, speaking of the Jews in 1937, put it like this: "Look, there is the world's enemy, the destroyer of civilizations, the parasite among the peoples, the son of Chaos, the incarnation of evil, the ferment of decomposition, the demon who brings about the degeneration of mankind" (quoted in Cohn 1969:204).

False accusations such as these result from the same kinds of movements of social time that lead to other genocidal conflicts. For example, warfare is an extreme movement of social time. As we have seen, when wars are interethnic, they may lead to conflict involving all those who share the antagonists' ethnicity. Wars may also lead to conflict with others. When a state loses a war, especially when this leads to a loss of territory, genocide becomes more likely. The Ottoman Empire had lost almost half of its territory during the two centuries prior to the 1915 genocide of Armenians in Turkey, and prior to the Holocaust, defeat in World War I had resulted in major territorial losses for Germany and the Austro-Hungarian Empire (Midlarsky 2005:135–62). Neither the Armenians nor the Jews were responsible, but in both cases these losses—a kind of downward mobility—not only exacerbated the already existing conflict with the losers' ethnic inferiors, but also led to new, and false, accusations against them. In the case of the Holocaust, World War II also threatened the Nazis' status, especially when the war with the Soviet Union began to prove much more difficult than expected. Hitler blamed the Jews for this war, and it was only after the invasion of the Soviet Union that the large-scale mass killing of Jews began. A state that loses a war, loses territory, or fights a war experiences a rapid loss or threat of loss to its status. These social upheavals cause so much conflict that they may result in the creation of new enemies, as socially distant ethnic groups that occupy an inferior position are accused of treason and other offenses regardless of their actual behavior.

GENOCIDE AND SOCIAL SPACE

The social changes that cause genocide do not always do so. They lead to ethnic conflict, but the presence and even the seriousness of a conflict do not in themselves determine how it will be handled. Whether genocide occurs, how severe it is, who participates, and who is targeted depend as well on the conflict's position in social space.

Genocide is a direct function of social distance and inequality. This means genocide is more likely when the antagonists are lacking in cultural similarity, interdependence, intimacy, and other forms of closeness, and when the aggressors are wealthier, more numerous, better supported, better organized, and otherwise higher in status than the targets.[12] Table 1 provides an overview of both parts of the theory, but in order to better understand the role of social distance and inequality, let us look more closely at two of the cases discussed above: the genocide of Indians in North America and the genocide of European Jews, or the Holocaust.

Table 1. The geometry of genocide

	SOCIAL TIME	SOCIAL SPACE
Theory	Movements of social time cause the ethnic conflicts that lead to genocide	Whether ethnic conflicts lead to genocide depends on their position in social space
Variable 1	Overdiversity: A society is ethnically divided, or previously separated ethnic groups have come into contact	Social distance: The aggressors and targets lack cultural similarity, interdependence, and intimacy
Variable 2	Understratification: A high-status ethnic group experiences a decline in or threat to its status, or a low-status ethnic group rises or attempts to rise in status	Inequality: The aggressors are wealthier, more numerous, better supported, and better organized than the targets

NORTH AMERICA

We have seen how social changes in the Round Valley of California led to genocidal massacres by white settlers against nearby Indians. Similar scenarios occurred elsewhere. In seventeenth-century New England, for example, the murder of Captain John Stone led to a retaliatory raid by white colonists against the Pequot Indians. When the

Pequots countered with a series of raids and ambushes resulting in the deaths of thirty whites, the colonists responded with a war resulting in the deaths of one-quarter to two-thirds of the tribe and the dissolving of the Pequots as a nation (Freeman 1995b:286–89; Katz 1991:208–213). In this case too we see an increase in diversity and a challenge by the Indians to the settlers' superiority—the predicted movement of social time. But their location and direction in social space was also as predicted: the settlers and Indians were separated by social distance, and the genocide had a downward direction, with higher-status whites exterminating lower-status Indians. Throughout the continent genocide was more likely to occur when these conditions—social distance and inequality—were present.

One type of social closeness comes about through cooperation. Political or economic cooperation, or functional interdependence, ties people together. Those who are not interdependent, who do not cooperate with one another, are more socially distant (Senechal de la Roche 1996:111). Cooperative ties may inhibit genocide even in situations of intense ethnic conflict. For instance, in South Africa under the apartheid regime, blacks, Indians, and the mixed-race people known as Coloureds made up an overwhelming majority of workers, and whites depended on their labor.[13] As political scientist Colin Tatz notes, whites would harass blacks, "arrest them, imprison them and sell them, beat them, relocate them, control their movements and regulate their lives, . . . but they always wanted more of them, not fewer of them" (2003:121).

We see something similar with European settlers and American Indians.[14] Where interdependence was greatest, genocide was absent. For instance, in the seventeenth century, the French—who established settlements to enable fur trading with the Indians—had more peaceful relations with Indians than the English did. In the French settlements, those who were not trying to trade furs were there to evangelize among the Indians, and both of these tasks required cooperation (Nash 2000 [1974]:44; see also Senechal de la Roche 1996:117). In the early eighteenth century, however, when the French established permanent settlements along the lower Mississippi, trade with the nearby Natchez was minimal, and conflicts became violent. Eventually the French killed at least one thousand Natchez and sold four hundred of them into slavery. Others fled to find refuge among other tribes, and the Natchez ceased to exist as a sovereign people (Nash 2000 [1974]:47–48).

Similarly, cooperative ties at first inhibited genocide in California. Prior to the Gold Rush, Indian laborers worked as near-slaves for Mexican and American ranchers. Ranch owner John Marsh noted that "throughout all of California the Indians are the principal laborers; without them the business of the country could hardly be carried on" (quoted in Sousa 2004:196). During this period, "despite the Mexicans' and Americans' debasing treatment of Indians, their cruelties stopped short of outright extermination" (Sousa 2004:196; compare Hurtado 1988:101). Even after the discovery of gold, ranchers at first found it profitable to use California Indians as miners, but during the Gold Rush immigrants sought wealth through their own labors (Sousa 2004:196–97). As relations between whites and Indians became less interdependent and less intimate, policies toward Indians became increasingly genocidal.

Still, as genocide became more common in California, whites with ties to Indians sometimes tried to stop it. In the Napa Valley in 1850, several employers of Indians worked together to prevent whites from killing the local Indians (Rawls 1984:183–84). And other employers of Indians opposed genocide more broadly: "Whites who perceived the Indians as a useful class of laborers objected to the actions of whites who regarded the Indians only as obstacles to be eliminated. . . . In the aftermath of the hostilities at Coloma in 1849, Theodore T. Johnson and others objected that 'wars of extermination' and 'indiscriminate revenge' had sacrificed the system of Indian labor exploitation in the mines" (Rawls 1984:183).

The Indians who were targets of genocide and the whites who targeted them were socially distant. They were also unequal. Conflicts that give rise to genocide normally have a downward direction—meaning those of higher status have grievances against those of lower status. And the farther downward the grievances travel—the higher the degree of inequality—the more likely genocide is. The aggressors' ethnic group is likely to be numerically larger than the targets' ethnic group. The aggressors are also likely to be wealthier—to possess more food, shelter, money, guns, and technology. They are likely to have more supporters than the targets, and they are likely to be more organized.¹⁵ It is often highly organized groups, such as governments, armies, and militias, that plan and conduct genocides. In such cases the individuals who initiate genocide tend also to have a high degree of authority—that is, to have high-ranking positions within their organizations. But a great deal of inequality is present even in less organized genocides, such as the killings of Indians by small groups of settlers.

The settlers' technology was always much more developed than the Indians', and they had higher levels of wealth, but the inequality between whites and Indians was not uniform throughout the continent. Native American groups had widely varying levels of social complexity. Some were small bands that subsisted on hunting and gathering, while others were large, hierarchical societies that grew crops and fought wars. The California Indians lived in simpler societies, and it was in California, where white miners and ranchers attacked hunter-gatherers, that genocide was most widespread and severe. In this respect California was similar to Australia, which, according to one historian, may have had more genocides than any other country (Moses 2000:93; see also Moses 2004:19). Like the California Indians, the Australian Aborigines targeted by British settlers were hunter-gatherers who lived in small groups and had low levels of technology. The Aborigines of Tasmania, whom the settlers hunted to near extinction, lacked even the technologies widespread among the Aborigines of mainland Australia and other hunter-gatherers. When first encountered by Europeans, they lacked "barbed spears, bone tools of any type, boomerangs, ground or polished stone tools, hafted stone tools, hooks, nets, pronged spears, traps, and the practices of catching and eating fish, sewing, and starting a fire" (Diamond 1999:312).¹⁶

Differences in the amount of inequality explain why genocide was greater in Australia than North America, and why within North America it was greatest in California. But such differences also explain why genocide was greater in some parts of California than others. The central and southern mining areas, for instance, were similar to one another except that Indians outnumbered whites in the southern area. After the onset of the Gold Rush, miners in the central region often indiscriminately killed Indians, and they prohibited them from working except in the most undesirable jobs (Hurtado 1988:101–11). In the southern mines, however, relations between whites and Indians mostly remained peaceful (Hurtado 1988:112–17).[17]

THE HOLOCAUST

Many German Jews were highly assimilated—culturally similar to and intimate and interdependent with German Christians. Why did this not protect them against genocide? The answer is that sometimes it did. For example, the Nazis initially exempted intermarried German Jews and their children from the Final Solution. Even though Nazi propaganda condemned all Jews and especially condemned intermarriage and miscegenation, they behaved more leniently toward German Jews who were socially close to other Germans. Later, on February 27, 1943, in what was meant to be the final roundup of Jews from Berlin, they began arresting intermarried Jews and Jews working in armaments factories. They separated the intermarried Jews (mostly men married to non-Jewish women) and held them at a welfare office. The intent was to deport them to the East, but after a massive protest from their wives and others, the men were released, and almost all of them survived the war (Stoltzfus 1996:xxii, 209–57).

Moreover, despite some assimilation, more culturally distant Jews were highly visible. Prior to the Holocaust, Eastern European Jews had immigrated in large numbers to the cities of Germany and Austria. In 1852, for instance, only 11,840 Jews lived in Berlin, compared to 108,044 in 1890 (Rubenstein 1983:146; see also Brustein 2003:104–7). And if Germans were distant from immigrants from the East, they were even more distant from those Jews who remained in the East—the first and most numerous of the genocide's targets. The mass killing of Jews began in Eastern Europe, along with the Nazi invasion of the Soviet Union. And most of those killed were Eastern European Jews, who made up the vast majority of European Jews. For example, three million Polish Jews were killed—half of all of those who died in the Holocaust—compared to only 165,000 German Jews.

Eastern European Jews were generally less assimilated than Jews in the West, and were thus more distant from the local populations of Christians, who often cooperated enthusiastically in the genocide. Local cooperation was less likely, though, where Jews were more assimilated. For instance, though Italy was allied with Germany in World

War II, genocide against Italian Jews did not begin until after Nazi occupation. Italy had experienced very little immigration from Eastern Europe, and the intermarriage rate between Jews and Christians was high.[18] Bulgaria, likewise, was allied with Nazi Germany, but the government resisted Nazi orders to deport Jews and successfully protected all Jews living in Bulgaria's prewar territory. Bulgarian Jews were socially closer to local Christians than were Jews in Germany and many other parts of Europe. They were an old community—largely the descendants of Jews who came from Spain after 1492—and they were highly assimilated (Brustein 2003:338). In the 1930s, however, Bulgaria had acquired territory from Rumania, Greece, and Yugoslavia. The Jews in these territories were more distant from Bulgarian Christians, and 96 percent of them were eventually deported (Fein 1979:159).

In the Holocaust the amount of inequality between the aggressors and targets was even greater than in the genocides of American Indians. It was a state-led genocide, as all of the major cases of genocide have been. This is consistent with the theory because modern governments are elevated along multiple forms of status, such as wealth, organization, and authority. Their status in comparison to their citizens increases when they become more centralized and when they involve themselves in multiple aspects of society. And as their status rises, they become more violent (Cooney 1997a:320; 1998:56–59; Rummel 1994:1–28; 1995). Thus, totalitarian regimes, such as the Soviet Union and Nazi Germany, have been much more violent toward their citizens compared to other authoritarian regimes, and more still compared to democracies (Rummel 1994:14–21).[19] The totalitarian nature of the Nazi regime made the conflict especially conducive to genocide.

GENOCIDE AND PHYSICAL SPACE

My theory deals with the social features of genocide—the social geometry. Certain movements of social time, overdiversity and understratification, cause ethnic conflicts, and when those conflicts have a certain position in social space—when the adversaries are socially distant and unequal—they may lead to genocide. But genocide is physical as well as social, so its position in physical space is also important. Even where the social environment is conducive to genocide, the physical environment might not be. Most obviously, genocide cannot occur if the killers are not physically close enough to their targets to carry out the violence. All violence—pinching and pushing, stabbing and shooting, bombing and burning—requires at least some degree of physical proximity, so anything that brings adversaries together in the same setting makes violence more likely. So does anything that prevents them from separating. Violence is common, for example, in prisons and day cares, where people cannot leave and thus cannot easily avoid one another (Baumgartner 1992b; Black 1998 [1993]:77; Senechal de la Roche 1996:115n22). Likewise, in ethnic conflicts genocide is more likely when fewer alternatives are available—when exit and expulsion become more difficult (compare Valentino 2004:5). In fact, the presence or absence of alternatives to genocide can explain much about the cases we have been discussing.

NORTH AMERICA

From the time of European arrival in North America, genocide and warfare against American Indians occurred sporadically, but as long as there was unsettled land available, Indians could emigrate when war was unsuccessful (Jennings 1975:186–227; Nash 2000 [1974]:25–138; Stannard 1992:104–46). For instance, in 1715 the Creeks and Yamasee fought an initially successful guerilla war against South Carolinians, but when the Carolinians allied with the Cherokees and began to launch effective counterattacks, the Creeks fled to their old homeland on the Chattahoochee, and the Yamasee fled to Florida (Nash 2000 [1974]:124–25). Whites forcibly deported other groups of Indians, and they did so more often as white settlers moved westward.

On the west coast, fewer areas were available for flight or deportation, and genocides in California were more widespread, numerous, and lethal than elsewhere. Many observers at the time recognized that the lack of a place to deport the Indians had altered the nature of the conflict. Among them were three federal treaty commissioners in California who published a message in the *Daily Alta California* on January 14, 1851. Articulating their fears of an Indian war, they noted that since there was "no farther west" for the Indians to go, the only alternatives were "extermination or domestication" (quoted in Hurtado 1988:135). Likewise, in 1860 the California state legislature issued the

Majority Report of the Special Joint Committee on the Mendocino War, which identified only two options concerning the Indians: "Shall the Indians be exterminated, or shall they be protected?" (California Legislature 1860:6). Expulsion was not an option since there was "no longer a wilderness west of us that can be assigned to them" (California Legislature 1860:3).

THE HOLOCAUST

Expulsion was not an option prior to the Holocaust either, at least not after previous plans fell through. In 1939 and 1940 the Nazis had planned to forcibly resettle the Jews under German control (Browning 1992:6; Gellately 2003:248; Valentino 2004:170–76). One idea was to deport them to the outskirts of the German empire—the Lublin region of Poland. When this proved impractical, they considered deporting Jews to the African island of Madagascar. Their inability to quickly defeat Great Britain, however, made this impossible, and they largely abandoned the idea by September 1940 (Browning 1992:19; Valentino 2004:172). War with the Soviet Union further reduced possibilities for resettlement, and in 1941 Nazi policies increasingly involved mass killings of Jews (Aly 2000:73–75; Browning 2004:187–188; Pohl 2000:86–90; Weitz 2003:129). Clearly any of the Nazis' schemes of mass deportation would have involved some genocide, but the degree of genocide reached unprecedented levels as separation became more difficult.

GENOCIDE AS A MATTER OF DEGREE

One thing that should be apparent from the discussion so far is that not all genocides are alike. Compare the genocides in America and Australia, on the one hand, with the Rwandan genocide and the Holocaust on the other. On the Australian frontier small groups of white settlers might massacre nearby Aborigines in response to some offense. For example, one settler in Queensland who had been troubled by nearby Aborigines invited an Aboriginal tribe to a great feast and upon their arrival had them shot by a party of men he had waiting (Palmer 2000:42). Other whites were not as successful in their attacks. Because of their superior bushcraft, the Aborigines could often get away, and they would sometimes even stop to make faces at the settlers who pursued them (Reynolds 2006:106–7). On other occasions Aborigines would gather in large groups and attack vulnerable settlers by surprise (Reynolds 2006:101–3, 105). Altogether, Aborigines killed as many as 2,500 Europeans. But European settlers, and later their allies in the Native Police, killed about 20,000 Aborigines (Reynolds 2006:125–27). The killings of Aborigines were genocides, but they were very localized, especially when conducted by settlers, and the settlers did not always kill all of those they targeted. Similarly, genocide by the Native Police often involved firing into groups of Aborigines to "disperse" them, a kind of indiscriminate killing that would nevertheless have left most members of the targeted groups alive. On other occasions the Native Police would intentionally spare some Aborigines, as when they killed all of the Aboriginal men living on Hinchinbrook Island but left the women and children (Palmer 2000:51).[20]

The genocide in Australia, which we might call a protogenocide, was similar to much of the genocide of Indians in North America, but it was very different from that in Rwanda, a more extreme case in which armies and militias, directed by state officials, worked every day for months attempting to kill every Rwandan Tutsi. And it was very different from the Holocaust, the most extreme case of genocide ever, which we might call a hypergenocide. But what does it mean to say that some cases of genocide are more extreme than others? It means they are more genocidal. Using the definition presented earlier, it means they involve more mass killing, they are more one-sided, and they are more ethnically based. Mass killing is greater when it is more intensive and when it occurs on a larger scale. Killing two-thirds of potential targets is more intensive than killing, say, 10 percent, and a genocide that targets an ethnic group throughout a nation or continent is larger in scale than one confined to a city or town. Mass killing that responds to violence by the targets, or where some members of the targeted group fight back, is less one-sided than the killing of unresisting people in a context unconnected to violence by members of the targeted group.[21] And a killing that targets only the men of an ethnic group, or only elites, is less ethnically based than one targeting all men, women, and children, since targeting is not solely based on ethnicity.[22]

Table 2 provides an overview of the dimensions of genocide, each of which can vary. My theory can explain this variation. It explains why some genocides are more intensive than others, why some are larger in scale, why some are more one-sided, and why some target people on the basis of ethnicity alone. For example, the most extreme genocides have been state-led genocides. This is because large-scale genocides must be highly organized. These are the cases where the conflicts are most unequal.

Table 2. Genocide as a matter of degree

DIMENSION	DEFINITION	PROTOGENOCIDE	HYPERGENOCIDE
Intensiveness	Proportion of targets killed	Killing ineffective or combined with non-lethal sanctions	Complete extermination
Scale	Time and territory over which killing operates	Small, local massacres	Coordinated national or regional massacres
One-sidedness	Extent to which violence moves in only one direction	Some violence by members of targeted group	No violence by members of targeted group
Ethnic basis	Extent to which killing is based on ethnicity alone	Only a portion of an ethnic group (e.g., men) are targets	All members of an ethnic group are potential targets

The case studies presented in chapters 3 through 7 feature almost the full range of genocidal violence, beginning with a protogenocide in North America and ending with the Holocaust, the most extreme hypergenocide ever. These chapters further demonstrate the theory's ability to explain these kinds of differences. But note too that since my theory explains genocide, it also explains the absence of genocide.

THE ABSENCE OF GENOCIDE

This theory of genocide is probabilistic rather than deterministic. It identifies what makes genocide more likely rather than what makes it certain. But in many cases it can predict the absence of genocide very precisely. Simply put, where the features conducive to genocide are absent, so is genocide. Genocide does not occur without large movements of social time that lead to ethnic conflicts, and even intense ethnic conflicts do not result in genocide when a conflict's location in social space is completely unfavorable to it. Where there is a grievance against members of a high-status ethnic group in a situation where ethnic relations are characterized by cultural similarity and intimate and cooperative relationships, genocide is inconceivable.

Something approximating this occurs whenever African Americans in the contemporary United States have grievances against whites. Such grievances are common. For instance, 62 percent of African Americans believe it is probably or certainly true that HIV and AIDS are part of a plot to kill blacks, and 73 percent believe the CIA has imported cocaine into the United States to distribute to black communities (Smith and Seltzer 2000; reported in Etzioni 2001:12). These fantastical beliefs in racist conspiracies are similar to the kinds of grievances that have led to genocide in other contexts, and sometimes such grievances even lead to calls for genocide—as when Kamau Kambon, an African American bookstore owner and occasional visiting professor at North Carolina State University, said to a panel at Howard University Law School, "We have to exterminate white people off the face of the planet . . . because they are going to kill us" (quoted in Sanders 2005). But such calls are ignored or unheeded. The geometry of the conflict is resistant to genocide.[23]

THE CIVIL RIGHTS MOVEMENT

In cases where most but not all aspects of the geometry of genocide are absent, conflicts do not lead to genocide. Thus the mostly downward grievances of whites against blacks in the contemporary United States do not result in mass killing. Nor did such conflicts lead to genocide in the recent past, though it seemed to some observers that they might. For instance, commenting in 1966 on a study of the attitudes of southern whites toward the civil rights movement, political scientists Donald Matthews and James Prothro stated that "only a significant change in White racial attitudes, awareness, and expectations [could ensure] the prevention of a racial holocaust and the preservation of political democracy in the South" (1966:365; quoted in Reed 2001:278). Yet as it turned out, only forty-four persons were killed in the whole of the civil rights movement (Reed 2001:279).

The theory presented here would predict that genocide would not occur in that situation. Sociologist John Shelton Reed (2001) notes that the cultural similarity of blacks and whites in the South—including a common evangelical Protestant heritage—played a role in reducing violence. Also, the political structure and the support among nonsoutherners for the civil rights movement meant that southern whites were opposed rather than supported by the national government, so white opponents of the movement had to confront federal marshals and a federalized National Guard (Reed 2001:280). Neither the social distance nor the inequality between blacks and whites was great enough for genocide.

Physical space also mattered. Genocide, remember, is less likely when some means of physical separation is available as an alternative. In this case, "many of the most vociferous opponents of desegregation withdrew in the wake of its accomplishment to private schools, to private clubs, and the like" (Reed 2001:282). Disgruntled whites were able to avoid blacks, and this acted as a "safety valve" in preventing violence (Reed 2001:283).

THE JIM CROW SOUTH

Earlier, when blacks in the South had fewer supporters and status differences were greater, grievances against blacks attracted more violence. Still, in many small towns the amount of intimacy and cooperation between the races was enough to prevent the most extreme forms of ethnic violence. In the late nineteenth and early twentieth centuries, for instance, numerous lynchings of blacks occurred in response to grievances that in other situations have led to genocidal attacks (Senechal de la Roche 1997:49). Lynching is much less severe than genocide in that the members of a lynch mob attempt to punish only individual wrongdoers. They might execute a black man, especially an outsider to the community who is accused of killing a white man, but they do not kill blacks indiscriminately.

The prevalence of lynching rather than violence directed at blacks more generally, then, was "a sign of the closeness between whites and blacks" (Senechal de la Roche 1997:63). Where there was greater distance and less cooperation between blacks and whites—in urban areas (many outside the South) or in cases where out-of-town whites attended a lynching—violence sometimes took the form of rioting, with whites targeting blacks simply for being black (Senechal de la Roche 1997:61–62). These riots involved little mass killing, but an extremely low degree of genocide sometimes occurred—such as when thirty-nine blacks were killed in East St. Louis in July 1919 (Horowitz 2001:19–20).

In these conflicts my theory predicts minimal if any genocide. Yet we can imagine alterations to the conflicts that would have made genocide possible. Had there been less similarity, intimacy, or cooperation, conflicts that led to lynching would have resembled the conflicts that often led to genocides of Native Americans in California. If grievances against blacks that led to rioting in cities had been formed by an authoritarian government rather than local white civilians, killing might have been larger in scale. If southern whites who opposed desegregation had attracted more outside support, the higher relative status of the aggressors would have made the genocide predicted by Matthews and Prothro more conceivable. In each situation, however, few of the conditions necessary for genocide were present.

As this chapter emphasizes, genocide is a response to ethnic conflict, a way of handling what the aggressors see as serious moral offenses by members of the targeted ethnic group. Once we understand what genocide is, we can begin to explain it. Just as we would explain law or any other way of handling deviant behavior, we must identify what gives rise to the conflicts and what determines the response to them. As we have seen, features of social life—particular patterns of culture, intimacy, and stratification—explain genocide just as they explain more ordinary responses to conflict. Genocide, like all conflict, is fundamentally social.

2 GENOCIDE AS PREDATION

We saw in the first chapter that genocide is a response to deviant behavior—a way for the aggressors to punish or eliminate those they see as evil. It is moralistic behavior, like law or any other form of social control. So are most other kinds of violence. Consider two fairly typical homicides in the United States. In one case a man shoots his next-door neighbor's visiting uncle because he has parked in front of his driveway and refuses to move. In another a man stabs his estranged wife, who when asked to consider what she is doing to their children, declares she does not "give a damn about the children" (Katz 1988:15–16). Such homicides, according to sociologist Jack Katz, can be seen as "righteous slaughters" arising from "moralistic rage" (1988:12). The killers, Katz says, are engaged in a "defense of the Good" (1988:15; see also Black 1983:36).

But not all violence is moralistic. Compare those righteous slaughters with the typical armed robbery. Armed robberies usually arise not out of conflict, but out of a "pressing need for cash" (Wright and Decker 1997:33). Robbers use violence not to "defend the Good," but to obtain money, often to buy recreational drugs. So while the logic of the righteous slaughter is moralistic—it involves punishing a wrongdoer—the logic of the armed robbery is predatory—it involves exploiting a victim. In these cases the two types of violence are distinct. The armed robberies involve no punishment, and the righteous slaughters involve no predation. But moralistic and predatory violence may overlap. They sometimes occur closely together, as when predatory violence, such as a robbery, leads to violent punishment (Cooney and Phillips 2002:93–94).[1] Other acts of violence are simultaneously moralistic and predatory, as when a robbery occurs in response to a conflict (Cooney and Phillips 2002:93; compare Cooney 1997b:180).[2]

One of the interesting aspects of genocide is that it is usually both moralistic and predatory. Like the killers in Katz's righteous slaughters, those who plan and carry out genocide see themselves as responding to evil, but unlike those killers they also exploit the targets for their own enrichment or pleasure. In the course of killing, the aggressors may gain land or other property, or they may force the targets to engage in labor or sexual activity. Why is this so? Political scientist Daniel Jonah Goldhagen says that it is "hardly remarkable that people slaughtering or expelling others they hate or see as threatening would also dispossess them. . . . Who would expect the many perpetrators, especially in poor countries, to, like ascetic monks, turn their backs on the possessions of the people they had just killed?" (2009:164).

Goldhagen is pointing out—correctly—that the killers believe the targets deserve to die. He sees predatory behavior as a byproduct of this moralistic aspect of the killing. I agree, but I do not see it as "hardly remarkable" and without need of explanation. As Katz's righteous slaughters illustrate, moralistic violence—even lethal violence—commonly involves no predation. People may define someone's behavior as wrong and worthy of punishment without recognizing any right to benefit at the wrongdoer's expense. To the extent that predation may involve disregarding morality, predation and social control even logically conflict with one another.[3] But the social geometries of predatory and moralistic behavior sometimes overlap.

THE GEOMETRY OF PREDATION

Predation is a form of economic behavior, like sharing, altruism, and exchange. Sharing is neither giving nor taking; it involves communal ownership. But when people do not share resources, they can transfer them through acts of altruism (giving without taking), exchange (mutual give and take), or predation (taking without giving) (compare Cooney and Phillips 2002:81; Jacques and Wright 2008:226; Michalski 2003:344–45). When people are intimate and otherwise socially close, sharing and giving are common (Black 1998 [1993]:142n6; 2011:89; Michalski 2003). But as sociologist Mark Cooney (2006) notes, predation is more common between strangers or between people from different cultures. Drug dealers, for example, are more likely to be robbed when they expand their businesses beyond their friends, and businesses are more likely to defraud customers who are members of different ethnic groups. And as social distance increases, predation involves larger amounts and becomes more violent (Cooney 2006: 59–60).

Just like predation, the handling of conflict becomes more severe as social distance increases. People who are intimate and otherwise socially close are more likely to tolerate one another's deviant behavior or try to deal with it in a way that preserves their relationship—such as with therapy or mediation. Their handling of wrongdoing shows concern for the wrongdoer (Black 1976:4–5; 1998 [1993]:16, 88–89, 155; 2011:148–49; Horwitz 1982:121–42; Tucker 1999:10–15). People who are more distant, though, are more moralistic in dealing with one another's deviant behavior—that is, they treat wrongdoers as enemies. Inequality matters, too, and people are especially moralistic toward those of lower social status (Black 1998:144, 151).

Genocide, as we have seen, occurs downwardly and across great social distances. It is highly moralistic, and in the most severe cases the aggressors treat the targets as enemies to be punished and eliminated without exception. That they also treat them as resources to be plundered is consistent with the theory of predation.[4] It is unsurprising, then, that in most genocides, and in all of the most extreme genocides, various forms of predatory behavior—usually land theft, looting, slavery, and rape—occur alongside the killing.

LAND THEFT

Genocidal conflicts often arise out of situations where two ethnic groups want to use the same land. Some scholars regard genocides of natives by colonists, for example, as "utilitarian genocide" (Dadrian 1975:209; Smith 1987:25; compare Chalk and Jonassohn 1990:29). But the term is misleading, since such genocides are largely moralistic. As we have seen, they usually occur in response to a theft, a killing, or some other offense by the natives. But the label utilitarian does point to an important secondary aspect of these and other colonial genocides: they materially benefit the colonists by enabling their complete control of the land they wish to use for economic activities such as growing crops, herding animals, or mining.

SETTLER COLONIALISM

Settler colonialism, whether genocidal or not, is inherently predatory. These situations are prone to genocide because, as historian Patrick Wolfe points out, they entail a "logic of elimination," according to which settler colonists seek to dissolve native societies and to build "a new colonial society on the expropriated land base" (2006:387–88). In many situations—such as where the settlers are farmers or herders and the natives are hunter-gatherers—the two groups have incompatible economic systems. The land cannot be used for both purposes, so settlement involves land theft. But the settlers do not necessarily view themselves as thieves.

For example, from a legal standpoint, the British viewed Australia as terra nullius, land that belongs to no one (Jones 2006:68; Moses 2000:94). In their view, they could simply claim the land without negotiating with the original inhabitants. This meant that they viewed any Aboriginal resistance to the colonists' predation as an act of wrongdoing. The Aborigines were the thieves and murderers; it was they who did not respect the colonists' property. Genocide against the Yuki Indians of northern California was similar. Hoping to make use of what one observer called "the best grazing ground in the State" (quoted in Miller 1979:45), white cattle ranchers began moving into the Round Valley, the Yukis' homeland, and they simply claimed the land and began fencing off thousands of acres. The Indians, with their land base restricted, now had difficulty obtaining food. They began killing the ranchers' cattle, and the ranchers responded with genocide (Carranco and Beard 1981; Miller 1979). In both cases the logic of the violence was both moralistic and predatory: the settlers punished the same people they were exploiting.

In some cases genocidal colonists speak forthrightly about the predatory nature of their actions, even if they still see them as justified. In South-West Africa, where Germans committed genocides against the Herero and Nama peoples, one military officer saw the conflict as an instance of a divinely ordained pattern in which the strong replace the weak: "Our Lord has made the law of nature such that only the strong of the world have a right to continuity, while the weak and purposeless will perish in favor of the strong" (quoted in

Madley 2005:436). Others did not bother justifying the taking of the natives' land. Another military officer, for example, gave a completely nonmoralistic endorsement of the annexation of South-West Africa: "That the natives [have] a right to the land and [can] do with it what they like . . . cannot be contested by talk, but only with the barrel of a gun" (quoted in Madley 2005:434).

Colonial genocides tend to have a partly predatory logic because they arise from attempts by one group to take the land of another. Similar situations have been present throughout human existence when societies with different economic systems have come into contact. As with the Australian and Californian cases, the most common targets may have been small groups of hunter-gatherers massacred by groups of men from more developed societies. Most such killings would have gone unrecorded and forgotten, yet evidence suggests their frequent occurrence beyond the context of nineteenth-century European colonialism. For one thing, we know that hunter-gatherers who survived alongside more developed societies occupied regions uninhabitable by others. Also, there are other examples of exterminations where hunter-gatherers lived on inhabitable land newly discovered by others. In 1835, for instance, the Maoris of New Zealand, upon learning of islands to the east, traveled to the Chatham Islands and over the next few years killed most of the hunter-gatherer inhabitants, the Moriori (Diamond 1999:53–57).

LIVING SPACE

So far we have discussed cases that many scholars would classify as utilitarian, but I am not reintroducing the previous typologies of genocide. The moralistic/predatory distinction is not a good way to distinguish genocides from one another, since genocides are both moralistic and predatory. Land theft has occurred in many contexts other than European colonialism and similar situations, and it does not just occur during small-scale genocides such as the ones we have discussed so far. It was also, for example, an important element of the Holocaust.

One of the aims of the Nazis' expansionary policy, which entailed both warfare and genocide, was to acquire lebensraum, or living space. The concept was developed not by the Nazis, but by geographer Friedrich Ratzel in 1897. His idea was that any successful *Volk,* or people, must spread out geographically as its population increases. In a struggle for living space, superior cultures would win, he believed, while inferior cultures would lose and die out (Madley 2005:432–33). Ratzel was a proponent of German colonialism and specifically of settlement in South-West Africa. The Nazis later used his ideas to argue for expansion into eastern Europe. They hoped that what would eventually result in the East was a "new, utopian social order, populated by Aryan farmers ruling over Slavic slaves" (Madley 2005:441). And there would be no place in the new social order for the large populations of Jews in the East. As one Nazi official explained, referring to the Holocaust, "We have forced them [the Jews] out of the *Lebensraum* of the people" (quoted in Madley 2005:435).

The pursuit of living space may even be a factor in genocides unconnected with any type of settler colonialism. Living space was a serious concern, for example, in Rwanda prior to the 1994 genocide. Rwanda was one of the most densely populated African countries. In this agricultural nation, farms were extremely small—averaging less than an acre in some places—and many Rwandans, especially the young, could not obtain farms of their own. Violence in the 1960s and 1970s, which led to the flight of many Tutsis into neighboring countries, had opened up land for landless Hutus, and many saw the same opportunity in the 1994 genocide (Diamond 2005:319–21; Mamdani 2001:201). Historian Gérard Prunier sees this as an important motive for participation in the genocide:

> Grim as it may seem, the genocidal violence of the spring of 1994 can be partly attributed to that population density. The decision to kill was of course made by politicians, for political reasons. But at least part of the reason why it was carried out so thoroughly by the ordinary rank-and-file peasants . . . was [the] feeling that there were too many people on too little land, and that with a reduction in their numbers, there would be more for the survivors. (Prunier 1995:4)

LOOTING

Genocide may also be accompanied by looting. Consider what happened during the Trail of Tears, the removal of the Cherokee Indians from Georgia in the early nineteenth century. This was a genocidal expulsion, resulting in the deaths of 8,000 of the 17,000 Cherokees rounded up by American soldiers and forced to move west. The Indians had to leave behind most of their property, and local whites moved in immediately to claim cattle and other possessions. They even robbed Cherokee graves of the silver pendants and other valuables buried with the dead (Stannard 1992:123–24). Similar behaviors have occurred during other genocides. In the 1915 Armenian genocide, as Turkish soldiers rounded up Armenians for execution or deportation, crowds of Turkish women and children would follow them around, in the words of one observer, "like a lot of vultures." They would "seize anything they can lay their hands on and when the more valuable things are carried out of the house by the police they rush in and take the balance" (quoted in Jones 2006:264). Later, when Armenian deportees would travel through an area, local Turks hoping to find gold coins would search through the piles of feces they left behind. The Armenians had begun swallowing the coins to keep them from being stolen (Bedoukian 1978:26).

LOOTING OPPORTUNITIES

The 1994 Rwandan genocide likewise opened up opportunities for predatory behavior. Many of those recruited to carry out the killing, according to Prunier, were among the poorest of the poor—"street boys, rag-pickers, carwashers, and homeless unemployed"—and "the genocide was the best thing that could ever happen to them" (1995:231). They were less concerned about political and ethnic conflict than with the material benefits that came from their participation: "They could steal, they could kill with minimum justification, they could rape and they could get drunk for free. This was wonderful" (Prunier 1995:232).

In many cases those who led the genocide recruited participants by giving them permission to loot. Sometimes they even promised specific items: "Everyone knew who had a refrigerator, a plush sofa, a radio, and assailants were guaranteed their rewards before attacking" (Des Forges 1995:44). One of the participants in the genocide says that because of the looting he felt "carefree and contented" during the genocide: "We drank very well with the money we were sniffing out. We ate the tastiest meat from the cows of those we had killed. . . . We slept comfortably, thanks to good nourishment and the fatigue of the day" (quoted in Hatzfeld 2005b:83). So eager were they to loot, said another participant of his colleagues, they might even neglect to finish killing someone: "For example, they gave the first machete blow and then spotted a bike, and—hop, they'd rather jump on the bike than finish the job" (quoted in Hatzfeld 2005b:131). One survivor said that the looting slowed down the genocide and enabled many Tutsis to survive: "If the Hutus had not been so worried about getting rich, they would have succeeded in exterminating every Tutsi in the country. It was out of good luck that they wasted much time pulling down sheet metal roofs, searching houses and squabbling over the spoils" (quoted in Hatzfeld 2005a:76).

Looting was a prominent feature of the Holocaust as well. In Poland, wherever the Nazis were in the process of executing or deporting Jews, locals would gather nearby waiting to rob the soon-to-be vacant apartments (Goldhagen 1996:551; Gross 2006:40; Gross and Gross 2012:42–43). Local Poles also visited synagogues and Jewish cemeteries and took the bricks, tombstones, and anything else they might find useful. They also took Jewish homes, sometimes by killing Jews whose property they wanted. One woman who tried to obtain an apartment that had belonged to Jews was told that she should have joined in the killing: "You could have killed 10 Jews and you would have gotten a house" (quoted in Gross 2006:45). In other cases Poles agreed to look after a Jewish neighbor's property and then refused to give it back after the war (Gross 2006:40–45).

LOOTING AS POLICY

The Germans looted too. Nazi official Hermann Göring summed up the government's policy when he said of Eastern Europe, "I intend to plunder it and do it thoroughly" (Madley 2005:452). And so the war in the East and the violence there against Slavs and Jews was to some extent predatory. Looting was such an important feature of the violence against Jews—in the East, in Germany, and everywhere under German control— that historian Götz Aly says the Holocaust can be properly understood only if "it is seen as the most single-mindedly pursued campaign of murderous larceny in modern history" (2006:285). By confiscating so much wealth, the Nazis were able to increase the level of economic equality and increase opportunities for upward mobility among Germans (Aly 2006:8). This, says Aly, is why Nazi policies received so much support—because ordinary Germans had become "well-fed parasites" (2006:324).

The large-scale looting of Jews began before the Holocaust, when in 1938 German Jews had to exchange most of their wealth for government stocks and bonds. That same year most Jewish businesses were "Aryanized," and German Jews had to pay 1 billion reichsmarks—collected through a 20 percent levy on their assets—as an "atonement payment" for the assassination in Paris of German diplomat Ernst vom Rath by a Jewish teenager (Aly 2006:19, 44; Melson 1992:227).[5] Jews who left Germany had to pay an additional emigration tax, and further confiscations followed. As an illustration of the effects of these and subsequent policies on Jews, even on those who escaped the Holocaust, consider the case of Emil and Henny Uhlmann, a wealthy Jewish couple who originally had assets worth 47,200 reichsmarks:

> After the emigration tax and the atonement payment, 21,350 reichsmarks of the original 47,200 remained. When they fled to Luxembourg in April 1940, they were allowed to take along only 10 reichsmarks each. A state-appointed trustee managed their assets after their departure and seized the money that came in from the rental of their property. As a result, the couple became dependent on a relative's financial support. Their house was officially transferred to the Reich and appears on a list of municipal property from February 18, 1941. Remaining assets were confiscated when the emigrants were stripped of German citizenship and when those who remained behind (relatives) had been deported. (quoted in Aly 2006:200)

This became a model for Nazi policy toward the Jews in Poland and other occupied countries, but the looting of Jews eventually went further. As the Nazis confined Jews to ghettos and deported them to labor or extermination camps, and even after they killed them, they continued to confiscate their wealth, including the smallest items of personal property—their clothes, their underwear, and their gold teeth (Melson 1992:228). At the Treblinka extermination camp, before they entered the gas chamber, Jews had to strip off and bundle their clothes, tie their shoes together, and give up any other valuables. Women had to hand over their wigs, and their hair was cut and later used to line slippers and stuff mattresses (Jones 2006:264; Snyder 2010:69–70). The Jews had nothing left now, except in some cases their gold teeth, which Jewish slave laborers removed from the corpses coming out of the gas chamber (Snyder 2010:270). If any items were overlooked, they were likely discovered later by local Poles, who after the war dug up the bodies buried at Treblinka hoping to find any remaining valuables (Gross 2006:41; Gross and Gross 2012).

SLAVERY

Slavery, or forced labor, is another form of predation that may occur alongside genocide. Though they sometimes occur close together, slavery and genocide are to some extent logically and theoretically contradictory. Whereas killing enables land theft and looting, it eliminates the possibility of enslavement. Furthermore, even though social distance makes predation, including slavery, more likely, slavery differs from land theft and looting in that it then leads to a reduction in social distance. Because slavery reduces social distance—by increasing intimacy and interdependence—it may reduce the likelihood of genocide (compare Payne 2004:49, 52). So we often see slavery during more limited genocides, where some people are killed and the rest are enslaved. Ancient and classical civilizations sometimes engaged in genocide after defeating enemies in war, but this seems to have involved both killing and enslavement rather than complete extermination (Jonassohn and Chalk 1987:12–13). In such cases genocide and slavery, though related, are distinct. The same individuals are not victims of both. But in other cases slavery itself may be genocidal. Slavery and genocide are not always contradictory. It is impossible to enslave those who have been killed, of course, but it is not impossible to kill those who have been enslaved. Slavery may even be the method of genocide, as when people are worked to death.

SLAVERY IN THE AMERICAS

We see both of these patterns—slavery alongside genocide and slavery as a form of genocide—in the various genocides of Native Americans by European colonists. Due to the natural tension between genocide and slavery, colonists often argued over which policy to pursue. In seventeenth-century Virginia, Governor William Berkeley came up with a solution: kill the adult males and sell the women and children as slaves. Selling the women and children, he said, would pay for the war of extermination (Stannard 1992:107–8). Conflict with Indians proceeded similarly elsewhere. In New England, following the colonists' war against the Pequots, some women and children were sold as slaves (Stannard 1992:115). Later, in California, whites sometimes massacred adult Indians and then sold their orphaned children (Hurtado 1988:145).

The Spanish conquistadors in Central and South America also engaged in both killing and enslavement. The killing was often direct and brutal. The Spaniards threw Indians into pits and impaled them on stakes embedded in the bottom; they burned them alive in their houses; they tied gourds to their feet and then tossed them into lakes (Stannard 1992:83). Or they enslaved them first and then killed them by overworking, underfeeding, and beating them. In the Andes, between a third and a half of the Incas who worked on coca plantations died within five months. Conditions seem to have been even worse in the silver mines. According to one observer, "If twenty healthy Indians enter [a mine] on Monday, half may emerge crippled on Saturday" (quoted in Stannard 1992:89). Another observer said that entering a mine was entering "a mouth of hell" (quoted in Stannard 1992:89). Here we see the hybrid form of slavery and genocide, where slavery is the means of death. But why in this case did interdependence not inhibit genocide? Why would the Spaniards kill people whose labor they needed? It was simply because there were so many Indians that the degree of interdependence was low. As historian David Stannard notes, "For as long as there appeared to be an unending supply of brute labor it was cheaper to work an Indian to death, and then replace him or her with another native, than it was to feed and care for either of them properly" (Stannard 1992:89; see also 217, 221). But when this began to change, colonists worried that an absence of laborers would eventually prevent the plantations and mines from operating, and the conditions of Indian laborers improved (Stannard 1992:90).

SLAVERY DURING THE HOLOCAUST

Slavery was also a feature of the Holocaust. Sometimes this was purely moralistic—a kind of punishment without material benefit to the Germans. Even labor that served no other purpose was, from the German perspective, an apt punishment for the Jews, a race of parasites who refused to do honest work. So Jewish slaves might have to build walls, tear them down, and rebuild them again, or carry mattresses back and forth from one barracks to another, or perform other pointless tasks (Goldhagen 1996:284–86, 304). But not all work was like this; many Jewish laborers worked in factories, sorted the shoes and clothing of Jews who had already been killed, and performed other important tasks. This was part of the Nazis' exploitation of the Jews—the attempt to extract as much as possible from them before killing them. As was true of the Indians in Spanish mines and plantations in Central and South America, the slaves worked with little food and under such harsh conditions that the work quickly killed them. Or in some cases their guards killed them outright. At the Lipowa labor camp in Lublin, Poland, guards shot a Jew for stealing a pair of woolen mittens, and there and elsewhere they executed Jews for other minor infractions: for stealing potato peelings, for stealing used undergarments, and even for accepting—not stealing—food from Germans or Poles who took pity on them (Goldhagen 1996:297, 306). Ultimately, even those who did not die from overwork, starvation, or abuse by the guards were still to be killed. Slavery only temporarily spared Jews from death. In late 1943, for example, the Nazis shot all three thousand Jews still alive at the Lipowa camp (Goldhagen 1996:295).

The interdependence created by Jewish slavery, then, was not enough to save Jewish workers indefinitely. But it did delay the closing of the work camps and ghettoes, so it delayed the genocide of some Jews for a few years—at a time when most European Jews had already died—and allowed others to survive the Holocaust. The enslavement of Jews also accounts for changes in the pattern of killing throughout the Holocaust. Mass killings of Jews first began with the Nazi invasion of Soviet territories, and at first, as in most genocides, adult males were most likely to be killed. Later the Germans began killing Jews indiscriminately, but when they began using Jews for labor, the targets were more likely to be women and children because men were more valuable as workers (Ringelheim 1993:391–400). Even at the extermination camps, the need for temporary laborers to run the camps kept many men alive. At Treblinka, for example, women were killed almost immediately, while men who were selected to work might live days, weeks, or months longer (Snyder 2010:270). And in the ghettoes, where the Jewish councils desperately tried to keep Jews working so the Nazis would spare them, men were more employable and therefore more likely to live than women and children. As the Jewish chief of the Vilna Ghetto in Lithuania explained, "I want to avert the end through work. Through work by healthy men. . . . The Germans wouldn't keep a ghetto for women and children for very long" (quoted in Ringelheim 1990:148).

RAPE

Rape, the use of force to compel sexual activity, is similar in its logic to robbery, the use of force to obtain wealth, and to slavery, the use of force to compel labor. Like robbery and slavery, rape is usually a form of predatory violence, an act of exploitation (compare Felson 2002:143–62). But as with robbery and slavery, occasionally rape is a way of punishing wrongdoing (Black 1983:35). For example, the Mehinaku people of Brazil would gang rape a woman as punishment if she saw the "sacred flutes" the men used in private religious rituals (Gregor 1990), and the Cheyenne people of the American plains might gang rape a woman for committing adultery (Black, 2011:45). Similarly, members of the Hells Angels, an American motorcycle gang, might gang rape a woman who "squeals" on one of them "or deserts him for somebody wrong" (Thompson 1996:191). In the aftermath of warfare and during genocides, both kinds of rape might occur. Wars and genocides create opportunities for purely predatory rapes, but mass rapes in these situations may be partly moralistic.

COLONIAL RAPE

In nineteenth-century California the rape of Indian women was a central part of the conflict between whites and Indians because the Indians' response to a rape sometimes led to genocidal massacres by whites. In 1849, for instance, gold prospectors from Oregon raped women at a Maidu Indian village and killed some of the men who tried to stop them. Later the Maidu responded by killing five of the whites, and the whites formed a mob and killed twenty Indians belonging to a different tribe (Trafzer and Hyer 1999:17). Whites during this time sometimes also captured Indian women and sold them as concubines or prostitutes or kept them for themselves. This sometimes led them to spare women's lives, as happened in 1861 during a genocidal expedition by a group of white hide hunters against Indians in northern California. The men attacked a group of sleeping Indians, and while pursuing those who fled, they came upon two Indian women, who immediately began running. One of the men, Bill Woods, yelled to the others not to kill the women, saying, "she's mine if I can ketch 'er" (quoted in Carranco and Beard 1981:181). Soon he lassoed one of the women, who "jumped up, scratching, biting, and spitting at Woods" (Carranco and Beard 1981:181). The other men, rolling around laughing as the Indian woman struggled to get away, yelled to Woods that he should keep her. He did, and the two spent their lives together on a nearby ranch (Carranco and Beard 1981:178–81).

RAPE AS POLICY

In Bosnia during the early 1990s, rape was more systematic, part of a deliberate policy on the part of the Serbs, who wished to drive Muslims from their homes so they could establish an ethnically homogeneous Serb state over much of Bosnia (Iacobelli 2009). Serb forces, often under direct orders, raped between 20,000 and 50,000 women (Gutman 1993:68; Stiglmayer 1994:85). As one Bosnian Muslim who witnessed the violence explained, "The people in authority all knew what was happening. . . . What mattered to them was that the people from our region should clear out, should never come back; and rapes are a splendid way to get that result" (quoted in Stiglmayer 1994:90).

The Serbs even set up rape camps, where they could repeatedly rape the women they imprisoned.

One Muslim woman, Ifeta, tells of being gang raped multiple times at a camp in Doboj. She estimates that over a period of five weeks she was raped by several men every other day. "And while they were doing it," she says, "they said I was going to have a baby by them and that it'd be an honor for a Muslim woman to give birth to a Serbian kid" (quoted in Stiglmayer 1994:118). At another camp a Muslim woman was told, "The next time we meet, you'll have one of our kids in your belly" (quoted in Stiglmayer 1994:92). Likewise, according to another woman, "They would say directly, looking into your eyes, that they wanted to make a baby" (Thomas and Ralph 1999:208). These statements point to a curious feature of the rapes in Bosnia: the Serbs wanted to impregnate the women, and in some cases they even made sure the women bore the children—sometimes by imprisoning them long enough to prevent them from having abortions. The idea was that these children would be Serbs, and so raping and impregnating Muslim women was one more way, along with the expulsions of Muslims and the massacres of Muslim men, of weakening the Bosnian Muslims as a people (Goldhagen 2009:453; Iacobelli 2009:275).

SADISTIC RAPE

In other genocides rape may be a prelude to or even a method of killing rather than an alternative to it. In such cases the raping and killing often involves an extreme degree of sadistic violence. During the Nanjing massacre of 1937 (often called the "Rape of Nanjing"), Japanese soldiers raped preteen girls, often slicing open their vaginas first; they raped pregnant women and ripped the fetuses out of their wombs; they raped old women; and they raped entire families (Chang 1997:91). In one case a group of Japanese soldiers raped a Chinese woman, Mrs. Hsia, stabbed her in the chest with a bayonet, and shoved a perfume bottle into her vagina. They then stabbed Mrs. Hsia's one-year-old baby, shot her parents, and took turns raping her two daughters, who were fourteen and sixteen years old. They then bayoneted both girls and shoved a bamboo cane into the sixteen-year-old's vagina (Chang 1997:92).

Rapes of Tutsi women in Rwanda during the 1994 genocide were also sadistic, often involving the removal of women's breasts (Mullins 2009a:25) and the mutilation of their vaginas with "machetes, knives, sticks, boiling water, and in one case, acid" (Nowrojee 1996). Somewhere between 250,000 and 500,000 Tutsi women may have been raped (Rittner 2002:94). Many of these women were killed, though women were more likely to survive the genocide than men. Most Tutsi women who survived had been raped, often multiple times, and many had severe injuries. One genocide survivor who was raped repeatedly and mutilated by the Hutu militia describes her experience after being rescued by the Rwandan Patriotic Front, the Tutsi-dominated army that was taking control of Rwanda:

> I told them to kill me because I didn't care anymore. . . . I was examined by a French doctor and was given medicine, food and clothes. When they gave me underwear, it was so painful that I could not even put it on. . . . I had to sit in medicated baths every day. . . . Since the war has ended, I have not had my monthly period. My stomach sometimes swells up and is painful. I think about what has happened to me all the time and at night I cannot sleep. I even see some of the Interahamwe [members of the Hutu militia] who did these things to me and others around here. When I see them, I think about committing suicide. (quoted in Nowrojee 1996)

The statements of the Hutu rapists make clear that these rapes often had a logic that was both predatory and moralistic. They sometimes emphasized that the genocide gave them the opportunity for exploitation. One Hutu militia member told his victim, "we have all the rights over you and we can do whatever we want" (quoted in Nowrojee 1996). Another said he had "never before had the opportunity to have sex with Tutsi women, but now they had all become available" (de Brouwer and Chu 2009:115). Others said things like "We want to see how sweet Tutsi women are," "We want to see if a Tutsi woman is like a Hutu woman" (quoted in Nowrojee 1996), and "We are going to rape you and taste Tutsi women" (quoted in Mullins 2009b:728; see also de Brouwer and Chu 2009:60, 112, 133). One Rwandan woman, attempting to explain the rapes, said, "Hutu men wanted to know Tutsi women, to have sex with them. Tutsi women were supposed to be special sexually" (quoted in Nowrojee 1996).

But the rapists also used moralistic language, expressing various grievances against the Tutsis generally or Tutsi women specifically. One woman says that her rapist "called me a snake and said that it was the end for all snakes" (de Brouwer and Chu 2009:54). Another man told a woman he was raping that he hoped in the future there would be only drawings to show that Tutsis ever existed. Other Hutu rapists would say things like "You Tutsi women think that you are too good for us," "You Tutsi girls are too proud" (quoted in Nowrojee 1996), and "Remember the past months when you were proud of yourselves and didn't look at us because you felt we were lower than you? Now that will never happen again" (quoted in de Brouwer and Chu 2009:114). Others made clear their punitive intentions by telling their victims that instead of killing them they would let them die from grief (Nowrojee 1996). In one case a woman begged a group of Hutus to kill her and her two daughters rather than rape the daughters in front of her, but the men replied that they intended to make them suffer (Mullins 2009b:729).

FORCED RELATIONSHIPS

In other cases during the Rwandan genocide, men forced women into ongoing sexual relationships. Sometimes Hutu militia groups held Tutsi women as prisoners for the duration of the genocide—or longer; they sometimes took the women with them to neighboring countries when they fled Rwanda—and raped them repeatedly. Individual Hutus might also keep Tutsi women for their sexual use, often hiding them from other Hutus to prevent them from being taken or killed. Sometimes these "forced marriages" lasted for years after the genocide, and sometimes the women voluntarily stayed with their captors. One such woman initially struggled against her captor, but, as her brother explained, "then she stopped struggling, she said 'I have nowhere to go'" (quoted in Fox 2011:294). Another said, "As long as he does not want to kill me, I will stay with him because I could not find another husband" (quoted in Nowrojee 1996). In general the women being held as sexual slaves and those forced into marriages with Hutus were allowed to live longer than other Tutsis, and they were more likely to survive the genocide. These long-term coercive relationships resemble slavery. Like slavery they involve a reduction of social distance, so they inhibit genocide to some degree.

A POSSIBLE EXCEPTION

Rape commonly occurs alongside genocide, sometimes as an alternative to killing some members of the targeted group and sometimes prior to the killing.[6] The Holocaust may be an exception as an extreme and large-scale genocide where mass rape was not as prevalent. According to Goldhagen (2009) the Nazis seldom raped Jewish women, in part because they genuinely believed Jewish women would pollute them: "They wanted to expose themselves to this danger no more than to intimate contact with a leper or, more precisely, a demonic leper" (Goldhagen 2009:457). But the rape of Jewish women was more common than Goldhagen suggests. Feminist journalist Susan Brownmiller (1975) notes that German law prohibited sexual relations between Germans and Jews, and she says that this did inhibit rape in some situations. One German soldier, for instance, prior to beating a Jewish woman with a whip, said, "I'll show you. But I can't have you, scum, because you're Jewish, and filthy" (quoted in Brownmiller 1975:51). But Brownmiller says Jewish women were nevertheless raped during the 1938 *Kristallnacht* riots in Germany, and that in Eastern Europe Jewish women were raped during the first phase of anti-Jewish violence—often dragged from their homes and raped in public—and later on when they were confined to the ghettoes. In one incident in the Warsaw Ghetto, forty Jewish women were beaten and raped after being taken to a house occupied by German officers. In another incident Germans brought the most attractive women in the ghetto to work at a mirror shop and then raped them after they finished their work. At one point the German Army tried to convince the Jewish Council in the ghetto to establish a brothel, stocked with Jewish girls, for German officers and soldiers (Brownmiller 1975:52).

The testimonies of Holocaust survivors mention other rapes too. In the Lviv region of the Ukraine, German soldiers forced Jewish girls to live with them and then turned them over to be killed after they became pregnant (Podolsky 2010:96–97). In Lithuania collaborators would rape Jewish women they had taken away for "work" (Sinnreich 2010:111). In the Skarzysko-Kamienna labor camp in Poland, men would rape and kill Jewish women serving as room cleaners or meal servers and drag others from their beds at night. Often these were gang rapes carried out in the open (Sinnreich 2010:114–15). At Auschwitz too Jewish women were sometimes raped and otherwise sexually abused. Several Jewish women have told of rapes or attempted rapes by the Auschwitz guards, including, in one case, a female guard, who wanted thirteen-year-old Halina Birenbaum to act as her sex slave in exchange for extra food rations (Shik 2009:231–32).[7] Newly arrived women were forced to undress while the male guards "made fun of their bodies, their breasts, and their genitalia, sometimes by 'playing' with their nipples and touching other intimate parts of their bodies" (Shik 2009:229). As one survivor explained, "It amused them to pinch the buttocks of the women who were young and pretty. When one of the men passed beside me and pinched my buttocks I felt really humiliated" (quoted in Shik 2009:230). Elsewhere the Nazis and their allies forced Jewish women into prostitution (Flaschka 2010:84–85; Sinnreich 2010:115–17).

Along with land theft, looting, and slavery, then, sexual predation was a feature of the Holocaust, even if it was not as common as in Bosnia and Rwanda. The geometry of genocide is conducive to rape and other forms of predation, so rapes occurred during the Holocaust even though Nazi ideology and German law were both hostile to sexual contact between Jews and Gentiles.[8]

The social conditions in which ethnic conflicts lead to genocide are the same social conditions that lead to extreme predation, so unlike most forms of violence, genocide is both moralistic and predatory. This explains the occurrence of land theft, looting, slavery, and rape alongside genocide, and it points to the asymmetric nature of extreme moralism. Downward, distant conflicts are handled severely. High-status parties are sensitive to wrongdoing from distant inferiors, yet at the same time they do not recognize any obligations toward these distant inferiors, whom they exploit at will. They do to others what they would punish severely if it were done to them.

Philosophers, theologians, and others commonly advance a universalistic morality. If something is right or wrong, it is right or wrong for everyone: for the rich as well as the poor, for strangers as well as friends, for ourselves as well as others. We see this in various ethical precepts, such as the Golden Rule and Kant's categorical imperative, which ask us to view our own actions the same way we view the actions of others.[9] These are moral prescriptions, of course, statements about what people ought to do rather than descriptions of what they actually do. When we look instead at patterns of moral behavior—what people condemn, what they punish—we find that morality is geometrical rather than universal: its application depends on its social location (Black 1998 [1993]:xxvi; Cooney 2009b:201). When disputants are close and equal, condemnation is weaker, predation is unlikely, and people may indeed do to others as they would like others to do to them. But toward distant inferiors, such as those who are targets of genocide, we see moral judgment without moral obligation (compare Fein 1979). So predation is compatible with genocide not because morality is absent during genocide, but because moralism is extreme.

3 INDIANS AND WHITES IN CALIFORNIA

In 1859, in the Round Valley of California, rancher H. L. Hall found the remains of a stallion and a cow, both apparently killed by nearby Yuki Indians. Hall and five other men responded violently: "We followed one of the trails about two miles and found the Indians; there were about thirty, all told. We killed at that time some eight male Indians; all the rest escaped. In this camp we found no evidences of stock having been killed." At the next camp they found everyone gone except for "one sick buck [Indian man]; we told him to tell the Indians . . . if they did not quit killing stock we would kill them." When they found another camp, only "three or four squaws [Indian women] and three or four children" were there (Hall 1860:41). They took them prisoner, intending to bring them to the nearby reservation, but only one made it. Hall explained why: "I did not see any killed, nor did I kill any of them; I saw one of the squaws after she was dead; I think she died from a bullet; I think all the squaws were killed because they refused to go further. We took one boy into the valley, and the infants were put out of their misery, and a girl ten years of age was killed for stubbornness" (Hall 1860:42).

"A WAR OF EXTERMINATION"

During the 1850s the population of California Indians declined by about two-thirds (Thornton 1987:107–9). Most of this decline was due to disease, but Indians also died at the hands of whites in numerous massacres on the California frontier—massacres similar to the ones described by Hall (Rawls 1984:176). When livestock were stolen or whites were killed, bands of settlers and sometimes more permanent militia groups held local Indians responsible and killed them indiscriminately. Throughout the state the pattern was similar. Disputes arose whenever whites settled in new areas and when, by making use of the land and other resources, they disrupted the Indians' traditional ways of obtaining food. For instance, mining interrupted the salmon runs, and cattle ranching depleted wild food crops (Hurtado 1988:122; Madley 2004:177; Miller 1979:47; Rawls 1984:176). Indians would then kill settlers' livestock, raid their settlements for food, or even attack them in retaliation for previous massacres or other offenses (Rawls 1984:177). The response by whites was often genocide—forthrightly called extermination by the settlers and many other Californians, who often spoke of the demise of the California Indians as unavoidable, necessary, or perhaps desirable. Governor Peter Burnett defended the genocidal settlers in his 1851 message to the state legislature: "The white man, to whom time is money, and who labors hard all day to create the comforts of life, cannot sit up all night to watch his property. . . . After being robbed a few times he becomes desperate, and resolves upon a war of extermination" (quoted in Hurtado 1988: 134–35).

Genocide in California led to the complete or near extinction of numerous groups of Indians. One of these groups was the Yuki Indians, who lived in and near the Round Valley of Mendocino County. The Yuki population declined from perhaps 12,000 in the mid-1850s to only 600 ten years later, and as demographer Russell Thornton notes, "the primary reason for their massive demographic devastation . . . was, without apparently any doubt, genocide" (1986:123).

In the next five chapters I apply the theory presented in chapters 1 and 2 to particular cases of genocide.[1] Each case study deals with a larger genocide, but it also focuses in detail on the killing in a smaller location. In this chapter I focus on the genocide of the Yuki Indians. We shall see that the evidence in this case strongly supports my theory of the geometry of genocide. The genocide was a response to ethnic conflict resulting from overdiversity and understratification—intercultural contact followed by a challenge to the dominant group. The genocide occurred across great social distances—between people who were dissimilar and unacquainted. And it occurred in part because some possible responses were physically unavailable. We shall see too that the theory explains other aspects of the genocide, such as why Indians living in the hills were the usual targets, why even serious offenses like the killing of whites by Indians were not always handled with genocide, why some whites intervened to protect Indians, and why the genocide in the Round Valley differed so much from the Holocaust and other more extreme cases of genocide. But let us begin by looking more closely at the background of the Yuki and their conflict with white settlers.

GENOCIDE OF THE YUKI

The Yuki, also called the Nome Cult Indians, referred to themselves as the Ukomno'm, which means "in the valley." The valley was the Round Valley, or the Nome Cult Valley, a lush, secluded place with branches of the Eel River surrounding three of its sides. The Round Valley was the setting of the Yuki's creation myth, and the Yuki had lived in the valley and the surrounding mountains since long before the arrival of whites (Miller 1979:12, 15). The isolated territory enabled their survival as a distinct people—different linguistically and physically from other California Indians. Their language was different from those of nearby groups, for example, and along with the nearby Wailaki, they were shorter and deeper-chested than other Indians (Miller 1979:9).

The area provided the Yuki with acorns, deer, and salmon, which made up the bulk of their diet. They were hunter-gatherers and they fished, but because of the steady food supply they were not nomadic like many such groups are. Fish were usually available in the Eel River, where the men would spear, net, poison, or trap them. The men killed deer with bows and arrows after using deer-head disguises to sneak up on them, or they would join in groups to drive the deer toward snares. Men, women, and children would join together to gather acorns, and the women were in charge of storing them, grinding them, and preparing various foods. The Yuki also gathered other foods, such as fungi and bird eggs, and killed and ate other animals, including rabbits, squirrels, and birds (Miller 1979:21–22). Most of the division of labor was sex-based and simple, with the men hunting and fishing and the women processing acorns, but some of the men had more specialized tasks. Shamans cured illnesses and were said to receive their power from Taikomol, or "he who walks alone," the Yuki's supreme being. Others, such as sorcerers and "singing doctors," who sang to cure victims of poisoning, also specialized in curing certain illnesses (Miller 1979:24–25).

The Yuki lived in villages, called *rancherias,* usually made up of several nuclear families and numbering at most about 150 persons. Several rancherias made up a *tribelet,* and tribelets were grouped together into six tribal subdivisions. Yuki government was weak. The leaders of the *rancherias* were respected men who were selected informally. More formal, but still weak authority existed at the *tribelet* level, where the men of the community elected a chief whose job was to exhort the people to do good, set dates for group functions, and maintain order (Miller 1979:18). The six tribal divisions had no governments, though they went to war against one another and other nearby Indians and maintained a strong sense of identity (Carranco and Beard 1981:95). Though Yuki as a whole identified themselves as a people, they were never unified politically.

The Yuki were unusual in that they had an elaborate ceremonial life—including religious ceremonies, puberty rites, and belief in a personal deity—but only simple tools and other technologies (Foster 1944:155, 223). Their political life, though not highly organized, was likewise much more elaborate than is usual in societies with no agriculture of any kind. This feature of Yuki life—material simplicity but more complexity in other areas—was enabled, it appears, by the abundance of food. The Yuki did not even have any tales of famine, and with plenty of game, fish, and acorns readily available, they could afford the idleness that would inhibit food extraction during times of ceremony (Foster 1944:223). "To the members of Yuki society," according to anthropologist George Foster, "life must have been full, interesting, and worth while" (1944:224). But this was not to last.

In May 1854 two parties of whites—one led by Samuel Kelsey and another consisting of brothers Frank and Pierce Asbill and their friend Jim Nephus—discovered the Round Valley. The Yuki inhabitants attacked them upon their arrival, but they fought back, killing thirty-two of the Indians (Miller 1979:36). In 1855 the Asbill brothers and Nephus returned, this time to gather up Indian girls to exchange for horses. Upon settling in the area, they captured two young Indians—a sixteen-year-old girl and a twelve-year-old boy—whom they intended to "tame" and to use to lure other Indian children. As other children came to visit—out of curiosity and to partake of beans and syrup—the men convinced thirty-five girls to come with them on a trip to another hunting ground, where they would receive plenty of beans and syrup. The men sold the girls in the Sacramento Valley, and they were loaded onto carts and driven to their prospective husbands (Miller 1979:38–40).

This kind of predatory behavior characterized the whites' behavior toward Indians in the Round Valley from the beginning. Like the Asbills, later settlers freely made use of the natural and human resources of the valley. White settlement in the Round Valley and elsewhere in California thus resulted in a disruption of the Indians' lifestyle and led to interethnic conflict. Whites saw this as the inevitable result of frontier settlement, but the authorities did try to improve the situation by establishing Indian reservations—places that would protect Indians from whites and also prevent them from interfering with white settlement. Initially the Round Valley was supposed to serve as such a reservation. In June 1856 Thomas Henley, superintendent of Indian affairs in California, sent Simmon P. Storms to investigate the Round Valley, and the Indians Storms met with on his visit agreed to allow him to establish a reservation—though it is likely they understood this to mean simply that a few whites would live in the valley to protect the Indians from other whites (Miller 1979:43–44). Actually Indians from many areas would be brought into the valley.

As Storms was attempting to establish the reservation—also known as the Nome Cult Indian Farm—white cattle ranchers moved in to make use of the land. Though white settlement conflicted with the use of the area as a government reservation, Henley encouraged it because he wanted to use his position as superintendent of Indian affairs to establish a large cattle empire (Carranco and Beard 1981:56; compare Bancroft 1963:490–91). Henley later became joint owner of a large herd of cattle in the area, and several members of his family were early settlers (Miller 1979:46). By the end of 1857, the cattle ranchers in the area—at least twenty-four of them at this point—had begun fencing off land (Miller 1979:46). This meant the Yuki were barred from much of what had always been their land, where they had previously found it easy to obtain food, so they began to kill stock belonging to the ranchers. In response the white settlers conducted numerous genocidal attacks on nearby Indians. One settler described the attacks as follows:

> In one thousand eight hundred and fifty-six the first expedition by the whites against the Indians was made, and they have continued ever since; these expeditions were formed by gathering together a few white men whenever the Indians committed depredations on their stock; there were so many of these expeditions that I cannot recollect the number; the result was that we would kill, on an average, fifty or sixty Indians on a trip, and take some prisoners, which we always took to the reserve; frequently we would have to turn out two or three times a week. (Laycock 1860:49)

Many of these attacks were responses to killings of the settlers' stock. Usually they were responses to very specific offenses—such as the killing of a particular cow, horse, or hog. In 1856, for example, settler John Lawson lost twenty hogs. After finding the meat in an Indian *rancheria,* Lawson and other settlers went after the Indians, shot three, and brought five to the reservation, where they were hanged (Lawson 1860:68). The same was true of larger massacres. H. L. Hall claimed to have started the conflict with the Indians in the valley when he refused to pay a group of Indians for working for him. In retaliation for the nonpayment, the Indians killed some of Hall's stock, and Hall and others "commenced killing all the Indians they could find in the mountains" (Scott 1860:22). At another time Hall and a group of settlers killed 240 Indians in response to the killing of a gray stallion (Carranco and Beard 1981:82; see also Garrett 1969:60). In yet another case W. J. Hildreth found three Indians skinning a steer. He then led a group of men to the offenders' *rancheria,* where they killed seventeen Indians (Hildreth 1860:32).[2]

Many of these killing expeditions involved small groups formed only to retaliate for a specific offense, but some groups were larger and more organized. For example, a large group of killers seems to have been involved for a period of time in 1858, at which time it was reported that "some twenty or thirty armed men" were "busily occupied during several months past in killing Indians" (quoted in Miller 1979:55). And in the summer of 1859, a more organized militia group—led by Walter S. Jarboe and authorized and funded by the state—began dealing with Indian offenses. Known as the Eel River Rangers, this group, which consisted of Jarboe and twenty other volunteers, operated until January 1860. During their few months of operation, the Eel River Rangers killed hundreds or perhaps more than a thousand Indians (Carranco and Beard 1981:95–97; Garrett 1969:70–71; Miller 1979:72). Their purpose was largely to continue the killing begun by the more informal groups of settlers, and like the other groups they also sometimes acted in response to specific offenses. On November 24, 1859, for example, a man reported that five horses had been killed. Jarboe himself described the response of the Rangers:

> The company came upon the Indians some 15 miles East of the Valley in a deep Canon on the waters of the Eel River. This was in the night and the Indians spies had discovered their approach. There was no time to lose, and the attack was made at once. Several were killed and 9 squaws & children taken prisoners. . . . The squaws were questioned, and revealed to them that the guilty party was $\frac{1}{2}$ mile distant in another Canon. They at once went as directed and found them in possession of the very horse flesh (identified by marks on the hides) that had been reported stolen. . . . Total killed 18 Bucks. (quoted in Miller 1979:71)

In other cases the Eel River Rangers, as well as the more informal groups of settlers, killed in response to Indian offenses more generally rather than to specific, single offenses. In November of 1858, for instance, after disappearances of stock became more frequent, settlers formed a party and attacked a *rancheria* in the mountains. There the settlers killed nine Indians, whose deaths they justified with the evidence of the remains of horses and cattle in the *rancheria* (Carranco and Beard 1981:73; Miller 1979:55). In another case a group of settlers—none of whom was missing any stock—attacked a *rancheria* on the Eel River and killed eleven Indians. Finding a horse's ear and two horses' tongues, they justified the expedition by saying "the Indians *had* killed stock and *would* continue to do so" (quoted in Miller 1979:67, emphasis in the original; see also Carranco and Beard 1981:90).

Often colonial genocides occur in response to the killing of settlers, but this was true of only a few cases in the Round Valley—mainly because the Yuki Indians so rarely killed whites. Genocide in the Round

Valley was mostly a response to theft, usually to a specific event such as the killing of a horse, but settlers frequently expressed more general grievances. The earliest visitors to the area described the Yuki in terms that were condescending but not hostile—as "well-formed naked Indians of small stature" or as "fat, brown, naked 'wild Injuns'" (Miller 1979:46). Later settlers, however, spoke of the Yuki with contempt—as "the most degraded specimens of humanity I ever saw" or as "the most shiftless, and the lowest mentally, of any tribe of which I have knowledge" (quoted in Miller 1979:46). Eel River Rangers captain Jarboe likewise expressed the view that the Yuki Indians were exceptionally inferior and contemptible: "The Yukas are without a doubt, the most degraded, filthy, miserable thieving lot of any thing living that comes under the head of the rank of human beings.... They are so inferior in intelect [sic] so devoid of feeling that they stand by coolly and unmoved and see their companions shot down by scores without evincing the least symptoms of sorrow and boldly avow their determination to continue their hostilities" (quoted in Carranco and Beard 1981:94).

Even those settlers with more favorable attitudes toward the Indians considered them their moral inferiors. One of these was George W. Jeffress, a physician on the reservation, who said reports of stock being killed by Indians were often exaggerated and that the Indians were nonhostile. But despite having some sympathy for the Indians, he considered them a "cowardly, thieving set of vagabonds." That the settlers massacred them so easily was evidence of their cowardice: "I do not consider they are brave when two white men can drive twenty-five of them, and shoot them down while they are running" (Jeffress 1860:64). Likewise Simmon Storms, who sometimes in his capacity of as supervisor of the reservation acted to protect the Indians, nonetheless described them as "an ungrateful, cowardly, treacherous, thieving set" (Storms 1860:37).[3]

GENOCIDE OF THE YANA

This chapter focuses on the genocide of the Yuki, but this behavior—mass killing in response to Indian thefts and killings—was not unique to the Round Valley. For example, in Butte County, east of the Round Valley and in the middle of the state, white miners and ranchers almost completely exterminated the area's Yana Indians. The circumstances were similar to those in the Round Valley. The settlers' animals grazed in the hills and depleted or destroyed the grasses and the acorn-bearing oaks the natives relied on. The settlers also polluted the streams, which affected the salmon runs in the Yana's territory. The Indians began stealing food and livestock from the settlers, and the settlers responded with forced migration and genocide (Kroeber 1961:48–50).

At first the settlers took many of the Indians to the Nome Lackee Indian Reservation twenty miles away, but by 1861 all the Indians there had died or escaped, and the reservation was abandoned (Kroeber 1961:63). Initially the killing expeditions were very simple, with whites responding to particular offenses and then disbanding. One such incident occurred in 1850, when a group of men went out to round up a rancher's cattle and oxen. The Indians later stole the animals, and the group, upon finding an Indian village they believed to be the home of the thieves, killed the Indians there and burned the village. In 1853 after Indians stole a cow, a group of whites killed twenty-five or more Indians (Kroeber 1961:60). Later expeditions were more organized. In 1859 white settlers collected $3,000 to fund their fights with the Indians, and Robert Anderson and Hiram Good, two men with tracking skills and prior experience killing Indians, began leading the expeditions, which now sometimes lasted weeks or months (Kroeber 1961:63, 66).

Anderson and Good continued to respond to Indian thefts, but they were sometimes also responding to killings. The Yana seem to have killed whites much more often than the Yuki did. In 1862 they killed a teamster, and soon afterward two teenage girls and a younger boy. Good and others then went into the hills and killed eight Indians (Kroeber 1961:68–69). In 1863 Indians kidnapped three white children and killed two of them, possibly in response to one of the frequent murders and kidnappings of Indian children. A group of whites immediately tracked down a group of Indians and killed one of them. A more organized group later captured hundreds of Indians and took them to the reservation in the Round Valley. In 1864, after the killing of two white women, Anderson and Good spent five months killing most of the Yana still remaining—about 2,000 of them. When this expedition was over, three of the four divisions of the Yana were almost completely exterminated, though the fourth group, the Yahi, lasted for many more years (Kroeber 1961:70–78).

The genocide of the Yana was similar to the genocide of the Yuki in the Round Valley. Both were predatory and moralistic—predatory since they arose from the settlers' attempts to exploit the Indians and take their land, moralistic since they arose from settlers' grievances. Most killing expeditions responded to Indian depredations against the settlers' stock, though when killings of whites occurred, they might elicit even more severe responses. But why was genocide the response in either case?

SOCIAL TIME

Prior to any genocide something must get the conflict started. Movements of social time—social changes—increase diversity and decrease stratification. Prior to the Round Valley genocide, diversity increased when white ranchers began moving into the valley in the 1850s. Later, thefts of livestock decreased stratification by lowering the settlers' status and raising the Indians'. As with most colonial genocides, the causes are straightforward and were understood at some level even by the participants. H. L. Hall and others who killed Indians explained their actions as a response to the thefts. They were correct: the thefts were the immediate cause of the killing. But not all interethnic contact leads to genocide; nor do all thefts. In this case social changes resulted in genocide because of the context in which they occurred.

INSEPARABILITY

Recall that one aspect of an ethnic conflict that determines whether it leads to genocide is geographical. Violence is impossible without physical closeness, and when adversaries are more accessible to one another, their conflicts are more likely to turn violent. They are especially more likely to turn violent when the adversaries are more inseparable—when exit and expulsion are impossible or difficult. The occurrence of genocide in California was partly due to the fact that it was not possible for whites to force Indians to move westward. But even though large-scale expulsion was not possible, whites did sometimes move Indians away from white settlements.

The Round Valley was at first intended as a reservation for Indians who were from the area or were moved there from other parts of the state. Subagent Storms had urged that the entire valley be set aside for the Indians, and he instructed whites coming into the area to go elsewhere (Carranco and Beard 1981:54). But due to various circumstances—mainly because of Superintendent Henley's personal plans for the valley—the whites did not leave. The government claimed only half of the valley, and ranchers moved in to make use of the rest of the land, which was not only adjacent to the reservation but also a central part of the land the Yuki were accustomed to using. Thus, as anthropologist Virginia Miller puts it, "two entirely opposing ways of life and value systems were vying for the same territory which each would exploit in a different way" (1979:99). The reservation policy failed to reduce conflict because it failed to keep Indians and whites apart.

Over time the difficulty of separating Indians and whites increased. The settlers invested substantial resources in building properties and developing the land for their own use, and the longer they were in the area the less feasible it became for them to move. Earlier settlers might have moved—and some did. Shortly after Storms established the reservation, for instance, the Asbill brothers and Nephus returned to the valley, but upon learning that other whites were settling in the area and that half the valley had been declared a reservation, they decided to go elsewhere (Miller 1979:45). Other early settlers might have moved on as easily as the Asbills if there had been a serious attempt to encourage them to do so. But by the time the government declared the whole valley a reservation in 1858, the settlers were unwilling to leave, and leaving had become more costly even for those who might want to. Residents formulated a series of petitions protesting the decision, and Henley did little or nothing to encourage settlers to move (Miller 1979:55–56). Settlers who were willing to leave first wanted reimbursement from the government for their buildings and improvements to the land (Miller 1979:55). After Henley had been replaced as superintendent, the government made further attempts to remove the settlers and agreed to pay them reimbursements. Years later, however, the reimbursements still had not been paid, the settlers still had not moved, and genocide continued in the area for some time (Miller 1979:83).

SOCIAL DISTANCE

In the Round Valley, then, movements of social time caused the kinds of serious ethnic conflict that may lead to genocide. And we have seen that one alternative way of handling ethnic conflict—separation of the groups in conflict—was largely unavailable. But these factors alone do not make genocide inevitable or even likely. As we saw previously, a conflict's position in social space also matters.

According to my theory, genocide occurs when the adversaries are socially distant from one another and when they are unequal. First consider social distance. Indians and whites in the Round Valley differed from one another concerning almost every aspect of culture, including language, religion, clothing, and diet. The adversaries were seldom very intimate either. In the many accounts given by settlers of their lives in the valley and their conflicts with Indians, for example, only once or twice was an Indian's name mentioned (Miller 1979:100). They also lacked cooperative ties. Since the Indians and settlers had completely different means of subsistence and attempted to use the land in different ways, competition over land use was a zero-sum game. The settlers fenced off land and allowed their cattle to graze at the expense of the Indians, and if Indians killed cattle to make up for the reduction in food supply, this would cut into the settlers' profits. Social distance thus separated Indians and whites in the Round Valley area, and the degree of social distance was greater in northern California than in other regions of the state. In the south, Indians had been in contact with whites much longer, and more of the Indians were "domesticated" (Hurtado:1988:121). Interethnic conflicts in the north—including those in the Round Valley area—thus became more violent than elsewhere.

INDIANS ON THE RESERVATION AND THE RANCHES

Whites were distant from Indians, especially those they killed, but the social distance between whites and Indians varied, and with it genocide. Most of the white ranches had Yuki *rancherias* on them, and the Indians on them often worked as servants and laborers in exchange for food and clothing (Miller 1979:47). Indians on the reservation sometimes worked too (Carranco and Beard 1981:60), though most pursued a traditional hunting and gathering lifestyle (Miller 1979:47). The Yuki who lived in the valley, especially those living on the ranches, were thus more intimate and interdependent with whites than those living in the mountains, so my theory would predict that they would be less frequent targets of genocide. And indeed killing expeditions were mostly directed toward Indians who lived in the mountains or in other locations outside the Round Valley.

Responses to offenses by Indians in the valley generally appear to have been treated less severely—with beatings or individual killings rather than genocide. For instance, the Eel River Rangers killed an Indian residing on a ranch because the man had previously deserted them (Shanon 1860:72). And when John Bland accused two reservation Indians of stealing articles of clothing, he abducted them in order to punish them (Dillon 1860:59). Later conflicts led to Bland's death at the hands of Indians, and the response to that killing also demonstrates the importance of social distance. In this case Jarboe and the Eel River Rangers attacked an Indian encampment outside the valley, where according to Jarboe they "killed eleven Buck Indians took six Bucks and twenty seven Squas prisners" (quoted in Miller 1979:69; see also Hildreth 1860:33). In addition, though, other settlers responded to the murder by taking a reservation Indian, cutting his throat, and shooting him (Carranco and Beard 1981:92; Garrett 1969:49; Miller 1979:69). So the offense that led to genocide against the more socially distant Indians in the mountains led only to a single revenge killing on the reservation.

CONTRADICTORY BEHAVIOR

One case of an expedition that was directed against Indians in the valley further demonstrates the importance of social closeness in that at least some of the Indians survived because of their employment with a local settler. This occurred on New Year's Day 1859 when a group of drunken ranchers spent the afternoon killing Indians. But when they arrived at the home of Isaac W. Shanon, they were turned away. Shanon described the incident as follows: "On the first of January . . . a party of citizens came to my house and said that they came to kill my Indians, because some Indians had been stealing; I told them that I wanted my Indians to work for me, and they must not hurt them.... They told me to pick out the Indians I wanted to work, and they intended to kill the remainder; they left my house without killing any" (Shanon 1860:73).

This was a case of contradictory behavior during genocide, where the same individual acts as a killer and a rescuer. Though Shanon rebuked the would-be killers this time and saved the Indians' lives, he had participated in killing expeditions on three previous occasions. In subsequent chapters we shall see behavior of this kind in other genocides, too. The occurrence of contradictory behavior challenges one of the fundamental assumptions of most studies of killers and rescuers: that killers and rescuers are very different kinds of people. But Shanon's behavior is what would be predicted by my theory of genocide. He killed those who were socially distant and rescued those who were socially close.

THE YANA

If we compare the Round Valley Genocide with the genocide of the Yana Indians in Butte County, we see that the role of social distance was similar in both cases. As did those in the Round Valley, settlers in Butte County targeted more distant Indians, and those with ties to Indians were most likely to aid them. As anthropologist Theodora Kroeber notes, though whites blamed Indians for thefts and murders, often without evidence, it was "never the close-by Indians, 'our' Indians: it was Indians at a distance, 'wild' Indians who had done the deed" (1961:50). They were especially likely to blame and target the Yahi, the most "wild" of the Yana's four branches. But when settlers did attack Indians who were close to whites, these whites objected and tried to help the Indians.

On one occasion expedition leaders Anderson and Good were unable to find any of the Yahi they were pursuing, so they went to Maidu territory and attacked a village there. The local whites "were much wrought up, for the Indians who had been killed were Maidu, 'tame' Indians, friends of the whites" (Kroeber 1961:67). Likewise, between August and December 1864, after the killing of two white women—and several kidnappings and killings prior to that—whites attacked the Yana without regard to their ties to other whites and despite the fact that many whites tried to protect them. Sometimes, Kroeber says, the killers "stole and ... literally tore children and half-grown girls from the arms of their white friends or employers, murdering them in view of anyone who was present except when enough men were at home and heavily enough armed to beat them off" (1961:76). In one case they killed three Yana men at work in a field while the rancher who employed them was gone. On this occasion the rancher's wife was able to save some of the Indians. When the men came inside looking for the Indians' wives, she put herself between them and the three Indian women. Later she and her husband helped the women escape to safety (Kroeber 1961:77).

INEQUALITY

Ethnic conflicts are more likely to lead to genocide when the adversaries are unequal—when the aggressors are higher in various forms of status than the targets. Although the Yuki outnumbered whites in the Round Valley area, they were vastly disadvantaged in terms of wealth and other resources. They were hunter-gatherers and fishers in contact with farmers and ranchers whose levels of wealth and technology far surpassed their own. When the settlers moved in, this inequality increased, as the Indians could no longer use the land they had previously used freely to obtain traditional food such as clover, roots, and acorns (California Legislature 1860:4). Many of the Indians, including many of those who came to live on the reservation, were reduced to hunger because the reservation did not have the resources to provide for them all or even to adequately compensate those who worked (Bourne 1860:20). When conflict came, the Indians' greater population was of little advantage to them. Indians could not own guns, and the Yuki had only bows and arrows to use on the few occasions when they fought back against whites (Madley 2004:178).[4]

UNEQUAL SUPPORT

Having supporters is an advantage in a conflict, and as is true of the targets of most genocides, Indians in the Round Valley area had fewer supporters than whites. When ranchers attributed the theft of their stock to the Indians, they received help from nearby whites, and later on from the state funded militia group. Indians received little help of any kind. The army might occasionally side with the Indians, but they did not stop the massacres. Nor did other Indians intervene to help those being attacked.

My theory predicts this pattern of unequal support, but what are the reasons for the pattern? Why did the ranchers but not the Indians have supporters? This we can begin to explain by using Donald Black's theory of partisanship. A partisan is a supporter, someone who takes a side in a conflict, and Black tells us that people tend to take the side of those who are socially close against those who are distant, and they tend to take the side of those who are high in status against those who are low in status (1998:125–43). In the Round Valley cattle ranchers were relatively high in status and socially close to other white settlers. They were culturally similar, and in a small area with few settlers they were well acquainted with one another. Some were related. For example, Superintendent Henley's four sons and his nephew lived in the valley (Miller 1979:46). The ranchers were also interdependent. Many were engaged with one another in business partnerships, and they sought to develop the valley for cattle ranching. So when a rancher suffered a loss, people were available to help. But because the Indians were low in status and distant from whites, even whites who were sympathetic to the Indians did not offer very strong support. For instance, some newspapers outside the region condemned the indiscriminate killings of Indians, but such support was weak. Outsiders did not actively join the conflict.[5] And though they outnumbered whites in the valley, groups of Indians failed to join together in part due to their social distance from one another. Some reservation Indians, for example, were from areas outside the valley. Subagent Storms had brought in a group of Nevada Indians who were loyal to him rather than to the Indians in the valley. But groups native to the valley were also distant from one another and had a history of warfare. The six subgroups of Yuki Indians thus did not attempt to form alliances among themselves against the settlers (Miller 1979:101). When they fought whites at all or resisted attacks, they did so as individuals or small communities (Bancroft 1963:477; Hurtado 1988:7).

KILLINGS OF WHITES

The presence of inequality helps explain why the Round Valley genocide occurred, but it also explains variation within the genocide.

The response to even the most serious offenses was not always the same. When Indians killed whites, for example, genocide usually followed, but not always. As my theory would predict, the settlers treated the killers of low-status whites less severely and the killers of high-status whites more severely.

Only a few killings of whites occurred, so we can examine each one. The first was in early 1857, and it seems not to have been avenged. In this case Indians killed two white frontier drifters and possibly two other men who went to search for the first two. Apparently they killed these the men in retaliation for their treatment of the Indians. Topographical officer A. G. Tassin noted that for one of the men "the provocation certainly justified the deed. His favorite amusement is said to have been shooting at the Indians at long range, and he usually brought down his game" (quoted in Carranco and Beard 1981:64; see also Miller 1979:50). In another case—which actually occurred in Sherwood Valley, about twenty miles southwest of the Round Valley—Indians killed a white man, Samuel Watts, who had killed an Indian apparently for no reason. In this case nearby settlers responded by killing a number of Indians and threatening to kill all of them (Carranco and Beard 1981:65; Tobin 1860:54).

In another incident—the only case where Indians in the area seem to have killed a white man who had not provoked them—they killed a man named William Mantel as he tried to swim his horse across the Eel River. A group of settlers from the Round Valley killed twelve to fourteen Indians in response (Carranco and Beard 1981:65–66; Miller 1979:50–51; Shanon 1860:72). In an 1858 incident Indians had supposedly committed a murder in nearby Sacramento Valley. Men from the valley formed a party and went to Eden Valley to attack a *rancheria*. On the way they stopped by the Round Valley and recruited more men to join them. In this case Simmon Storms, the subagent in charge of the Round Valley reservation, seems to have thwarted what would otherwise have been a genocidal massacre. Having learned of the expedition, Storms sent one of his employees along to try to prevent the massacre. Instead of attacking the *rancheria* as they had planned, the settlers demanded that four Indians accused of the killing be surrendered. The Indians handed these men over, and the settlers shot them immediately (Carranco and Beard 1981:67; Miller 1979:51).

The final case was the killing of John Bland. Like several of the other cases, it involved the killing of a white man in retaliation for his treatment of the Indians. Bland had captured an Indian girl and forced her to live with him. When members of the army came to arrest Bland for another offense, they took her away and placed her on the reservation for her protection. Bland quickly found out where she was staying, came to the house, and "took the squaw by the arms and pulled her out the door" (Dillon 1860:59). When she escaped again, this time to the mountains, Bland spent months harassing the Indians and searching for her. Eventually, while he was out searching for the girl, Indians captured him and burned him at the stake (Carranco and Beard 1981:92; Dillon 1860:59). After finding Bland's body, Jarboe led the Eel River Rangers against an Indian encampment, where, as mentioned earlier, they killed eleven Indians and took thirty-three captive.

It is no surprise that most of these killings led to additional violence. Men who engage in genocide in response to cattle theft are unlikely to ignore homicide. But they do seem to have ignored the first case, the 1857 killing of two whites, and one observer even described those killings as justified. What was different about it was that the victims were frontier drifters—low-status men viewed as "course and repulsive" by the other whites in the area (Miller 1979:50).[6]

THE ROUND VALLEY GENOCIDE AS A MATTER OF DEGREE

Any case of genocide can be more genocidal or less so. Many of the genocides of natives in Australia and North America were low on the intensiveness and scale of the mass killing, low in one-sidedness, and low in the degree to which the killing was ethnically based. These least extreme cases are protogenocides, and they are very different from the most extreme cases—hypergenocides such as the Holocaust. The Round Valley genocide is the first of our five cases of genocide, and it is the least extreme case, a protogenocide low in every dimension other than its one-sidedness—a variable on which it differed from other northern California genocides. But why was this case less genocidal than many others? It is largely because of the social geometry of the conflict; the same theory that explains the occurrence of genocide and various other aspects of it can also, with some elaboration, explain the degree of genocide.

INTENSIVENESS

The intensiveness of the Round Valley killings was very low overall, though certainly this was not always the case. H. L. Hall, for example, was reported to have said that he did not want anyone to hunt Indians with him if he "would not kill all he could find" (Scott 1860:22). And even when the settlers took prisoners, they sometimes later killed them, as we saw in the case at the beginning of the chapter, in which Hall's men ended up killing their captives (Hall 1860:42). Still, settlers often brought Indians to the reservation instead of killing them. This was the pattern elsewhere in California as well. As historian James Rawls notes, "the volunteers often aided in the work of concentrating Indians on reservations while at the same time they waged a 'war of extermination.' It was not uncommon for their operations to produce an equal number of Indian homicides and candidates for the reservations" (1984:178).

That some genocides are more intensive than others, more thorough, is likely due to a number of factors both social and physical. In some cases the physical aspects of the conflict may allow for alternatives to genocide or make them more difficult to pursue. If it is possible to separate the conflicting ethnic groups, the aggressors may expel the targets instead of killing them. But sometimes separation occurs alongside rather than instead of genocide, so it is related to intensiveness as well. In the Round Valley some Indians could be confined to the reservation, so when groups of settlers joined together to punish nearby Indians, they killed some and took others to the reservation.

SCALE

The scale of the killing in northern California was also low. Like the genocide of the Australian Aborigines and many other colonial genocides, the Round Valley genocide consisted of a series of unconnected or loosely connected genocidal events (compare Moses 2000:93). To some extent the scale of genocide is related to the extent of the settlers' organization. Genocidal aggressors are usually organized, nearly always more so than the targets, and the more organized they are, the more capable they are of operating over larger territories and longer time periods. In the Round Valley the killers were not very organized, especially at first, but they became more organized with the formation of a more permanent militia group, the Eel River Rangers, and then the scale increased somewhat.

But why did the degree of organization increase? Why did whites form the Eel River Rangers? By drawing from other sources, we can begin to answer this. First, according to historian Roberta Senechal de la Roche (1996:118), collective violence tends to be more organized when the continuity of deviant behavior is higher. Whenever deviant behavior is ongoing, those who have been dealing with it on a piecemeal basis are likely to want it dealt with more routinely. So one reason for the formation of the Eel River Rangers is that the thefts continued. Second, Black's theory of partisanship tells us that people are likely to support those who are high in status and those with whom they have social ties, so attempts to find more effective ways of dealing with wrongdoing may come about after offenses occur against very high-status, well-connected people.

This is what happened in the Round Valley. As the Indians kept killing cattle, the settlers pushed for the formation of a more permanent group to deal with them. Also, the conflict changed with the increasing involvement of an extremely high-status and well-connected rancher. The triggering event for the formation of the Eel River Rangers seems to have been the killing of a prized black stallion belonging to Serranus Hastings—a wealthy landowner and former chief justice of the California Supreme Court (Carranco and Beard 1981:83–84; Garrett 1969:60). An absentee landowner, Hastings had hired H. L. Hall to supervise his stock. Hall had previously organized genocidal parties in response to offenses against Hastings's stock, but with this new offense Hastings himself became involved. Along with Superintendent Henley and nine other settlers, he petitioned the governor of California—a personal friend—to raise a company of volunteers to deal with Indian theft and aggression. In letters sent after the petition, Hastings told the governor that the soldiers in the area were not adequate, as they "are friends of the Indians and appear to be engaged in a campaign against the American citizens settled in this country" (quoted in Carranco and Beard 1981:85). Eventually the governor authorized the formation of the group, and though he at times protested the indiscriminate killings they conducted, he allowed the Rangers to continue without interference until at least several hundred Indians had been killed. Then at the beginning of 1860, the governor disbanded the group and thanked them for doing "all that was anticipated," and "for the manner in which it [the campaign] was conducted" (quoted in Carranco and Beard 1981:97 and Miller 1979:73). Hastings's involvement altered the geometry of the conflict. With a higher status than the other aggrieved parties and with social ties to prominent citizens, he was in an ideal social location to attract stronger support. The aggressors thus became more organized, and the scale of the genocide increased.[7]

ETHNIC BASIS

The ethnic basis of the genocide in northern California was also low. All genocides involve killing on the basis of ethnicity, but ethnicity alone does not always determine the targets. In this case the killers often spared women and children by taking them to the nearby Indian reservation. To some extent this was the Rangers' official policy, as can be seen in one captain's orders to his men to "kill all the bucks they could find, and take the women and children prisoners" (Scott 1860:23). This aspect of genocide becomes more extreme when the ethnic groups involved become more polarized—as the social distance and inequality separating the two ethnic groups increases.[8] In the Round Valley some interethnic relationships involved closeness. Some of the Yuki Indians lived on the ranches or on the Round Valley's reservation, and many of these worked for the whites as servants and laborers (Carranco and Beard 1981:60; Miller 1979:47). And on the occasions when the killers spared the more distant Indians living in the mountains, they brought them to the reservation, where they would be physically and socially closer. Also, the status differences between the Indians and the settlers were not extreme on all dimensions, since the Indians outnumbered the settlers and since the settlers' degree of organization was low.

ONE-SIDEDNESS

Most of the killings in the Round Valley seem to have had a high degree of one-sidedness. Massacres almost always occurred in response to the killing of stock. Indians in the valley rarely attacked whites, and in the handful of cases where they did, the violence was usually limited to one death at a time (Carranco and Beard 1981:64–67, 92; Miller 1979:50–51). The one-sidedness of genocide is usually related to the degree of inequality between the adversaries, but in this case, it is not entirely clear why the Indians did not attack whites more often. It may be that the Yuki did not have any of the advantages some other natives had with respect to white settlers. Also they had conflicts with one another and were unable to organize except in small groups. When they finally did fight back, their attacks were ineffective (Miller 1979:72).

The high degree of one-sidedness in the Round Valley deviates from many of the genocides of California Indians, such as that of the Yana Indians. These killing expeditions, especially the most severe ones, were often a response to the killings of whites. And sometimes the Yana successfully resisted their attackers. In 1857, for example, a group of whites looking for Indians went directly into Yahi territory, where they were ambushed and forced to retreat (Kroeber 1961:60). On another occasion the Yahi were able to gain an advantage over their attackers, but only temporarily. A group of twelve whites had attacked a group of Indians and killed five or six of them. The others had begun to run, but eventually they gained a stronghold in the mountains, attacked the whites who were pursuing them, and killed two of them. In the two-day siege that followed, the white attackers killed eighteen more Indians (Kroeber 1961:58). The killing here was still one-sided in the sense that it was much greater in one direction than the other. One estimate, probably based on an undercount of killings by whites, is that one white person was killed for every thirty to fifty Indians (Kroeber 1961:46). Still, with significant violence from both sides, the degree of one-sidedness was low beyond the Round Valley. As is often the case, inequality was situational. When Indians had the advantage, they attacked, but whites had the advantage more often.[9]

To explain the degree of genocide in the Round Valley, we have had to elaborate and add to the theory by specifying connections between particular variables and particular features of genocide and by drawing from other theories to show how some of the explanatory variables might themselves be explained. The result, summed up in table 3, is a theory of the differences between cases of genocide. The next four chapters deal with genocides of increasing severity, and this theory

Table 3. Explaining the degree of genocide

DIMENSION	DEFINITION	THEORY
Intensiveness	Proportion of targets killed	Decreases with the separability of the adversaries
Scale	Time and territory over which killing operates	Increases with the organization of the aggressors
One-sidedness	Extent to which violence moves in only one direction	Increases with inequality between the aggressors and the targets
Ethnic basis	Extent to which killing is based on ethnicity alone	Increases with the polarization of the adversaries

can explain how these cases differ from the genocide in California and how they differ from one another.

This chapter has examined the genocide of Indians in California, particularly the killing of the Yuki Indians of the Round Valley. As we have seen, my theory of genocide explains numerous facts about the killing, including most aspects of its variation. Movements of social time—the cultural contact between the settlers and Indians, and the Indians' theft of cattle—led to conflicts between people who were socially distant, unequal, and unable to easily get away from one another. My theory explains why genocide occurred; why the killers targeted mountain-dwelling Indians more than those in the valley; why a white rancher and participant in the killing intervened to protect certain Indians; why offenses against some whites did not lead to genocide; why, compared to more extreme cases of genocide, the killing was limited in intensiveness and scale; why the scale increased somewhat over time; and why the killers so often spared Indian women and children. The theory can also explain other California genocides, such as the killing of the Yana in Butte County. The genocides in California were protogenocides, but in many ways they were like any other genocide. A small group of settlers attacking an Indian settlement after the killing of cattle differs from the Nazis' systematic killing of Jews throughout Europe, but to a family of Indians or a family of Jews threatened with annihilation, the experience may be much the same.

4 MUSLIMS AND HINDUS IN INDIA

In 2002, in a neighborhood in Ahmedabad, India, hundreds of Muslims took refuge in the home of a prominent Muslim politician, seeking protection from a crowd of thousands of Hindus. The Hindus set the house on fire and attacked those who tried to leave. Mehboob Mansoori, a 38-year-old Hindu who survived the attack, remained in hiding as he watched the attackers kill his family:

> Eighteen people from my family died. All the women died. My brother, my three sons, one girl, my wife's mother, they all died. My boys were aged ten, eight, and six. My girl was twelve years old. The bodies were piled up. I recognized them from parts of their clothes used for identification. They first cut them and then burned them. Other girls were raped, cut, and burned. First they took their jewelry, I was watching from upstairs. I saw it with my own eyes. If I had come outside, I would also have been killed. (quoted in Human Rights Watch 2002:18–19)

GENOCIDE IN GUJARAT

Ethnic conflict involving Hindus, Muslims, and Sikhs has been a recurring feature of Indian society since independence. The most severe episode occurred in 1947 and 1948, just after the partition of the state and the division of the Punjab between India and Pakistan. The partition left large minority populations in both countries, and it led to mass flight, forced expulsion, and rioting resulting in the deaths of hundreds of thousands or perhaps millions of Sikhs and Hindus on the Pakistani side and Muslims on the Indian side. Ethnic conflict in India has never again been this violent, but numerous "deadly ethnic riots" have occurred since the partition.[1] For instance, anti-Sikh ri-

Muslims and Hindus in India 73

ots following Indira Gandhi's assassination by her Sikh bodyguards in 1984 led to thousands of deaths. And from 1950 to 1995 hundreds of Hindu-Muslim riots resulted in a total of more than 7,000 deaths (Varshney 2002:95, 104–5).

This chapter discusses the anti-Muslim violence that occurred in early 2002 in the Indian state of Gujarat, particularly the violence in the city of Ahmedabad. This violence was more extreme than prior Hindu-Muslim riots, and a number of observers have argued that it was not a riot at all, but rather a pogrom (Ghassem-Fachandi 2006:140; Varshney 2004), an ethnic cleansing (Chenoy, Nagar, Bose, and Krishnan 2002; Dagli 2006:8–9), or a genocide (Brass 2004; Ghista 2006; Guzder 2002; People's Union for Democratic Rights 2002:7; "Genocide—Gujarat 2002" 2002).[2] Using the definition given here, this was a case of genocide—one-sided, ethnically based mass killing. This means it can be explained with my theory. We shall see here that the triggering event for the violence was the killing of Hindu activists, allegedly by Muslims. This event was a movement of social time, an instance of understratification similar to the thefts and other victimizations of whites by Indians that led to genocide in California. And it occurred in the right social context for genocide—where Hindus and Muslims were socially distant from one another and where Hindus were higher in status than Muslims. Like genocide in California it was the result of a particular kind of social change occurring in a particular social context, but the genocide here was more extreme for several reasons, including the fact that the aggressors here were much better organized.

"JAI SHRI RAM"

The Sangh Parivar is a family of organizations dedicated to Hindu nationalism, or *Hindutva* ("Hinduness"). It consists of the Rashtriya Swayamsevak Sangh (RSS); the Viswa Hindu Parishad (VHP), which was formed to cover the social aspects of RSS activities; the Bajrang Dal (BD), the militant youth wing of the VHP; and the Bharatiya Janata Party (BJP), the political party (Ghista 2006:20; Human Rights Watch 1999; 2002:39–40). One of the long-term goals of the Sangh Parivar—referred to hereafter as the Hindutva movement or Hindu nationalists—has been the rebuilding of a temple dedicated to the Hindu god

Ram. In the sixteenth century, the Hindu nationalists say, Muslims destroyed a Hindu temple built on the site of Ram's birthplace in Ayodhya and established the Babri mosque in its place. In 1992 nationalists destroyed the Babri mosque so the Ram temple could be rebuilt.

Ten years later, in early 2002, Hindutva volunteers began traveling to Ayodhya to aid in building the temple. One group of volunteers traveling aboard the Sabarmati Express clashed with the Muslims they encountered on stops along the way. At their stop at the Dahod railway station, they vandalized the wares of Muslim vendors, and at the Rudauli station they stabbed Muslims, pulled their beards, and forced them to shout "Jai Shri Ram" ("Praise Lord Ram"). This continued on the return from Ayodhya several days later. At each station the Hindus shouted slogans such as "Muslims, Quit India. Go to Pakistan" and "Ask for milk and we'll give you kheer (pudding), But ask for Kashmir and we'll cut you up" (quoted in Concerned Citizens Tribunal 2002b:12).

Shortly after 7:30 a.m. on February 27, the train stopped in Godhra. At the station the volunteers forced a Muslim tea vendor off the train, and they refused to pay several other Muslim vendors. They climbed on top of the train and made obscene gestures toward Muslim women residing nearby. Some of them tried to pull a seventeen-year-old Muslim girl onto the train but were unsuccessful. By the time the train departed, a large mob of perhaps 2,000 Muslims from the surrounding area had gathered, and they began to throw stones and possibly fire bombs at the train. Less than a kilometer from the railway station, the train stopped after someone pulled the emergency chain. Shortly afterward, Coach S-6 was on fire, and fifty-eight passengers died—most of them Hindutva volunteers. It is unclear exactly what happened—why the train stopped and exactly what and who caused the fire—though it is clear that the killings were not preplanned (Chenoy, Shukla, Subramanian, and Vanaik 2002; Concerned Citizens Tribunal 2002a:23–25; 2002b:12–16; Ghista 2006:8–14; "Genocide—Gujarat 2002" 2002; Human Rights Watch 2002:13–14; Jaffrelot 2011:377–378; Nussbaum 2007; People's Union for Democratic Rights 2002:5).

News of the massacre spread quickly, and so did disinformation and anti-Muslim propaganda. The vernacular press reported incendiary rumors—such as a report in the Gujarati daily *Sandesh* that Muslims had abducted, raped, mutilated, and killed Hindu women on the train (Chenoy, Shukla, Subramanian, and Vanaik 2002). Hindutva organizations published false reports—such as that Muslim passengers left the train before it arrived at Godhra, and that Muslim teachers and students were absent from Godhra schools on the day of the massacre (Concerned Citizens Tribunal 2002b:21). Hindu nationalists, the vernacular press, and state officials also repeatedly described the fifty-eight deaths on the train as acts of terrorism (Ghassem-Fachandi 2006:147–56). For instance, Narendra Modi, who was the chief minister of Gujarat and has since become prime minister of India, called the incident an "organized terrorist attack" and suggested that Pakistani agents had orchestrated it (Chenoy, Shukla, Subramanian, and Vanaik 2002; Ghista 2006:11; Human Rights Watch 2002:13).

Rumors and rhetoric drew attention to the killings and helped inspire outrage toward Muslims. So did other actions on the part of the state government and of the Hindu nationalists and their supporters. First, on the evening of the killings, the government had the bodies transferred to Ahmedabad, where large crowds gathered to receive the remains and to display them in a public procession. Second, Hindu nationalists called for a general strike—called a *bandh*—on February 28 to protest the killings. Subsequently this strike was endorsed Chief Minister Modi and by the BJP—the Hindu nationalist party and the ruling party in Gujarat (Chenoy, Shukla, Subramanian, and Vanaik 2002; Concerned Citizens Tribunal 2002b:18). Violence began on the day of the strike. Large crowds of Hindus, usually numbering in the thousands, forced Muslims to flee their homes; mutilated, raped, and killed many others; burned Muslim homes and businesses; and destroyed or looted Muslim property. Although estimates vary, it is likely that by the time the violence was over nearly 2,000 Muslims were dead (Chenoy, Nagar, Bose, and Krishnan 2002; Jaffrelot 2011:389; Sethi 2002).

"WHEREVER THERE ARE MUSLIMS, THERE IS A PROBLEM"

The violence in Gujarat was a response to the deaths of Hindus on board the Sabarmati Express. Hindutva leaders blamed the Muslim community and justified the violence as a reaction to those killings. Chief Minister Modi, for instance, told reporters that the violence resulted from "the natural and justified anger of the people" and declared that "every action has an equal and opposite reaction" (Human Rights Watch 2002:34). And Indian prime minister Atal Bihari Vajpayee, a member of the Hindu nationalist political party, declared to a meeting of the party's national council, "If the passengers of the Sabarmati express, innocent, unblameworthy, had not been deliberately burnt alive . . . [the violence] could have been avoided. But this did not happen. People were burnt alive" ("Genocide—Gujarat 2002" 2002).

But as with other genocides, the grievances were broader. Much of the preparation for the violence preceded the events in Godhra, so the violence was more than just a response to the deaths on the train. For years in fliers and speeches and at youth training camps, the Hindutva movement had depicted Muslims as an alien presence in a "country of Hindus" (Human Rights Watch 2002:43; see also Concerned Citizens Tribunal 2002b:57). Muslims had invaded India by force, compelled Hindus to convert, and destroyed sacred places such as the Ram temple (Concerned Citizens Tribunal 2002b:57). As politicians pandered for their votes, the argument went, they had become a privileged minority while Hindus had become second-rate citizens (Dagli 2006:23, 29). But despite their privilege, the nationalists said, Muslims were disloyal to the state and hostile to Hindus. The portrayal of the Godhra incident as Pakistani terrorism connected the local Muslims' alleged treachery to Islamic terrorism throughout the world. Similar charges appeared in other contexts. One Hindu nationalist pamphlet said that local Muslims had been armed by more than fifty Muslim nations and that they were ready to revolt when Pakistan attacks India (Concerned Citizens Tribunal 2002b:63; see also Dagli 2006:40). Likewise, one Hindutva leader said that Muslim schools served as factories manufacturing Islamic militants, and he compared the construction of the Babri mosque to the September 11, 2001, attack on the World Trade Center in New York. Both were "symbols of Islamic jihad" ("Genocide—Gujarat 2002" 2002).

Hindu nationalists also condemned Muslims for sexual relations with and marriage to Hindu women. One 1998 flier described Muslims as "trapping Hindu girls," and another portrayed them as "making Hindu girls elope" (Human Rights Watch 2002:43), while Hindutva volunteers learned that Muslims "spoil our Hindu daughters" (Concerned Citizens Tribunal 2002b:57).[3] And Hindus condemned Muslim cultural and religious practices such as polygyny and cow slaughter. The practice of polygyny, Hindu nationalists said, led to high birthrates, which in turn led to poverty and a Muslim population explosion in Gujarat and throughout India (Dagli 2006:30). Chief Minister Modi frequently would say of Muslims that "five of [them] produce 25 offspring" and "from five to 25 and from 25 to 625" (Dagli 2006:30).[4] Cow protection is one of the main aims of the Hindutva movement, and it was a priority for the nationalist government in Gujarat. In the first week of February 2002, Modi announced a drive against illegal slaughterhouses all over the state (Ghassem-Fachandi 2006:536). The Hindutva movement also opposed bull sacrifices performed in Muslim religious festivals. For example, just four days before the Godhra incident, activists tried to stop a sacrifice in the village of Tankaria. When the local Muslims resisted, the activists returned with the police, who attempted to arrest the Muslims for their supposedly illegal sacrifice.[5] The villagers again resisted, and the incident ended with one Muslim killed by police fire (Ghassem-Fachandi 2006:530–31).

Many Hindus described Muslims' treatment of women as misogynistic and otherwise offensive. At the training camps for the Hindutva youth movement, the young volunteers learned that Muslims "don't let their daughters out in public" and that while all the top heroes in Hindi films are Muslims, "there are no Muslim heroines" (Concerned Citizens Tribunal 2002b:57). The wearing of the burqa was also considered offensive—and even a threat to Hindu safety. Anthropologist Parvis Ghassem-Fachandi reports that many times while he lived in Ahmedabad, Hindus told him that during curfews—when police often allow only women to move about—Muslim women used the burqa to arm Muslim men by smuggling in guns, knives, and acid bulbs under their robes. Another belief was that Muslim criminals would disguise themselves as burqa-clad women to escape the police (2006:117).

Hindu nationalists ascribed to Muslims numerous other undesirable characteristics. Muslims were uneducated, poor, incompetent, ill-mannered, unemployed, backward, and burdensome to the rest of society (Dagli 2006:28–30). In addressing his party's national council, Prime Minister Vajpayee summed up the view of Hindu nationalists: "Wherever there are Muslims, there is a problem" (quoted in "Genocide—Gujarat 2002" 2002).

GENOCIDE IN AHMEDABAD

The Gujarat genocide was one way of dealing with the "problem" of Muslims. As a tract given out during the violence put it, "When there were kings, the Muslim kings forced Hindu brethren to convert and then committed atrocities against them. And this will continue to happen until the Muslims are exterminated" (quoted in Jaffrelot 2011:389). The genocide, which eventually spread to nineteen of Gujarat's twenty-four districts, began in Ahmedabad and Vadodara (People's Union for Democratic Rights 2002:1). The violence lasted until early May, but it was most severe during the first phase, from February 28 to March 5, in particular during the first three days (Concerned Citizens Tribunal 2002a:19, 193–94; Dagli 2006:2). Here we concentrate on the killing in Ahmedabad during the first phase of the violence.

GULBERG SOCIETY

On the morning of February 28, the day of the strike, a crowd of perhaps 25,000 gathered around the Chamanpura area of Ahmedabad.[6] From 7:30 a.m. until about 4:30 p.m., the Hindu crowd engaged in a siege of a Muslim housing development known as the Gulberg Society, where they destroyed property, raped women, and mutilated and killed people. By the end of the day approximately seventy Muslim residents were dead—forty-nine Gulberg Society residents and eighteen to twenty Muslims from other neighborhoods nearby.

The Gulberg Society was a small, enclosed middle-class compound consisting of eight buildings and fifty-five dwelling units. Its most prominent resident was Ehsan Jafri, a member of Parliament belonging to the Congress Party. As the attackers surrounded the area, and later as they burned houses and attacked residents in the compound, Muslims from the Gulberg Society and surrounding areas took refuge in Jafri's home. Attempting to ensure that the residents would be protected, Jafri requested that the police send in enough force to deal with the mob or aid them in leaving. At 10:30 the police commissioner visited Jafri and assured him that reinforcements would be coming soon and that Jafri and the others should not attempt to leave. Despite the commissioner's assurances and Jafri's repeated requests, however, the police did not arrive for another six hours, although the nearest police station was less than a kilometer away.

After the police commissioner left, shortly after 10:30, the crowd became more violent. They first burned a bakery and an autorickshaw just outside the Gulberg Society and then began attacking the compound from several directions. From one side Chunilal Prajapati, a worker for the Hindu nationalist party, led a group shouting, "Kill! Slaughter! See what they did in Godhra. They killed our Hindus so now kill them all, destroy their society" (Concerned Citizens Tribunal 2002a:29–30). From the rear a group of about 5,000, led by Jagrup Singh Rajput, a former deputy mayor of Ahmedabad and a nationalist party member, threw stones, acid bottles, and petrol bombs. From yet another side ex–Congress Party municipal councilor Meghsingh-Dubsingh led a group in throwing stones. Next, Hindus began throwing heavy stones from the terrace of an adjacent bungalow where they had gained access. This was the only Hindu residence in the Gulberg Society, and its owner, Dayaram Mochi, had turned his home over to the crowd and fled with his family—allowing for a direct frontal attack from within the colony. At the rear of the neighborhood, Hindus later managed to break down the gate, and the people in Jafri's house and elsewhere were left defenseless as the attackers assaulted anyone outside and bombarded the residences with burning tires, acid, and kerosene cloth balls. Those inside Jafri's house desperately tried to keep the house from burning. They removed carpets to keep them from catching fire and singed their hands as they threw back burning tires. They had no water because the attackers had emptied the water tanks.

As the attack continued, Jafri began making calls for help—including calls to the police commissioner, the home commissioner, and Chief Minister Modi. Receiving a callous response from Modi, Jafri began to lose hope, and at some point shortly after 2:00 the phone was disconnected. Jafri then began asking the attackers for forgiveness and asking them to allow the residents to leave without their belongings. The attackers responded, "You burnt our parents, our sisters, so we will not spare you" (Concerned Citizens Tribunal 2002a:29).

At 1:00 the attackers killed, cut up, and burned a neighborhood resident named Yusuf. At about 2:45 they did the same to Anwar, another resident. During this time they also seized Jafri, either after he gave himself up or after they dragged him out of the house. They stripped him, paraded him naked, and told him to say "Jai Shri Ram." When he refused, the attackers cut off his fingers and again paraded him around the neighborhood. Later they cut off his hands and feet, dragged him down the road, decapitated him, poured kerosene on his body, and threw his body into a fire. They also killed three of Jafri's brothers and two of his nephews, and they burned alive another man, Shafi Mohammed Munawar Sheikh.

At approximately 3:30, after Jafri's death, the attack on his home intensified. The attackers broke the windows and doors of the house, threw chemicals on the floor, and brought gas cylinders from the nearby abandoned homes to use as ammunition. Soon all but one room of the house was on fire, and many of those inside died of asphyxiation. The crowd robbed, mutilated, and burned anyone who tried to leave. Later they went into the house to find those who were still alive. Rosam Bibi, one of the refugees in Jafri's home, describes this: "I was on the ground floor. The mob came in and threw petrol and started a fire. There was heavy smoke. They told us to give them our jewelry. They took everything. Then they hit everyone and I got burned. Then they pulled people outside and cut them and burned them" (quoted in Human Rights Watch 2002:19).

It was during this time that Mehboob Mansoori watched the attackers kill his family. They attacked women and children—even babies—as well as men. One witness notes that "they pulled the babies out with the men, then poured petrol over them and burnt them" ("Genocide—Gujarat 2002" 2002). They even made a special effort to kill unborn children (Ghassem-Fachandi 2006:135). The husband of one pregnant woman describes her fate as follows: "Her house was attacked by a large mob. Her womb was cut open with a sharp weapon and the unborn baby was taken out and both mother and child were burnt dead" (quoted in Human Rights Watch 2002:19). The attackers also raped women before killing them—often after first promising the women safety to get them to come out of the house. And they mutilated these women's bodies—for example, by shoving iron rods into their vaginas and otherwise injuring their genitals (Ghassem-Fachandi 2006:135).

The killings continued until some time between 4:30 and 5:00 p.m., when the Rapid Action Force of the central government arrived. At this time most of the attackers fled, but those who remained began stoning the police. At about 5:15 the gas cylinders inside Jafri's house burst, killing the thirty to thirty-five women who remained. At 7:00 p.m. the police began escorting the survivors out of the area, and the attackers threw stones at the van that was transporting them. In response the police began firing into the crowd. This quickly dispersed them and prevented them from killing the remaining residents (Concerned Citizens Tribunal 2002a:29). Later on in the evening, the attackers played cricket with the skulls of the dead.

NARODA GAON AND NARODA PATIYA

The neighborhoods of Naroda Gaon and Naroda Patiya had a Muslim minority of about 1,000—many of them daily wage earners who had migrated from Karnataka and Maharashtra.[7] On the day of the strike, in one of the most severe massacres of the genocide, Hindus attacked the area's Muslims and burned and looted their homes.

The Hindu attackers consisted mostly of youths dressed in khaki shorts and saffron vests with black bandanas tied around their heads, but they were led by prominent members of the Hindutva organizations. They gathered shortly after 9:00 a.m. and began by destroying the local mosque, using gas cylinders, kerosene, petrol, and burning tires. In defense of the mosque, Muslim youths threw stones at the Hindus, and four of them were killed when they were fired on by the Special Reserve Police in the area. Between 10:00 and 10:30 the crowd destroyed the minaret of the mosque and began attacking nearby Muslims. They chased down several who fled for safety, doused them with petrol, and set them on fire. Some Muslims, though, made it to their homes and remained there until the afternoon. During this time dozens of Muslims called the police commissioner's mobile phone requesting that forces be sent in to stop the violence. After a few calls the phone was turned off, and there was no response.

A second wave of attacks began around 2:30 p.m., when the crowd—now numbering 5,000 to 10,000—surrounded the area and attacked residents with fuel and burning balls of cloth. During the attacks the leaders waved around copies of the newspaper and shouted that this is what Muslims did to Hindus at Godhra. When distressed Muslims called out "Allah! Allah!" the attackers responded, "No, say Jai Shri Ram!" (quoted in Concerned Citizens Tribunal 2002a:37). As in the earlier attacks, police officers refused to help those who asked for protection. "No, today we have orders from above that you are not to be saved," was the response one woman received after begging a police officer for help (quoted in Concerned Citizens Tribunal 2002a:37). Another Muslim, seeking shelter with the police, was told, "We won't allow you in today, today you have to die" (quoted in Concerned Citizens Tribunal 2002a:41). The police also helped the attackers find Muslims who were hiding, and they deliberately directed fleeing Muslims toward danger. Some police officers were more directly involved in the violence. For instance, police shot a man named Mohammed Hussain in the head as he tried to cross the road to get to his wife and children. When his wife then tried to reach him, the police beat her and her children with the butts of their rifles. As this was going on, the Hindus put kerosene and tires on the man's body and set it on fire.

For hours the crowd continued looting and burning Muslim homes and killing the residents. As in the Gulberg Society the violence went beyond mere killing. The attackers often quartered their victims or severed their limbs before burning them, and they stripped, paraded, raped, and mutilated many women before killing them. Eleven men raped a woman named Khairunissa and then burned her and her family alive. Kauser Bano, nine months pregnant, was also raped and burned, but first the attackers cut her open, impaled her unborn child on a sword, and then tossed the child onto the fire. The treatment of many more women and girls was similar, and some even threw themselves on the fire to avoid sexual abuse. The attackers also killed young children in exceptionally violent ways. For instance, they poured petrol into the mouth of a six-year-old boy and then blew him apart by throwing a match into his mouth.

Men, women, and children were all targets, and in many cases whole families were nearly or completely destroyed. One woman describes the attack on her family, which resulted in the deaths of eight of eleven family members:

The mob caught hold of my husband and hit him on his head twice with the sword. They threw petrol in his eyes and then burned him. My sister-in-law was stripped and raped. She had a three-month baby in her lap. They threw petrol on her and the child from her lap was thrown in the fire. My brother-in-law was hit in the head with the sword and he died on the spot. His six-year-old daughter was also hit with the sword and thrown in the fire. My mother-in-law had with her the grandson who was four years of age and he was burnt too. We were at that time hiding on the terrace of a building. . . . My mother-in-law told them to take away whatever money she had but to spare the children. They took away all the money and jewelry and burnt the children with petrol. (quoted in Human Rights Watch 2002:17)

In all, the killing, arson, and looting lasted for over seventeen hours. At least 150 and perhaps over 300 Muslims were killed, including at least eighty whose bodies were thrown into a well. The attacks ended at 2:30 a.m. when the remaining Muslims were rescued and taken away under police escort.

GOMTIPUR AND SUNDARAMNAGAR

On February 28, the same day as the attacks on the Gulberg Society and on Naroda Gaon and Naroda Patiya, several groups of Hindus numbering about 10,000 each launched a sustained, thirty-six-hour attack on Gomtipur and Sundaramnagar—areas of Ahmedabad known as Muslim ghettoes or strongholds.[8] As in the other areas the Hindus used gas cylinders and chemicals to destroy Muslims' homes and property, looted homes and businesses, indiscriminately killed Muslim men, women, and children, and raped women and girls. The police were involved to a larger extent than in Naroda Gaon and Naroda Patiya. They would tell the Hindus to attack Muslims and destroy their property, and then they would fire at the Muslims who resisted the attacks (Shani 2007:170). It was mostly police officers—rather than Hindutva leaders—who led the crowds, and many more of the deaths here seem to have been a result of police shootings.[9]

One of the most severe and sustained attacks occurred near the

Bapunagar locality in the area surrounding the madrassa, the Islamic school. The daily wage earners who lived nearby had taken refuge at the school, and from there they tried to resist the Hindu crowd. The police opened fire on the resisting Muslims, and the attackers sent numerous messages to the school to determine how many people were still alive. They used gas cylinders to cause explosions inside the buildings and a truck to break down the compound wall. The attackers then entered the school, where they drank alcohol and wrote slogans on the walls such as, "We will kill. Long live the Bajrang Dal, long live Narendra Modi," and "The inside story is, The police are with us in this" (quoted in Chenoy, Nagar, Bose, and Krishnan 2002; Concerned Citizens Tribunal 2002a:53–54). They then burned the buildings in the compound, along with scooters, bicycles, and autorickshaws. The remaining Muslims fled.

Gomtipur and Sundaramnagar continued to experience sporadic violence for months afterward, but the most extensive damage occurred on February 28 and March 1. The deaths numbered at least into the hundreds. One witness alone said he saw four hundred to five hundred badly burned corpses—including the bodies of about a hundred children.

OTHER ATTACKS

Severe violence—but not mass killing—occurred in other areas of Ahmedabad. On February 28 Hindus destroyed the seventeen Muslim-owned wholesale fruit businesses at the Naroda Fruit Market. They also attacked a nearby mosque, and before they reduced it to rubble, they tore up and defecated on the Koran, wrote "Jai Shri Ram" on the walls, and placed a photograph of a Hindu idol in the spot where the imam normally stands during religious services (Concerned Citizens Tribunal 2002:43; "Genocide—Gujarat 2002" 2002). Hindus also destroyed 225 shops and killed the two security workers on duty in the Kabadi Market (Concerned Citizens Tribunal 2002:43; "Genocide—Gujarat 2002" 2002).

In Vatwa, where about 30 percent of the population consisted of Muslims, most of whom were poor, the attacks were similar to those in other areas. Huge crowds led by Hindutva leaders burned down buildings, shouted anti-Muslim slogans, and attacked residents with guns, stones, fire, and bombs. The damage to property was as extensive as in other areas, but violence against persons in Vatwa was minimal—limited to about thirteen deaths and sixty injuries (Concerned Citizens Tribunal 2002:45–46). The same was true of the violence in Paldi, an affluent area where Hindus attacked six housing societies that were home to about a thousand Muslims. The attackers completely burned homes and buildings, and they injured many Muslims and forced others to flee, but they killed very few if any (Concerned Citizens Tribunal 2002:48–52).

SOCIAL TIME

These events illustrate the potential longevity of cultural conflict. Just as the crucifixion of Jesus still sometimes causes conflict between Jews and Christians, just as slavery still causes conflict between whites and African Americans, the sixteenth-century destruction of the Ram temple still causes conflict between Muslims and Hindus. This rejection of Hindu culture was an extreme cultural change—a movement of social time—and it affects the social world even today. The immediate causes of the Gujarat genocide, though, were the same as the causes of other genocides: overdiversity and understratification. Overdiversity, remember, occurs whenever two cultural groups come into contact with one another, as in the Round Valley, or when a society is ethnically divided, as was the case here. The Hindu nationalists objected to the very presence of Muslims; indeed, it was because of the Muslims' presence that Hindus over and over again were confronted with unwanted diversity in the form of cow slaughters, burqas, and other Muslim practices. But overdiversity seldom causes genocide by itself. In this case the trigger was the fifty-eight Hindu deaths on the train in Godhra. This was understratification—an event that reduced stratification, even if only slightly. It threatened the status of the dominant ethnic group, just as killings of whites by California Indians had done.

INSEPARABILITY

As previously noted, whatever the movement of social time, genocide is less likely when physical separation is an alternative. In this case any comprehensive expulsion of Muslims would not have been feasible. Neither the state government nor the local Hindutva organizations could have driven Muslims entirely out of Gujarat without the cooperation of neighboring states and the Indian government, or in an even less likely scenario, the government of Pakistan.

One type of physical separation can occur when the aggressors expel the would-be targets of genocide; another occurs when the targets flee. In the areas where the violence was most severe it was particularly difficult for Muslims to flee because Hindu attackers surrounded and trapped them. In the Gulberg Society Hindus surrounded all sides of the neighborhood and set fire to the home where the residents took refuge. They also surrounded Muslims in Naroda Gaon and Naroda Patiya, and one of the most severe incidents in Gomtipur and Sundaramnagar occurred when the crowd surrounded Muslims who had taken refuge in the Islamic school. On the other hand, in many of the places where the violence was less severe, it seems to have been for the simple reason that the attackers were unable to prevent Muslims from leaving. In Vatwa, for instance, the residents of many neighborhoods left for relief camps "out of sheer fright" as soon as the crowds gathered (Concerned Citizens Tribunal 2002a:46). The low number of deaths in Vatwa is no doubt due in part to this mass flight. Unsurprisingly, when it is physically possible for people to escape genocide, they usually do.

SOCIAL DISTANCE

Movements of social time in Gujarat—especially the killing of the Hindu volunteers—created intense ethnic conflict. And they did so in a situation where violence against Muslims was possible while many alternatives were not. But remember that according to my theory that is not enough. The conflict must have the right social location if genocide is to occur. Genocide is greater with social distance, and in Gujarat, as we would expect, Hindus and Muslims were socially distant. Ethnic riots in 1969, along with the success of the Hindutva movement, helped to kick-start a process of Muslim ghettoization and residential segregation that continued throughout the years prior to the 2002 violence (see Chenoy, Nagar, Bose, and Krishnan 2002; Concerned Citizens Tribunal 2002b:156–57; Nandy 2002; Parekh 2002; Sethi 2002). In Gujarat even well-off professionals typically lived in segregated areas, and people commonly referred to some Muslim areas of the state as "Pakistan" (Parekh 2002; Sethi 2002). Muslims and Hindus often went to different schools, and many elite and middle-class schools would not admit Muslim children (Concerned Citizens Tribunal 2002b:156–57; Sethi 2002). Muslims were also underrepresented in the police and civil service, and generally in political and civic life (Parekh 2002). And of course, because they had different religions, Muslims and Hindus participated in different religious observances and festivals.[10] Not only that, they worshiped different gods, practiced different rituals, dressed differently, ate different foods, and had different names. And although some members of the two communities cooperated economically, economic separation was common. In Modasa, Sabarkantha, for example, two cooperative banks—one Hindu and one Muslim—each served mainly Hindus or Muslims (People's Union for Democratic Rights 2002:29). Additionally, previous riots had contributed to a weakening of economic cooperation as rioters attacked Muslim business establishments (People's Union for Democratic Rights 2002:29).

GENOCIDAL CITIES

Social distance also explains why genocide would occur in Ahmedabad rather than in other areas of India. Generally ethnic violence has been uneven across India. Rioting has been almost entirely an urban phenomenon, and even most cities have had little violence. In fact just eight cities, one of which is Ahmedabad, accounted for almost half of all deaths from ethnic rioting between 1950 and 1995 (Varshney 2002:7). Political scientist Ashutosh Varshney explains this variation with the presence or absence of local networks of interethnic civic engagement. Where organizations such as political parties, voluntary social associations, business associations, and labor unions are both strong and ethnically integrated, they act as "institutionalized peace systems" that dispel rumors and take various other actions to prevent conflicts from becoming violent (Varshney 2002:11). But in cities lacking such organizations, conflicts quickly polarize and become violent. These integrated civic institutions reduce violence because they increase intimacy and interdependence among ethnic groups. In the cities of India, stable economic and relational ties between Hindus and Muslims do not form in the absence of such institutions. Interestingly, such organizations are not necessary to produce interethnic social ties in the rural areas, where there is more everyday, face-to-face engagement between Muslims and Hindus (Varshney 2002:10). So most ethnically based killing occurs neither in rural areas nor in most cities; rather, it occurs mainly in a few cities—such as Ahmedabad—where the social distance between ethnic groups is extreme.

In general the 2002 violence in Gujarat occurred in cities with little interethnic civil engagement, the same places less severe ethnic violence has occurred in the past. Ahmedabad, along with Vadodara and Godhra, the two other cities most prone to ethnic violence in the past, experienced severe violence in 2002.[11] In Surat, a historically peaceful city where Hindus and Muslims belong to integrated business associations, violence was minimal (Varshney 2004; see also Sethi 2002). One key difference from the past, though, is that the violence within Ahmedabad did not occur in the "traditional trouble spots" that were previously the sites of the most extensive rioting. Instead, most of the initial violence occurred beyond the city walls in places where Muslim residents were either vastly outnumbered or where they were migrants from outside the state (Ghassem-Fachandi 2006:122–23). Even more social distance and inequality separated Hindus and Muslims in these areas than in areas where violence had previously been more frequent.

NEIGHBORS AND OUTSIDERS

Social distance separated Hindus and Muslims generally in the areas where the violence happened, but even greater social distance separated the specific aggressors and targets. In each area where genocide occurred, the attackers were mostly outsiders—organized members of the Hindutva organizations who arrived in trucks and buses and had to rely on prepared lists to identify the homes and businesses belonging to Muslims. Many of them were not even from Gujarat, but were brought in from states such as Uttar Pradesh and Maharashtra (Ghista 2006:29). In some cases neighbors also participated in the attacks (Concerned Citizens Tribunal 2002b:31–32), but this seems not to have been the case to any large extent in the genocidal attacks in Ahmedabad, and everywhere the attackers seem to have overwhelmingly been outsiders.[12]

The Gulberg Society had only one Hindu family, the Mochis, from whose home the Hindu crowd was able to attack the compound. Though some have condemned Dayaram Mochi and his family as accomplices, the family maintains that the attackers forcibly took control of the residence. In any case, the Mochis were not participants in the killing. At most they allowed the attackers into their home before they themselves fled from the area. And although some Hindus lived in the Bhagwatinagar Society just opposite Gulberg, none of them participated in the violence (Concerned Citizens Tribunal 2002a:32). The violence in Naroda Gaon and Naroda Patiya likewise seems mainly to have been the work of outsiders—many from the nearby Gopinath and Gangotri housing societies (Concerned Citizens Tribunal 2002a:36; "Genocide—Gujarat 2002" 2002). Some local Hindus may even have left the area before the attacks began. One witness told of a Hindu family living in Naroda who she believed knew of the attacks beforehand because they left the previous night (Concerned Citizens Tribunal 2002a:41). In Gomtipur and Sundaramnagar, the pattern of social distance was especially notable. In these areas the police acted as crowd leaders and were generally more directly involved in the violence than elsewhere. And here the police were all distant outsiders: they came not from the Bapunagar station, which normally covers the area, but from Amraiwadi. The Bapunagar police, meanwhile, had gone to Amraiwadi. This has been described as a "deliberate attempt to ensure that people would not be able to recognize them as local policemen" (Concerned Citizens Tribunal 2002a:57). Whatever the intent, this meant the police were socially distant from the Muslims they killed.

ALTRUISM TOWARD MUSLIMS

In the previous chapter a case of contradictory behavior illustrated very clearly the importance of social distance between the aggressors in and the targets of genocide. A white settler in California acted as a killer of socially distant Indians on one occasion and as a rescuer of socially closer Indians on another. As that case suggests, the theory explains rescuing as well as killing, and it can do so even in cases where there is no contradictory behavior. Aiding the targets of genocide is the opposite of killing them, so if social distance explains genocide, social closeness explains rescue. Nearly everyone who has studied rescuers during the Holocaust has noticed that ties between particular Gentiles and Jews were important (Gushee 2003:134).[13] Social closeness has been important in rescues during other genocides, too, and it was important in the few cases in which Hindus helped Muslims during the Gujarat genocide.[14]

During the violence in the Gulberg Society, one Muslim woman caught by the mob was saved by a neighbor who claimed the woman was a Hindu servant held against her will (Ghassem-Fachandi 2006:130; Sharma 2004). Likewise Noor Mohammed Rasool Bhai Vora, a resident of Naroda Patiya, was aided by his Hindu landlord, who initially allowed the Muslim and his family to take refuge in a room in his own house. When a crowd demanded that he hand over the tenant, the landlord said he did not know where he was (People's Union for Democratic Rights 2002:25). Also, in Naroda Patiya the management and staff of the nearby state transport workshop helped their Muslim workers get out of the area. As one witness recounts, "At about 4 p.m., the ST management made arrangements for us to leave by bus. . . . Just as we came out of the ST workshop at Naroda, a 2,000 strong mob stopped the bus and asked 'Are there any Muslims inside?' The staff was supportive and said there were no Muslims" ("Genocide—Gujarat 2002" 2002). This is especially notable given that many Hindu workers from the workshop were involved in the violence, and workers there supplied the attackers with diesel fuel that they used to burn both people and property (Concerned Citizens Tribunal 2002a:38; "Genocide—Gujarat 2002" 2002). This may have been a case of contradictory behavior, if any of these same individuals also aided in the rescue.

INEQUALITY

Hindus were generally higher in status than Muslims. Muslims were a minority group, and they were vastly underrepresented in education and in the formal job market (Sethi 2002). Economic changes, such as the collapse of Ahmedabad's textile industry, had worsened their situation. As unemployment rose, many Muslim youths gravitated to illegal activities such as illicit distillation, drug pushing, protection rackets, and petty crime (Nandy 2002). Muslims were also underrepresented in the state government. Their representation in the Gujarat legislative assembly was never above four percent—a third of their proportion of the population—and they were underrepresented in the police force and the civil service (Parekh 2002; see also Dagli 2006:10). The rise of the BJP, the Hindutva political party, further decreased the role of Muslims in the Gujarati government: when the party gained power in 1998, the new government began to stack the ranks of government with Hindu nationalists and to systematically assign Muslim police officers to desk jobs and away from the field (Dagli 2006:22; Human Rights Watch 2002:41; Jaffrelot 2011:386).

UNEQUAL SUPPORT

Muslims also had few supporters. The military only belatedly attempted to curb the violence, for instance, and officials of the central government—with the Hindu nationalist party leading the governing coalition—often expressed support for the Gujarati government's handling of the attacks. On numerous occasions L. K. Advani, the deputy prime minister and home minister, praised Chief Minister Modi, even referring to him as "the best chief minister in 50 years" (quoted in Concerned Citizens Tribunal 2002b:51). And within Gujarat, the police were mainly inactive and often aided the attackers.

The importance of their support can be seen in the few instances where police did intervene on behalf of Muslims. In Kutch, Vivek Srivsatava early on ordered the arrests of the crowd leaders, including a Home Guard commandant and nationalist party member who attacked a Muslim woman. These actions effectively ended the violence, and Kutch remained mostly peaceful ("Genocide—Gujarat 2002" 2002). Likewise, in Bhavanagar, Rahul Sharma fired on a crowd of Hindus trying to set an Islamic school on fire and imprisoned the leaders—thus saving four hundred lives ("Genocide Gujarat" 2002).[15] Elsewhere, however, genocide proceeded in the absence of support for the targets. As sociologist and clinical psychologist Ashis Nandy puts it, the "entire state machinery, except for some courageous dissenters . . . turned against the minorities" (2002).

OUTNUMBERED TARGETS

One difference between the genocide in Gujarat and earlier ethnic rioting there was that the most severe violence occurred in areas where Hindus vastly outnumbered Muslims or where Muslims were migrants from outside the state. The attacks on migrants illustrate the role of social distance, while the attacks on outnumbered Muslims illustrate the role of inequality. In the case of the Gujarat genocide, inequality at the local level was greater than in prior episodes of violence, which occurred in areas with "sizable populations of both communities sharing space" (Ghassem-Fachandi 2006:123). Ghassem-Fachandi connects this difference to the fact that the violence this time was not "communal violence," in the sense of "groups clashing all over the city in fierce combat," but instead a "pogrom" (2006:124). Where it was more genocidal—more one-sided, for instance—it occurred under conditions of greater inequality.

THE GUJARAT GENOCIDE AS A MATTER OF DEGREE

The 2002 violence in Gujarat was more severe than most previous episodes of ethnic violence in India. Some of it was one-sided, ethnically based mass killing—genocide. It was also more severe than the genocides in California, even if the degree of genocide was still fairly low. This was an intermediate case of genocide—low in its intensiveness and one-sidedness, and to some extent its scale, but high in the extent to which the killing was based on ethnicity. In chapter 3 we saw that by adding to and elaborating my theory of the geometry of genocide, we can explain differences in each aspect of genocide. Genocides tend to be less intensive when some amount of separation is possible—when the targets can flee or when the aggressors can expel them. Genocides tend to be larger in scale when the aggressors are more organized. Genocides tend to more one-sided when the inequality between the aggressors and targets is greater. And the targeting tends to become more ethnically based when the groups involved become more polarized.

INTENSIVENESS AND ETHNIC BASIS

In this case the intensiveness, or the proportion of the targets killed, was especially low, but the extent to which the targets were chosen on the basis of ethnicity alone was very high. The intensiveness was low because expulsion and flight were much more common than killing. More than 200,000 Muslims were displaced from their homes as a result of the violence, compared to about 2,000 who were killed (Sharma 2004). Overall the separability of the groups was limited because it was not possible for Hindus to deport all Muslims from Gujarat. This was a factor that led to the genocide, but some separation was still possible because Hindus could expel many Muslims from their homes and because Muslims could flee their homes to avoid violence. So the attackers directed most of the violence at Muslim homes and Muslim-owned businesses rather than Muslims themselves. The killing that did occur, though, tended to be indiscriminate—based on ethnicity alone. When Hindus killed Muslims, they killed men, women, and children. This is associated with polarization, and ethnic relations here were highly polarized, meaning a high degree of social distance and inequality separated Hindus and Muslims.

SCALE

The scale of the killing, though fairly low, was much higher than in the genocidal expeditions in Australia and California. The killing occurred in places throughout Gujarat, most of it over a period of three days. Just as the scale was intermediate, so was the organization of the attackers, as we would expect. Those carrying out the violence were mostly part of a private, trained militia led by leaders of the Hindutva organizations. The leaders coordinated their operations using cell phones, and they selected targets using computer printouts of the locations of Muslim homes and businesses (Concerned Citizens Tribunal 2002b:29; Human Rights Watch 2002:23). The attackers themselves were well armed and well prepared for their tasks. Many carried gas cylinders, swords, or backpacks filled with chemicals for starting fires—all distributed well in advance of the violence. There was even a division of labor, where some militia members, for instance, would work only on loading guns (Concerned Citizens Tribunal 2002b:30).

The severe violence against persons and property—the arsons, the bombings, the killings, and the rapes—was carried out, then, mostly by well-organized Hindutva activists. Less organized crowds usually only looted (Concerned Citizens Tribunal 2002b:30).

The largest-scale genocides have been carried out by states, but here state involvement was too weak to have facilitated a genocide occurring over a larger area or over a larger time period. Nevertheless the state was more involved than in previous episodes of violence. This time, as political theorist Bhikhu Parekh notes, the Gujarati government "gave up all pretense of neutrality and openly encouraged Hindu violence" (2002). Several government ministers helped lead the attackers, and many more government officials helped plan the violence. At a meeting on the evening of February 27, for instance, two cabinet members met secretly with about fifty Hindu nationalist leaders at a home in Lunavada, where they made detailed plans concerning the manner and methods of the violence (Concerned Citizens Tribunal 2002b:76; "Genocide—Gujarat 2002" 2002). The high degree of state complicity was perhaps most important in that it ensured that police would not attempt to stop the violence. In many cases the police were more directly involved—either in killing Muslims themselves or in aiding the Hindu attackers—but even where this was not the case they mostly refused to intervene on behalf of Muslims. That this was a high-level policy decision has been demonstrated subsequently by the punitive transfers of the few police officers who did take action to stop the violence (Chenoy, Shukla, Subramanian, and Vanaik 2002).

Still, the democratic nature of the government limited its power, and political divisions prevented the aggressors from gaining much support beyond Gujarat. Though the Gujarat state government and the Hindutva movement had personal and organizational ties to members of the national government who often gave them expressions of support, representatives of the central government eventually did intervene to some degree to stop the violence (Pandit 2002). Two factors explain this. First, while national government officials' social closeness to the aggressors in Gujarat was conducive to support, their higher status was not. As Donald Black's theory of partisanship predicts, lower-status parties are more likely to support higher-status parties, not the other way around. Second, the BJP—the Hindu nationalist party—had not consolidated its power at the national level as it had in Gujarat. It had formed a coalition government (the National Democratic Alliance) that included twelve other parties, and it had ties with people both inside and outside of India who opposed the violence.

ONE-SIDEDNESS

The one-sidedness of the genocide in this case was low. It certainly was one-sided, but the killing was a response to what was thought to be—and may have been—the killing of Hindutva volunteers by Muslims. Hindus and Muslims in Gujarat also had a long history of violence, most of which was less one-sided than the Gujarat genocide. Also, in a democratic state where Muslims still had political rights and some support from outsiders, the inequality separating Hindus and Muslims was not extreme. Particularly in locations where Muslims were not vastly outnumbered, they could engage in some violence against Hindus.

The 2002 Gujarat genocide resulted from movements of social time—in particular the killing of Hindus on board the Sabarmati Express. As my theory predicts, this occurred in the context of social distance and inequality in a situation where the complete physical separation of the groups would have been difficult or impossible. The theory explains a number of other facts about the genocide too. It explains why genocide would occur in early-twenty-first-century Ahmedabad, a city where Hindus and Muslims were not civically engaged and where inequality between Hindus and Muslims was greater than it had been previously. It explains why the violence was more severe in certain areas of the city, such as where Muslims could not flee, where they were migrants, and where they were outnumbered. It explains why some Hindus who had ties to Muslims avoided the violence or even helped rescue Muslim neighbors or employees. And the theory of the degree of genocide explains why this case was greater in its scale and ethnic basis than the Round Valley genocide but lower in its intensiveness and one-sidedness.

This chapter confronts us again with the moralistic nature of violence that we view as evil. We read of entire families killed, men cut into pieces, women raped and mutilated, babies set on fire, unborn children ripped from wombs, and a six-year-old boy blown apart. At the same time we notice the complete moral confidence of the attackers. Waving the newspaper, they confronted their Muslim victims with what Muslims had allegedly done in Godhra. "You burnt our parents, our sisters," said others. The attackers were moved by "natural and justified anger," said Chief Minister Modi. It would not have happened if the "innocent, unblameworthy" passengers in Godhra "had not been deliberately burned alive," said India's prime minister. For the Hindu attackers and their supporters, the Godhra incident was the true atrocity. They—Hindus—were the ones who had been wronged, and their consciences were clear. As sociologist Randall Collins points out, "The more intense the feeling of our goodness, the easier it is to commit evil" (2012:5).

5 MUSLIMS AND SERBS IN BOSNIA

At a prison camp in Bosnia in 1992, Serbian guards ordered ten Muslim men to undress. One man refused. A guard put a gun to the man's neck, but he still refused. Two guards began using their knives to take off the man's clothes. By the time they finished, blood was everywhere, and the Muslim prisoner, screaming in pain, struggled to stand up:

> One guard took a water hose from a nearby hydrant and directed the strong jet at the poor prisoner. A mixture of blood and water flowed down his exhausted, gaunt, naked body as he bent down repeatedly, like a wounded Cyclops, raising his arms above his head, then lowering them toward the jet of water to fend it off; his cries were those of someone driven to insanity by pain. . . . The guards had cut off the man's sexual organ and half of his behind. . . . The poor man, after succumbing to torture, was taken to a garbage container, doused with gasoline, and burned. (Hukanovic 1996:35)

GENOCIDE IN BOSNIA

Following the breakup of Yugoslavia in the early 1990s, Serbs, Croats, and Bosnian Muslims engaged in various kinds of interethnic violence. In Bosnia-Herzegovina (hereafter, simply Bosnia) most of the violence was by Serbs against Bosnian Muslims (also called Bosniaks, or simply, as I refer to them hereafter, Muslims) and to a lesser extent against Croats.

This chapter focuses on the violence in the Prijedor district in northwest Bosnia from April to October 1992. We are looking at increasingly genocidal cases, and here we have a genocide where the killing was extreme in its scale. The scale was much greater than in the previous two cases, and it is the aggressors' much greater organization that accounts for this. As in the previous cases, my theory of the geometry of genocide also accounts for the occurrence of the genocide and for many of the patterns within it. In this case the movement of social time that triggered the genocide was the secession of Bosnia from Yugoslavia. This was a challenge to Serbian dominance occurring in a context of great inequality, as Yugoslavian Serbs together with their co-ethnics in Bosnia were vastly more powerful than Muslims. Not all Serbs were killers, though, and not all Muslims were killed; as the theory predicts, killing was greater with social distance. The theory thus explains not only the occurrence of killing in Bosnia, but also who killed whom and who rescued whom. This chapter examines all of this in detail, but first let us look at the general features of the genocide in Bosnia and the ethnic divisions that gave rise to it.

ETHNICITY IN BOSNIA

The ethnic history of Bosnia and the surrounding area is complicated. By the early seventh century, a population of Slavs lived in Bulgaria, Serbia, and probably Bosnia, and soon afterward two more distinct but closely related groups of Slavs arrived—the Croats and Serbs. These groups settled in areas corresponding roughly to modern-day Croatia and modern-day Serbia, and they likely intermingled with the larger Slav populations already there. Distinct groups known as Croats and Serbs were in the area since ancient times, then, but the ancient Serb and Croat populations do not necessarily correspond to the modern ethnic groups of the same name. This is especially true of the people now called Serbs and Croats in Bosnia, who probably descend mainly from the earlier Slav populations (Malcolm 1994:2–8).

In Bosnia it was only after the Turkish conquest in 1463 that the population began to diverge along lines that eventually led to separate ethnic identities. Prior to this time most Bosnians were either Catholic or adherents of the schismatic Bosnian Church. But under Turkish rule Bosnians began converting to Islam—and also to Orthodoxy as the area began to receive an influx of settlers from Orthodox lands. At least by the seventeenth century, the population was mostly Muslim, but with substantial numbers of Orthodox and Catholic Christians (Cigar 1995:14–15; Malcolm 1994:51–81). With Bosnian society divided along religious lines, the Christians eventually came to identify themselves with their co-religionists in Serbia and Croatia. The Orthodox became Serbs, while the Catholics became Croats. By the early twentieth century, Bosnia's Christians had ethnic identities that united them with people outside Bosnia but separated them from one another and from Muslims (Bringa 1995:28; Malcolm 1994:156–73).

The ethnic identity of Muslims was for some time more ambiguous. Muslims might sometimes identify as Croats or Serbs, but this was mostly arbitrary, since the division between Croats and Serbs was based entirely on religion (Malcolm 1994:200). Thus Bosnia's Muslims came to form another distinct ethnic group. This became official in 1971, when the Yugoslavian state for the first time recognized Muslims as a national group—alongside Serbs, Croats, Macedonians, Albanians, and others. But they differed from other national groups in that each of the others was connected with a particular territory. Though Muslims lived in Bosnia, their nationality was not Bosnian, and they shared the territory with Serbs and Croats. And unlike Bosnian Serbs and Croats they did not share an identity with larger national groups living outside Bosnia's borders. Muslim was a category referring only to Muslims in Bosnia. Bosnia's Muslims did not identify ethnically with Albanians, who were also Muslim by religion but whose nationality was Albanian (Malcolm 1994:198–200; Sells 1996:15).

ETHNIC CONFLICT IN BOSNIA

The conflict in Bosnia, then, involved three ethnic groups distinguished mainly on the basis of religious affiliation. The religious divisions were centuries old—the result of political developments, conversions, and in-migrations. Over time, as Bosnians came to identify ethnically as Croats, Serbs, and Muslims, they became involved in larger conflicts. For example, in the Serb-dominated Yugoslavian state established after World War I, Croats supported greater regionalism and Serbs supported greater centralism. Bosnian Croats and Serbs divided along ethnic lines, while Muslims sided with the Croats against Belgrade.[1] Ethnic conflict intensified following the Nazi invasion of Yugoslavia, when the Germans dismantled the Yugoslavian state and incorporated Bosnia into the new Independent State of Croatia (NDH). Now free from Serb domination, the Croats conducted genocide against the Serbs, Jews, and Gypsies within the new Croatian state. In some Bosnian towns they arrested Serbs, shot many of them en masse, and put others in concentration camps. In the largest of the concentration camps, at Jasenovac, the Croat regime killed between 70,000 and 100,000 Serbs, Jews, and Gypsies. Serbian villagers resisted the Croatian government, and in areas where they took control they executed Croats and Muslims as collaborators with the NDH. Serbs associated with the royalist Chetniks, members of one of the two main Serb-led resistance movements, attacked Muslim villages. During World War II, then, Bosnia was the site not only of civil war, but also of numerous genocidal massacres of Serbs, Croats, and Muslims. This would become an important component of the continuing interethnic conflict, as Serbs and Croats accused one another of collaboration and genocide and disputed each others' claims about the killings (Cigar 1995:18–19; Gutman 1993:xxi; Malcolm 1994:156–92).

Ethnic conflicts continued—though without violence—following World War II and the establishment of the Socialist Federal Republic of Yugoslavia, referred to here as "the federation." Disputes over how to share power continued—with Croats and other ethnic groups opposing what they saw as Serbian domination of the state, and Serbs opposing what they saw as unwarranted privileges given to other national groups (Cigar 1995:19–21; Gagnon 1994–1995:140–43). In the 1980s these conflicts became more pronounced with a resurgence of nationalism among Serbian intellectuals. In 1986 members of the Serbian Academy of Arts and Sciences drafted the *Serbian Memorandum,* which outlined a number of ethnic grievances. The Communist state, they argued, had thwarted Serbian nationalism while encouraging nationalism among other peoples. This had made it difficult for the government to function, especially since the Serbian provinces of Kosovo and Vojvodina had received autonomy, and it meant that Serbs outside of Serbia were persecuted. Overall the *Memorandum* claimed that Serbs possessed rights regardless of geographic or political boundaries, and it argued for a strengthening of federal institutions and popular sovereignty to secure these rights (Cigar 1995:23; Malcolm 1994:206–7; Mann 2005:364–65; Sells 1996:56). Others went further, advocating not only greater centralization and the protection of Serb minorities, but also the formation of a "Greater Serbia" to include all areas where Serb minorities lived (Gutman 1993:18; Mann 2005:365).

Soon after publication of the *Memorandum,* Slobodan Milosevic brought nationalism into the political mainstream as he and his supporters gained power within the Serbian League of Communists. Once he gained political power, Milosevic abolished the autonomy of Kosovo and Vojvodina and took various actions toward the nationalist goal—expressed in the *Memorandum*—of reforming the federation so it would be more centralized, more Serb dominated, and more protective of Serbian interests. But here the nationalists clashed with the other republics, which already resented Serbian influence and opposed greater centralization. Eventually the other republics began to withdraw from the federation—Croatia and Slovenia in June 1991 and Bosnia in March 1992. This left a rump Yugoslavia consisting of Serbia and Montenegro. It also left large populations of ethnic Serbs residing outside Yugoslavia. Slovenia, with few Serbs, left peacefully, but in both Croatia and Bosnia, secession led to warfare, ethnic cleansing, and genocide (Cigar 1995:24–33; Malcolm 1994:203–33; Mann 2005:370–72).

As conflict escalated, and even before secession, Serbs began designating majority-Serb areas within Bosnia and Croatia as autonomous regions. When Croatia seceded, Serbs in the autonomous regions in Croatia also proclaimed independence and formed the Serb Republic of Krajina. Yugoslavian forces, along with militia groups, then intervened on behalf of the Serbs in these areas. Much of the violence was conventional warfare, with clashes between Croatian and Yugoslavian forces. But some ethnic cleansing, carried out mainly by the irregular forces, helped to link together majority Serb areas by driving out the Croats living in between. By the time the fighting ceased in January 1992, 10,000 people had been killed, and Serbs controlled one-third of Croatian territory (Maass 1996:27; Malcolm 1994:226).

In Bosnia the pattern was similar. In May 1991 Bosnian Serbs declared three Serb Autonomous Regions. They also began arming local Serbs and provoking minor incidents of violence. When Bosnia declared independence in early 1992, the federal army and Serb paramilitaries moved in immediately. After just five or six weeks, Serbs controlled more than 60 percent of Bosnia, and by the end of 1992 the newly declared Republika Srpska covered 70 percent of what had been Bosnia (Judah 1997:239; Malcolm 1994:224–38).

By the end of 1992 Croats and Muslims were largely gone from Bosnian Serb territory. This was accomplished through mass killings, imprisonment, gang rapes of women, deportations, and the destruction of mosques and other cultural artifacts (Mann 2005:356–57). Genocide was thus only one component of the larger campaign of violence against Croats and Muslims, their property, and their symbols. Some of the killing occurred as part of several large-scale massacres. The largest of these was in Srebrenica, where in July 1995 Serb forces killed more than 7,000 Muslim men over a period of three days (Gendercide Watch 2002). There were also smaller massacres of villagers, fleeing refugees, and prisoners in the concentration camps. In all, 200,000 to 250,000 Bosnian Muslims were killed—more than 10 percent of their population (Gutman 1993:xxxi).

USTASHAS, ISLAMISTS, AND TRAITORS

Serbs were acting upon grievances against Muslims and Croats. Serb nationalists made charges of discrimination against and unfavorable treatment of Serbs in the Yugoslav federation. Most important were the secessions of Croatia and Bosnia, which were opposed by Croatian and Bosnian Serbs, who did not wish to be ruled by non-Serbs. Political leaders in Serbia also opposed the secessions unless the Serb minorities within those states were allowed to break away. Serbs argued that as a minority in these states they would be the targets of persecution and perhaps extermination (Maass 1996:27).

In the 1980s Serb nationalists had begun excavating pits containing the bones of those massacred by Croatian fascists—known as Ustashas—under the Nazi-allied Croatian state, and they often referred to all Croats as Ustashas. Serbs argued that Croats were genocidal by nature and were preparing for another genocide against Serbs (Pervanic 1999:xix–xx; Sells 1996:61–62, 75). They called Bosnian Muslims Ustashas as well, and they associated them with the earlier genocide. The Nazis had recruited Bosnian Muslims into two SS divisions—evidence, according to Serb nationalists, of Muslim collaboration during World War II (Sells 1996:62). Serb nationalists also called Muslims Turks and associated them with all of the alleged offenses of the Ottoman Empire against the Serbs. They believed that Bosnian independence would roll back everything Serbs had died for, and that Muslims would again rule over Serbs. Additionally, they called Bosnian Muslims fundamentalists. They said that Muslims would impose an Islamic state based on religious law and that they would take Serb women and put them in harems (Judah 1997:199; Malcolm 1994:217; Sells 1996:23, 41, 66–67, 118–19; Vulliamy 1994:48; Weiss 1997).

Serbs had broader grievances too. Bosnian Croats and Muslims, they believed, were the descendents of Serbs who had converted to Catholicism or Islam, thus betraying their race (Cigar 1995:25–26). This was especially the case with Bosnian Muslims, whose betrayal of Prince Lazar in 1389 was said to have brought about Islamic rule. The nationalist literature compared this act to Judas's betrayal of Christ, and Bosnian Muslims were thus Christ killers as well as race traitors. By converting to Islam they had destroyed Christian Bosnia (Cigar 1995:29; Sells 1996:31, 37). Others spoke of Muslims as having various other undesirable characteristics. The Serbian nationalist Dragos Kalajic, for instance, described them as lazy, prone to stealing, lacking ethics, and lusting for power but incapable of ruling themselves. He also said that they were alien. Bosnia's Muslims belonged not to Europe but to a "semi-Arabic subculture" (Cigar 1995:26–27; Sells 1996:83). Finally, Serbs charged Muslims with breeding like rabbits. Their high birthrates threatened Serbs and were part of a calculated strategy to obtain power (Cigar 1995:28; Judah 1997:199; Oberschall 2000:991; Sells 1996:22, 65; Vulliamy 1994:49; Weiss 1997).

"WE TRIED VERY HARD TO LIVE WITH THEM"

Political leaders, novelists, and others associated with Serbian nationalism articulated a number of grievances, and many of them were repeated at the local level by those involved in or close to the violence. For example, after Serbs attacked a village in the Prijedor region and detained its inhabitants, the Serbian guards asked their prisoners, "Did you have to vote for . . . independent Bosnia? Wouldn't it have been better for all of you to live together with us in the new Yugoslavia?" (quoted in Pervanic 1999:24). Likewise a regional police chief, when asked about a massacre of Muslims in Bosnia, said, "We tried very hard to live with them as human beings and brothers, but they thought they could create an Islamic state" (quoted in Battiata 1992). Those less involved in the violence also expressed grievances. A journalist asked one peasant Serbian woman why Muslims had been arrested in her village. "Because they were planning to take over the village," she replied. "They had already drawn up lists. The names of the Serb women had been split into harems for the Muslim men" (quoted in Maass 1996:113).

During the genocide continual anti-Muslim propaganda not only restated the broader grievances, but also accused Muslims of more specific offenses. For example, a document put out by Bosnian Serbian leaders, called "Lying [sic] Violent Hands on the Serbian Woman," alleged that Muslims and Croats in Bosnia were placing Serbs in detention camps, starving them, and separating out Serbian women for rape and impregnation (Gutman 1993:ix–x). Serbs in Bosnia also claimed to have found proof that Muslims were planning to circumcise Serbian boys, kill the men, and place the women in harems (Gutman 1993:113). In Prijedor Serbs claimed that Muslims were circulating a list called "The Silent Night," which had the names of Serbian leaders and community figures to be targeted by Muslims (Weiss 1997). And after the seizure of Prijedor, the radio announced that Muslims were trying to establish an Islamic state, that they would have annihilated the Serbs, and that a Croatian doctor was castrating Serbian infants and sterilizing Serbian women (Wesselingh and Vaulerin 2005:39). The Serb-controlled media also broadcast misinformation regarding the attacks. For instance, after Serbs had cleansed the unarmed village of Kevljani of its inhabitants, a Belgrade television station reported, "A few hundred Green Berets were captured in the Muslim village of Kevljani in north-western Bosnia, together with one thousand guns" (quoted in Pervanic 1999:34).

GENOCIDE IN PRIJEDOR

Prijedor—now part of the new Republika Srpska—was an administrative district in northwest Bosnia. The main town in the district was also named Prijedor, and there were two smaller towns, Kozarac and Ljubija, as well as about seventy villages and hamlets. Prior to 1992 approximately 112,000 persons lived in the district, and the population was 42.5 percent Serbian, 44 percent Muslim, and 5.6 percent

Croatian.² By 1993 only about 65,000 remained. Of these, 81.8 percent were Serbs, 9.3 percent were Muslims, and 4.8 percent were Croats. By 1995 hardly any Croats remained in Prijedor, and only 1 percent of the population was Muslim (Greve 1994:7, 14; Human Rights Watch 1997; Oberschall 2000:984; 2001:122; Wesselingh and Vaulerin 2005:35). These changes were almost entirely the result of the killings and expulsions of non-Serbs in the area, most of which occurred from April to October of 1992.

Prijedor was not one of the declared autonomous regions and thus was not part of the independent Serb republic declared by Bosnia's Serbs in April 1992. Bosnian Serb leaders considered it to be strategically important, though, in establishing a corridor between Serbia proper and the Croatian Krajina, which was at that time controlled by rebel Serbs. But with Muslims in Prijedor slightly outnumbering Serbs, and with Serbs in the district politically divided,³ Serbs were unable to hold onto political power. Elections in 1990 gave the majority of seats in the Prijedor Assembly to the SDA (the main Muslim party), making it the only part of Bosnia's Krajina region not under the control of the SDS (the main Serbian party). In response to the elections, the SDS walked out of the assembly and organized a "Crisis Committee" to act as a parallel government for Serbs. They also set up a parallel police force and with outside help began arming the local Serbian population. Then, on the night of April 29–30, 1992, claiming an imminent Muslim takeover, Serbs took control of the city of Prijedor (Battiata 1992; Greve 1994:13–19; Human Rights Watch 1997; Judah 1997:199; Oberschall 2000:985; 2001:122–23; Wesselingh and Vaulerin 2005:37–38).

After the coup, the Serbian party took control of the local radio and newspaper, set up roadblocks, limited travel, introduced a nightly curfew, required non-Serbs to turn in their weapons, and dismissed most non-Serbs from their jobs. They required non-Serb policemen to sign a pledge to abide by Serbian law. Few did so, and non-Serbs were soon removed from the police force (Greve 1994:44–48; ICTY 1998; 2002). Additionally, mass violence began shortly after the coup, as Serbs started shelling Muslim areas and rounding up or killing the inhabitants.

HAMBARINE

On May 22, 1992, four members of a Serbian paramilitary unit forced a Croat to drive them to the Hambarine area. On a road held by Muslims they were stopped at a checkpoint and asked to give up their weapons. One of the Serbs opened fire and killed the checkpoint commander. The other Muslims returned fire and killed two of the Serbs and wounded the other two. Following this the Crisis Committee issued an ultimatum to Hambarine's leaders. They were to turn over a former policeman—a Muslim who lived near the checkpoint—and all the inhabitants were to surrender their weapons. When these demands were not met, Serbs began shelling Hambarine with artillery. Tanks, infantry, and paramilitary units then followed, and the Serbs looted homes and detained or killed the inhabitants. They also set a number of houses on fire, destroyed the mosque, and continued pillaging the area for two weeks. Many of the villagers fled to nearby areas when the shelling began, and some of these later came under artillery fire when they tried to return. This was the first mass killing in the district. Five hundred persons were killed, and many others were rounded up and taken to the camps (Greve 1994:49–50; Pervanic 1999:11–12; Wesselingh and Vaulerin 2005:42–43).

KOZARAC

Kozarac was a heavily Muslim area east of the town of Prijedor. After the takeover in Prijedor, Serbs began collecting weapons from Kozarac's inhabitants, and on May 9 Serbian authorities gave Kozarac's leaders seven days to sign an oath of loyalty to the Bosnian Serb republic. On May 14 Serbs disconnected the town's telephone lines, and the Serbian army surrounded the area. On May 24 the army began shelling the town with heavy artillery, tanks, grenades, and firearms. A few hours later they stopped the shelling and announced that no one would be harmed if they surrendered. Then, as the people filled the streets, the Serbs resumed their attack. The shelling continued the next day, and at this time Serbs killed thousands as they attacked convoys of cars attempting to leave as well as crowds of people waving white flags in an attempt to surrender. Next Serbian tanks and infantry moved in, along with paramilitaries and local armed Serbs, and they went from house to house rounding up men, women, and children. Using lists of names, they selected prominent citizens—politicians, judges, police officers, and other influential people—to be brought forward and killed immediately. They herded the other Muslims into columns and took most of them to the camps, though they selected some for roadside executions and killed others by throwing grenades into the columns. Altogether the Serbs killed at least 2,500 and perhaps as many as 5,000 of the 27,000 non-Serb inhabitants of the Kozarac area, and the rest they expelled from their homes. Afterward they pillaged the town and destroyed those homes that had not caught fire in the previous attacks. Less organized looting and killing continued for weeks in the surrounding villages (Battiata 1992; Greve 1994:50–54; Hukanovic 1996:88; ICTY 1995; Maass 1996:38–39; Pervanic 1999:44–45; Weiss 1997; Wesselingh and Vaulerin 2005:43).

THE TOWN OF PRIJEDOR

On May 30 a small group of poorly armed Muslims and Croats who had been hiding on Kurevo Mountain attempted to retake the town of Prijedor. They received no support from the people of Prijedor, and the Serbs quickly defeated them. The Serbs then began an attack on Stari Grad—the old part of the town, where many Muslims lived. As in other areas they first shelled the homes and mosques and then rounded up the inhabitants, separated the men from the women, and transported them to camps. Later they attacked other areas of Prijedor in the same way. In many of these areas, once they killed or expelled the inhabitants they leveled the buildings (Greve 1994:54–58; ICTY 2002; Wesselingh and Vaulerin 2005:43).

VILLAGES ON THE LEFT BANK OF THE SANA RIVER

On July 20 Serbs began attacking an area of villages located on the left bank of the Sana River, where about 20,000 Muslims and Croats lived. The attacks here were similar to those in Kozarac and Hambarine, except that they involved little artillery. As elsewhere, Serbian soldiers, paramilitary fighters, police, and armed locals went from house to house beating, killing, and rounding up non-Serbs for deportation. Sometimes they later killed those initially chosen for deportation. For example, when the camps did not have room for a bus full of male prisoners, Serbian soldiers ordered them out and shot them dead. By the end of the first day, the attackers had killed more than 1,500 persons (Greve 1994:58–60).

Many of the attacks in the following days also involved large massacres. In the village of Biscani, Serb forces gunned down at least 150 persons at close range, and the attack against the village of Carakovo resulted in more than 760 deaths. Serbs surrounded the area early in the morning of July 23, then attacked from all directions with bombs, grenades, and machine guns. The Serbs killed hundreds this way, but they also sought out specific persons and families. For example, they killed everyone with a particular surname—one hundred persons in all—because they believed it was the name of the Muslim party's local leader. In Carakovo and elsewhere they also engaged in predatory behavior. They raped fifty women from the settlement Donja Mahala. And as in the other areas, once they removed the inhabitants, they pillaged the property and destroyed many of the buildings (Greve 1994:58–63; Gutman 1993:62).

THE OMARSKA CAMP

After the attacks on the towns and villages, Serbs continued to kill, deport, and detain Muslims and Croats in smaller-scale operations. Torture, gang rapes, and mass killings continued at Prijedor's three concentration camps, located at Omarska, Keraterm, and Trnopolje. The prisoners at Omarska were mainly intellectuals, political leaders, and other elites. Keraterm housed other non-Serb men, and Trnopolje housed mainly women, children, and elderly men (Greve 1994:66; Human Rights Watch 1997; Wesselingh and Vaulerin 2005:44).

The camp at Omarska held several thousand men at any given time and perhaps as many as 13,000 altogether.[4] Of these, perhaps 4,000 or 5,000 died as a result of mass executions, individual torture and beatings, or the general living conditions (Gutman 1993:xiv, 145; see also Greve 1994:68–69). At the camp the guards crowded the prisoners together into rooms without beds and kept them in unsanitary conditions without medical care. Infectious diseases, dysentery, and lice were common, and the prisoners suffered severe weight loss due to their meager diets. Once a day the guards took them to the canteen and gave them only two or three minutes to eat their only meal—usually consisting of cabbage leaves, a few beans, and a piece of bread. On the way to and from the canteen, guards would pour water or wax on the floor to make it slippery, and when a prisoner would fall they would beat him with whips made of electrical cable (Greve 1994:71–73; Hukanovic 1996:27, 71–72; ICTY 2001b; Wesselingh and Vaulerin 2005:51–52). The conditions for some prisoners were even worse. For example, 160 men from Kozarac were packed into a garage so tight that they had to sleep standing up. Except for the occasions when the guards would throw in a plastic container full of water and let the men struggle with one another to get a few drops, the men had no water, and they began drinking one another's urine (Hukanovic 1996:29–32). Other prisoners had to stay outside and lie face down all day long (Gutman 1993:90).

Each day the guards would call out men for torture and interrogations. At first they chose prisoners from lists of "extremists" or "fighters," but later the selections were random. The guards took the men to either the "White House" for torture and interrogation or the "Red House" for certain death. At the White House, under the supervision of inspectors from the Prijedor police station, the guards beat the prisoners with shoes, brass knuckles, baseball bats, rifle butts, rubber hoses, and iron rods, and they coerced the prisoners into making confessions—usually that they had carried out attacks on Prijedor, owned firearms, or were part of a plan to liquidate Serbs (Greve 1994:74–75; Gutman 1993:90; Hukanovic 1996:28; Maass 1996:51; Pervanic 1999:127; Wesselingh and Vaulerin 2005:52–53). These interrogations normally resulted in death—usually after severe torture and even mutilation, such as in the case described at the beginning of the chapter, in which guards cut off a man's penis before dousing him with gasoline and setting him on fire. In another incident the guards tied a wire around a Muslim man's testicles, attached the other end to a motorcycle, and then sped off (Maass 1996:50). In another they forced two men to have sex with one another, then castrated them, hung them from a crane, and beat them until they died (Vulliamy 1994:108). In other incidents they forced prisoners to bite off the testicles of other prisoners (Greve 1994:77).

The interrogations at Omarska normally resulted in the deaths of about five to ten men each day (Gutman 1993:92). The guards also engaged in more sporadic killings, such as on one occasion when a guard suddenly fired a machine gun into the garage where the men from Kozarac were held (Hukanovic 1996:32). On another occasion when a group of prisoners were confined to the canteen, the guards ordered a man who stood up and protested to sit down, and when he refused, they shot him with a rifle (ICTY 2001b). Additionally, the camp administrators allowed local Serbs and members of paramilitaries to enter the camps to insult, beat, and kill the prisoners (Greve 1994:76; Maass 1996:52–53; Pervanic 1999:80; Wesselingh and Vaulerin 2005:52).

Starting in late July the authorities began conducting mass executions by firearms, resulting in approximately one thousand deaths over a ten-day period (Pervanic 1999:162–63). Shortly thereafter, on August 6, the camp effectively closed (Greve 1994:70).

THE KERATERM CAMP

Like Omarska, the camp at Keraterm held non-Serb men mainly from the Prijedor area. These tended to be men of lower status than those held at Omarska, but not in every case, as assignment to one camp or another often depended on where room was available. Holding 1,000 to 1,500 men at a given time, Keraterm Camp was also much smaller than Omarska. Otherwise the two camps were similar. Prisoners at Keraterm lived in crowded and unsanitary conditions and received very little to eat. The camp guards beat the prisoners, and professionals from outside the camp conducted tortuous and usually lethal interrogation sessions with the guards' assistance. People from outside the camp abused and killed the prisoners too. These were people such as soldiers back from the front and members of paramilitary groups, who were able to enter the camp and do what they liked (Greve 1994:81–85; Wesselingh and Vaulerin 2005:61). The interrogations, as well as the less organized acts of violence, resulted in at least two or three deaths each day, but two massacres were much larger. The largest of these occurred on July 24 after 250 newly arrived prisoners were locked into a storage space known as Room Three without food, water, or fresh air. When some of the prisoners tried to force their way out, guards began firing machine guns into the room. By the next morning

100 to 150 of the men had been killed (ICTY 2001a; Greve 1994:84–85; Vulliamy 1994:111–112; Wesselingh and Vaulerin 2005:61–62). Another massacre occurred on July 26 when about fifty prisoners were killed with submachine-gun fire (Wesselingh and Vaulerin 2005:62). Along with Omarska, Keraterm Camp closed in early August (Greve 1994:83).

THE TRNOPOLJE CAMP

The camp at Trnopolje, which held between 4,000 and 7,000 prisoners at a given time, was for the most part a detention facility for women, children, and elderly non-Serbs prior to deportation. No formal interrogations took place here, and killing was much less frequent than in the other camps. The living conditions were also better—less cramped and with fewer sanitation problems, mainly because of the higher turnover rate. But guards and outsiders still beat, raped, and killed prisoners. On one occasion Serbs killed five boys who had been ordered to load some timber. On another they bound a group of inmates, forced them to lie down on the ground, drove tractors over their legs, and then shot those still alive. Groups of soldiers would enter the camp at night to rape women. On June 6, for instance, a group of Serbian tank drivers entered the camp, took thirty to forty female prisoners, raped them, then returned them to the camp (Greve 1994:86–89; Wesselingh and Vaulerin 2005:56–58). In another incident guards stopped a group of women and girls when they attempted to return to the prison after a trip to get water from a well. They took six of the girls and four other female detainees to the yard of a nearby house, where a group of thirty Serbian soldiers had gathered. The soldiers then raped the girls after first forcing them to strip and parade in a circle (Maass 1996:53–54).

When the camps at Omarska and Keraterm closed in early August, many of the prisoners were taken to Trnopolje. Once they arrived, Serbs often beat them and interrogated them, but after this conditions in the camp improved somewhat. By late August most of the prisoners from the Prijedor area who still had homes were released, though many later returned after being registered for deportation. Some even bribed guards to allow them to enter the camp so that they could receive safe transportation outside of Prijedor. In October, with all the detainees released or deported, the camp closed (Greve 1994:89; Wesselingh and Vaulerin 2005:57–58).

SOCIAL TIME

Social time, remember, is a concept developed by sociologist Donald Black (2011). It refers to social changes—in diversity, stratification, and intimacy—and these changes cause conflict. Something has to happen—something has to change—to get a conflict going. For conflicts that lead to genocide, normally two movements of social time have to occur. The first is overdiversity—that is, an increase in diversity. An increase in ethnic diversity occurs when ethnic groups live alongside one another and constantly increase the diversity in their lives through intercultural contacts. It also occurs when ethnic groups come into contact for the first time. The second kind of social change that normally must happen before genocide will occur is understratification, a decrease in stratification. This occurs when a subordinate ethnic group rises or attempts to rise, or when a dominant ethnic group falls or is in danger of falling.

Multiple movements of social time often precede genocide. These lead to multiple ethnic conflicts, some of them centuries old. But something triggers particular cases of genocide; even when conflicts are old, something intensifies them. In the Round Valley of California the cause of the genocide was the overdiversity that occurred when whites and Indians came into contact and the understratification that occurred with the Indians' destruction and theft of whites' livestock. In Gujarat the conflict between Hindus and Muslims was much older. Multiple movements of social time, going far back, caused the genocide, but the immediate cause was again overdiversity, this time of the kind that comes simply from living in a multiethnic society, and understratification, which occurred with the deaths of Hindu volunteers—deaths attributed to Muslim attackers.

As in the Gujarat genocide, some of the conflict leading to the Bosnian genocide resulted from movements of social time in the distant past, such as the rejection of Christianity by the ancestors of Bosnian Muslims. Others were decades rather than centuries old—the massacres of Serbs during World War II, for example. But again the immediate causes were overdiversity and understratification: Bosnia was an ethnically divided society, and Muslims were increasing their status. Bosnia's secession from Yugoslavia in 1992 would have given Bosnia's Muslims political power over less numerous Serbs and Croats. Serbs were the dominant ethnic group in the Yugoslav Federation, and the Serbs in Bosnia refused to become subordinate in an independent, Muslim-led Bosnia.

INSEPARABILITY

The secession caused conflict, but one of the reasons the conflict led to genocide was the lack of other alternatives. In the other republics political separation worked to reduce conflict by severing ties between the parties. This was true of Slovenia, and it was even true to some extent of Croatia, where the Serbs' main objection to secession had to do with Croatian control over Serbs in one part of the republic. But unlike in Slovenia, where 88 percent of the population was Slovene, or Croatia, where 78 percent of the population was Croat, no ethnic group in Bosnia had a majority. Bosnia was thus the only republic that could not conceivably be organized as a predominantly monoethnic nation-state (Mann 2005:363). The political breakup of Yugoslavia did not separate Bosnia's three ethnic groups from one another, and neither could a simple breakup of Bosnia. Any division of Bosnia would have left large ethnic minorities in each area (Mann 2005:366). Separating the ethnic groups without violence would have been difficult or impossible.

SOCIAL DISTANCE

The first part of my theory—the idea that genocidal conflicts result from overdiversity and understratification—is well supported in this case. In a society with ethnic divisions, members of a subordinate ethnic group attempted to increase their status, in this case through secession. We have seen that this occurred in a context where many ways of separating the adversaries were impossible or extremely difficult to achieve. This is important to pay attention to because the kinds of conflicts that lead to genocide may be handled in other ways when possible. But what about the second element of my theory? Remember that even though movements of social time cause conflict, a conflict's location and direction in social space help determine how the conflict will be handled. Did the Bosnian genocide occur in the social location predicted by the theory—one characterized by social distance and inequality? With regard to social distance it might seem at first that the evidence is not supportive. Indeed some observers of the genocide in Bosnia have emphasized the social closeness of the killers and victims. They call the conflict an "intimate war" or say that it occurred in a climate of "monstrous intimacy" (Maass 1996:149; Wesselingh and Vaulerin 2005:77). But Bosnia's ethnic groups were in fact socially distant.

Ethnicity was important in the organization of the Yugoslavian state, and its importance to civil society had increased during the 1990 elections, when political parties divided almost entirely along ethnic lines. In the past people had belonged to multiethnic social organizations such as Communist youth leagues, trade unions, and professional associations, while ethnic organizations coordinated cultural activities but kept out of politics. But in the 1980s the multiethnic organizations began to decline in importance, and the monoethnic cultural organizations began to act as mobilizers for ethnically based political parties (Mann 2005:375). Combined with government control over the economy, the ethnically based and decentralized political system also ensured that the groups were involved in zero-sum economic conflicts. Privatization only increased this, since it was often those with political connections who received state-owned assets (Mann 2005:364; see also Malcolm 1994:203). Ethnic competition rather than cooperation characterized both the political and the economic spheres.

According to some scholars, Yugoslavia, and especially Bosnia, had high intermarriage rates (see Maass 1996:11, 205; Malcolm 1994:222). But in fact they were relatively low in Yugoslavia and even lower in Bosnia. Demographer Nikolai Botev found that in Yugoslavia as a whole, only 12 to 14 percent of all marriages and only 8.6 percent of intact marriages were mixed (Botev 1994:468). In Bosnia Croats and Serbs were even less likely to marry outside their group than they were elsewhere. Muslims in Bosnia were somewhat more likely to intermarry than in most of the other republics, but their rate of intermarriage was still low (Botev 1994:474–75). While often cited to demonstrate social closeness, the intermarriage rates in Bosnia actually indicate a high degree of distance between Muslims, Croats, and Serbs in Bosnia and elsewhere. As Botev notes, "Although geopolitically the East and the West meet in what used to be Yugoslavia, they were rarely meeting in front of the marriage altar" (1994:477).[5]

Discussions of intermarriage in Yugoslavia tend to overemphasize what was uncommon overall. Intermarriage rates varied, though, and this variation explains variation in genocide. In Bosnian cities relations among the ethnic groups were generally closer than in the countryside, and intermarriage was higher (Malcolm 1994:222; Mann 2005:366). A key aspect of the cosmopolitan societies of the cities was a Muslim intelligentsia, the result of migration of dispossessed Muslim landowners to urban areas. But in the 1950s and 1960s, Serb and Croat peasants had begun migrating to the cities as well, and rather than assimilate into the multiethnic urban culture, they brought with them their rural customs of ethnic separateness. In accord with my theory, these newly urbanized Serbs and Croats were much more involved in anti-Muslim violence than the older inhabitants. For instance, when Sarajevo was under siege, 60,000 of the 150,000 Serbs—mainly those who had lived there before the 1950s—remained in the city alongside the Muslims (Vulliamy 1994:39–40; 1998:78; see also Maass 1996:159).

OUTSIDERS AS AGGRESSORS

Those who organized and initiated the violence were especially distant from those they killed (Malcolm 1994:234–35, 251; Mann 2005:387). Though Bosnian Serbs were also involved, the conflict was mainly "an invasion of Bosnia planned and directed from Serbian soil" (Malcolm 1994:238; see also Maass 1996:252). Especially at the outset, the Yugoslav military (the JNA) was directly involved. Later, with the formation of a rump Yugoslavia consisting only of Serbia and Montenegro, the JNA was ostensibly removed, but the Serbian forces already in Bosnia simply became the Bosnian Serb army. This was at first just an adjunct of the JNA, and the Yugoslav ministry of defense continued paying the salaries of former officers who transferred (Judah 1997:230; Malcolm 1994:237–38). Serbia-based militias also worked in close cooperation with the army and were responsible for many of the large-scale killings (Cigar 1995:54). As historian Noel Malcolm puts it, these were "young urban gangsters in expensive sunglasses from Serbia" carrying out "a rational strategy dictated by their political leaders" (1994:252). It is also noteworthy that these paramilitary groups avoided killing the socially closer Muslims who lived alongside them. As political scientist James Ron points out, Muslims were safer if they were inside Yugoslavian territory (2000:609–10). For example, the Sandzak region, where many of the militias were based, had a large Muslim population, and ethnic cleansing would have been a conceivable response to Serb fears of the thriving Muslim secessionist movement there. But in the Sandzak region violence never rose to the level of ethnic cleansing (Ron 2000). Instead the paramilitaries traveled to attack more socially distant Muslims in Bosnia.

In the Prijedor region most of the genocide occurred either during assaults on the villages or in the camps later on. Consider first the initial attacks. Locals were involved in many of them, but the main participants were military and paramilitary troops. These were not primarily attacks of neighbor against neighbor, and normally the attackers were distant enough that they were unknown. For instance, an analysis of seventeen attacks on villages in the Prijedor district from May to June 1992 revealed that in fourteen of these the survivors had not recognized any of the attackers (Oberschall 2000:982–83; 2001:119–20).

Outsiders also played a dominant role in each of the major attacks on villages discussed above. Yugoslavian army troops and paramilitaries carried out the assault on Hambarine in response to the killing of members of the White Eagles, a militia group based in Serbia (Greve 1994:49; Wesselingh and Vaulerin 2005:42–43). In Kozarac, Serbs from Serbia and Knin controlled the main weapons, and the army and paramilitaries, along with local Serbs from Prijedor, carried out the violence (Greve 1994:50–52). Even the local Serbs, however, were not neighbors; they were from areas outside of Kozarac. The attackers were unfamiliar enough with the residents that they had to rely on one local Serb who was from one of only a handful of Serb families in the area to identify prominent citizens for arrest and possible elimination (Battiata 1992). The attack on the town of Prijedor also relied on outsiders. Serbian police units were called in, along with a unit with tanks and canons from Banja Luka. These assisted the military forces already in Prijedor, along with Serbs from Prijedor town (Greve 1994:55). Likewise, Serbian infantry and paramilitaries conducted the attacks on the villages on the left bank of the Sana River (Greve 1994:58).

This is not to say local Serbs were never involved. The Prijedor government that took control in the coup cooperated closely with Serb authorities in Bosnia and in Serbia proper, and many ordinary local Serbs participated in the violence. One observer estimated that 30 percent of the local Serbs disagreed with the ethnic cleansing but remained quiet, while perhaps 60 percent agreed or were at least willing to go along. He said that they were led by the other 10 percent, "who have the guns and control the television towers" (quoted in Maass 1996:107). Those willing to go along often joined directly in the violence or assisted the attackers by providing information (Cigar 1995:64). But outsiders played a central role in all of the attacks. This was less the case in the camps, where the guards were locals and where non-Serbs might be "beaten by their former teachers, murdered by their old customers, robbed by their ex-colleagues" (Wesselingh and Vaulerin 2005:40; see also Sells 1996:13). But even there the involvement of outsiders was necessary to spur the guards to genocidal violence. At Omarska, for instance, the local guards were at first hesitant to engage in violence, but soon a special police squad from Banja Luka came to show them how to run the camp. One former prisoner describes the guards as "eager pupils" and says that after the visit from Banja Luka "everything changed" (Pervanic 1999:74, 64).

CONTRADICTORY BEHAVIOR

The guards' behavior varied, however, and certain guards might aid some of the prisoners. For example, Damir Dosen and Dragan Kolundzija, both guards at Keraterm whom the International Criminal Tribunal for the Former Yugoslavia (ICTY) later indicted for their role in the violence, would at times try to improve conditions for some of the prisoners (Clark 2009:435–36). And at Omarska a prisoner named Hamdija received help from a guard with whom he had attended a work retraining program many years before. This guard would periodically call Hamdija out of the room to give him food. Another guard knew Rezak Hukanovic, a Muslim detainee at Omarska, and proclaimed upon seeing him, "you're the prisoner and I'm the guard, but you were my friend before and that's how you'll stay." After this he secretly passed food to him and brought him messages from home (Hukanovic 1996:78). Hukanovic also tells of an incident during his transfer from Omarska to a camp in Banja Luka, when a group of Serbs came onto the bus asking for Muslims from Kozarac. One of the Serbs was about to shoot a man named Djemo when another Serb, a former waiter in Djemo's café, intervened to stop him (Hukanovic 1996:105). These incidents mostly conform to the pattern we have seen previously. Where Serbs aided Muslims, social closeness was involved, and even killers might engage in contradictory behavior, killing those who are distant and aiding those who are close.

Guards in camps outside of Prijedor also sometimes engaged in contradictory behavior, and when they did, we see the same pattern. Dragon Nikolic, commander of the Susica Camp in Vlasenica, engaged in especially sadistic behavior. When detainees would beg to be shot rather than beaten any more, he would reply, "A bullet is too expensive to be spent on a Muslim" (quoted in Clark 2009:436). But at other times he would give food and milk to the prisoners. Goran Jelisic, a guard at the Luka Camp in Brcko who referred to himself as the "Serbian Adolf," helped a Muslim friend escape across the border. And Ranko Cesic, a guard at the Luka Camp who pled guilty to ten murders, nevertheless saved the lives of other Muslims, including some of his neighbors (Clark 2009:436–37).

INTIMATE KILLINGS

The pattern of genocide in Bosnia is as my theory predicts, but people sometimes did kill those who were more intimate. These killings tended to differ from the others in that they often involved personal settling of scores. In such cases the aggressors expressed individual rather than ethnic grievances against the targets. For example, Abdullah Puskar, a math teacher and inmate at Omarska, was singled out by a guard who was his former student. When they first met in Omarska, the guard declared, "I listened to you long enough, now you'll listen to me for a while." Later the guard would call Puskar out and beat him severely. Once, while beating him over the head with a club, the guard yelled, "I'm gonna beat that math out of you or die trying" (quoted in Hukanovic 1996:74–75). In another case a Serb believed a Muslim judge had given him an unfair sentence. Another Serb was offended that a Muslim had once failed to offer him a drink. And yet another Serb targeted a Muslim man because of an old grudge he had against the man's father (Pervanic 1999:101, 120, 157). In such cases the genocide opened up opportunities for other kinds of killing. Every Serb had license to kill without fear of sanction, and many took advantage of the situation to kill individuals who were personal rather than ethnic enemies (Pervanic 1999:156–57). The Serb visitors allowed into the camps were especially likely to use the opportunity to target particular inmates for private reasons: "They wanted to settle old scores. . . . A poor Serb might search for the wealthy Muslim who refused to give him a job five years earlier; a farmer might try to find the Croat who, a decade before, refused to lend his tractor for a day; a middle-aged man might look around for the Muslim who, twenty-five years ago, stole away his high school sweetheart. Petty quarrels were settled with major crimes" (Maass 1996:53).

More intimate killings did occur, then, but these were disproportionately likely to involve score settling. These were genocidal in the sense that those who organized the violence and ran the camps allowed them to occur, but in these cases those who carried out the killing were not selecting targets on an ethnic basis.

INEQUALITY

The genocide also occurred, as my theory predicts, in a context of ethnic inequality. Serbs were the largest of Yugoslavia's ethnic groups and the best organized politically and militarily. They were overrepresented in the police force, interior ministries, and the armed forces, and they dominated the army's officer corps (Gutman 1993:xxxiii; Mann 2005:363). The state's headquarters were in Belgrade, and with the breakup of Yugoslavia, Serbs were in an ideal position to seize state assets. Yugoslavia had one of Europe's largest armies, along with immense stockpiles of weapons that had been intended for defense against a Soviet attack (Gutman 1993:xxxiii). But while Serbs were the strongest of Yugoslavia's ethnic groups, Bosnian Muslims and Kosovo Albanians were the weakest, and they were the main targets of genocide (Mann 2005:410; see also Maass 1996:25).

As journalist Tim Judah notes, before the violence in Bosnia many people believed that a "balance of terror" would ensure peace. But the

Bosnian Serbs' alliance with Belgrade tipped the scales. Armed and assisted by the Yugoslavian army, the Bosnian Serb leadership came into the possession of weapons that greatly increased their power (Judah 1997:194). The Serb army had somewhere between a 20:1 and a 100:1 advantage in heavy weaponry over the Bosnian Muslims, and the United Nations arms embargo, which was enacted in September 1991 and continued for several years, locked this disparity into place (Sells 1996:117).

THE BOSNIAN GENOCIDE AS A MATTER OF DEGREE

Like the 2002 Gujarat genocide, the Bosnian genocide was highly genocidal in some respects but less so in others. Whereas the Gujarat genocide was highly genocidal only in its ethnic basis, the Bosnian Genocide was highly genocidal only in its scale. My theory of the degree of genocide explains why.

SCALE

In Prijedor the violence occurred at multiple locations throughout the district, and similar violence occurred throughout the Bosnian areas under Serbian control. As my theory predicts, the large scale of the genocide was related to the aggressors' high degree of organization. Those who planned the violence were mainly state elites in Serbia and in the Serb-controlled areas of Bosnia, and those who carried it out were mainly members of the military or militia groups (Cigar 1995:15).

Factors conducive to organization were present, including the continuity of deviant behavior. When the deviant behavior that genocide and other forms of violence are responding to is ongoing, organized groups may form to deal with it. Here the triggering offense, the secession of Bosnia, was by nature continuous. Though a secession is, in a sense, a one-time act, it results in permanent separation, and the problems secession created for Bosnian Serbs, including a loss of political power, were ongoing. Accordingly, already-existing organizations like the Yugoslavian state responded, and new organizations—such as militia groups and newly formed Serbian governments within Bosnia—arose. Also conducive to organization was the fact that the offended parties were high in status and well-connected in comparison to the deviants. Black's theory of partisanship tells us that people are most likely to take sides in a conflict with those to whom they are socially close and with those who are higher in status. Here it was important that the leaders of Serbia and other Serbs outside of Bosnia supported the Bosnian Serbs—to whom they were culturally close—against the Muslims.

INTENSIVENESS, ONE-SIDEDNESS, AND ETHNIC BASIS

Although high in its scale, the Bosnian genocide was low in its intensivenessness, one-sidedness, and ethnic basis. Intensiveness refers to how thorough the genocide is—the percent of the targets killed. In this case the attackers killed only a small portion of Muslims, and even a small portion of the men. All told, they killed about 10 percent of Bosnia's Muslims, and in locations of intense mass killing, most people survived. At the Omarska Camp, for example, the Serbs killed about 4,000 to 5,000 men out of perhaps 13,000 (Gutman 1993:xiv, xxxi, 145).

Furthermore, although the violence was certainly one-sided in Bosnia,[6] it was much less so than in many cases of genocide. The killing in Bosnia mainly involved Serbs killing Muslims. To a lesser extent Serbs killed Croats, and Croats killed Muslims, but Muslim violence against Serbs was rare (Maass 1996:32). Still, anti-Serb violence by Muslims did occur. The Bosnian army, for example, committed a small number of atrocities, and one Muslim warlord killed hundreds of Serbs (Vulliamy 1998:76).

The ethnic basis of the killing—the extent to which it was based on ethnicity alone—was also low, as the attackers focused on portions of the targeted groups instead of killing anyone who happened to be a Muslim or Croat. In the attack on Kozarac, for instance, the Serbs chose prominent citizens to be brought forward and killed immediately (Battiata 1992; Hukanovic 1996:88; Maass 1996:38–39; Wesselingh and Vaulerin 2005:43). And the concentration camps at Omarska and Keraterm, where most prisoners were Muslim men, were much more deadly than the camp at Trnopolje.

That these aspects of the genocide were limited is also consistent with my theory for two reasons. We have seen before that genocides tend to be less intensive if the adversaries have some way of separating. Again we are talking about a matter of degree. If expulsion is easy, genocide likely will not occur at all, but any possibility of expulsion—even if difficult—may limit a genocide that does occur. In this case the fact that Serbs and Muslims lived throughout all parts of Bosnia closed off some options for peace. It meant that initially there was no way to divide the state to resolve the ethnic conflict (Mann 2005:366). But ultimately Bosnia did break up, and the violence subsided after it had altered the ethnic composition of the areas that would become two separate political entities. Most of the violence that brought this about involved expulsion rather than genocide. Expulsion was possible because areas controlled by the Muslim-dominated Bosnian government were available as close-by destinations for Muslims who had been living in Serb-controlled territories. It was easier to deport rather than kill these people—especially women, children, and elderly men who would not add to Bosnia's military force.

Another factor that limited the genocide was the degree of inequality between the adversaries, which was not as great as it would otherwise have been due to the Muslims' numerical advantage over Serbs within Bosnia. Where inequality is limited, so is the one-sidedness of genocide; the targets engage in some violence against the aggressors. And because extreme inequality is an aspect of the social polarization of ethnic groups, which leads to genocides in which people are targeted on the basis of ethnicity alone, this aspect of genocide was limited as well. Still, though inequality was limited due to the Muslims' numbers, the Serbs had an overwhelming advantage in heavy weaponry (Sells 1996:117). In these respects, the conflict was similar to many of the conflicts between European settlers and the native inhabitants of Australia and California, where the natives were superior in numbers and the Europeans superior in military technology. The attackers' overall superiority thus led to genocide, but because inequality was limited, the genocide was limited in its one-sidedness and ethnic basis.

In the Bosnian case some degree of separability and equality limited genocide even as the organization of the aggressors intensified it. Extremely genocidal in some ways but not in others, the Bosnian case lies in the middle of a continuum between protogenocide and hypergenocide, genocide's minimal and maximal forms.

Most of the violence in Bosnia was ethnic cleansing, and some of it was genocide. Like the other cases of genocide, it occurred in response to conflict caused by movements of social time and occurring in a context of social distance and inequality, and where separating the groups was difficult. These variables explain where the genocide occurred, who participated, and who was targeted. We saw, for instance, that newly urbanized Serbs—more distant from local Bosnians—were more involved in anti-Muslim violence in Sarajevo. Likewise, the organizers of the violence and the actual attackers in Prijedor were mainly outsiders socially distant from their targets. Many of these people went to Bosnia to kill Muslims while leaving Muslim populations near their homes in Yugoslavia untouched. We also saw that during the violence Serbs might spare particular Muslims, and that even guards at the concentration camps might engage in contradictory behavior—helping Muslims who were close to them while killing those who were distant. And we saw that social geometry explains the particular features of the Bosnian genocide in comparison to the other cases—why it was extremely genocidal in some ways but not in others.

It should also be clear from this chapter that ethnic conflict in Bosnia was deeply rooted, even as the genocide was contingent on very particular recent events. Misleading accounts of the conflict in Bosnia tend to emphasize one of these aspects at the expense of the other. Journalist Robert Kaplan, for example, describes the Balkans as a "region of pure memory: a Bosch-like tapestry of interlocking ethnic rivalries where medieval and modern history thread into each other" (Kaplan 1993b; see also Kaplan 1993a:3–6). Following this line of thinking, some journalists and other observers have portrayed the conflict as simply part of a centuries-old dispute—ancient, irrational, and perhaps intractable.[7] At the other extreme, some deny that it was the result of ethnic conflict at all.[8]

The problem with the first view is that while many of the grievances were certainly old, ethnic conflict had not been continuous for hundreds of years or even throughout the twentieth century. Ethnic identities changed, ethnic alliances shifted, and ethnic conflict was absent or minimal for long periods of time. History was not enough.

Something else had to happen to intensify conflict and produce genocide. What happened was the secession of Bosnia and the breakup of Yugoslavia. But this does not mean that history and ethnicity were unimportant. The second view fails to understand how ethnicity facilitates and collectivizes conflict. As discussed in chapter 1, conflicts across cultural boundaries easily become conflicts involving all those who share the antagonists' culture. Whites in California side with other whites against Indians; Hindus in India side with other Hindus against Muslims; Serbs in Bosnia and Serbia side with other Serbs against Muslims and Croats. People may even side with fellow ethnics in far off conflicts, including conflicts far off in time—from centuries past. And current conflicts are likely to revive ancient ones as people become aware of past offenses against their own ancestors that were inflicted by the ancestors of their ethnic enemies. Ethnicity connects people to the past, to their ancestors (real or imagined), and to their ancestors' conflicts. And their conflicts are immortal. Those who are willing can still collect any debt or avenge any atrocity. Any conflict not forgotten is never really dead.

6   TUTSIS AND HUTUS IN RWANDA

For several days in April 1994, Hutus in Nyakizu, Rwanda, attacked Tutsis gathered in and around the Cyahinda Catholic Church. At one point the attackers fired machine guns into a crowd of Tutsis in the church's courtyard. As one survivor pointed out, the attack left no bullet holes in the walls of the courtyard because "the crowd was so dense that the bullets went into their bodies. Even if the bullets passed through one person's body, they went into the body of another person" (Des Forges 1999:393). Several days after the end of the massacre, the burgomaster (Nyakizu's political leader) ordered locals to start burying the corpses: "He told them participation in the burial was required as *umuganda,* a kind of labor tax which people were customarily obliged to perform for the commune. In the course of the clean-up, a group of dead children were tossed into a hole. One young girl, wounded but still alive, was thrown in with the others. She cried out for help and, for more than a week, was kept alive by water brought to her by other children. When the burgomaster learned of this, he ordered the hole sealed" (quoted in Human Rights Watch 1994b:7).

ETHNIC CONFLICT IN RWANDA

The 1994 Rwandan genocide was more genocidal than any of the three previous cases. The Hutu killers targeted men, women, and children, and in only three months they killed somewhere from 500,000 to 800,000 Tutsis—about three-fourths of the Tutsi population (Des Forges 1999:16; Straus 2006:51; United Nations 1999:3). In chapters 1 and 2, I discussed the broad characteristics of the Rwandan genocide, including the nature of the conflict, its causes, its social geometry, and its predatory aspects. This chapter expands on those discussions, but like the other case studies it also focuses on the violence in a particular location: the Nyakizu commune in the prefecture of Butare.

The events here and elsewhere in Rwanda further support my theory. For example, the idea that genocide increases with social distance helps to explain why genocide began later in parts of Rwanda where there were interethnic ties such as interethnic marriage. We shall also see that Hutu refugees from Burundi, who would have been socially distant from local Tutsis, were heavily involved in the early killings in Nyakizu. And we shall see that social ties often led Hutus—even those involved in the killing—to spare Tutsis who otherwise would have been killed. Before discussing this further, though, let us look more closely at the events that led to the reemergence of ethnic grievances in Rwanda in the early 1990s and eventually to a highly genocidal campaign involving the massacre of Tutsis throughout all areas of government control.

ETHNICITY IN RWANDA

Discussions about ethnicity in Rwanda are sometimes similar to those about ethnicity in Bosnia. With the outbreak of the Rwandan genocide, many reports inaccurately depicted the violence as something that had been going on for centuries. One such report, by journalist Elaine Sciolino of *The New York Times,* described Rwanda as a "failed central African nation-state with a centuries-old history of tribal warfare" (1994). Since then many accounts have more accurately, but still misleadingly, characterized the ethnic divisions and conflict in Rwanda as a more recent development—the product of colonialism or the machinations of political elites. Political scientist Mahmood Mamdani, for instance, presents the historic Hutu-Tutsi distinction as a political rather than ethnic distinction that was created by the precolonial Rwandan state (2001:74). Later, under colonialism, this distinction became racial: Hutus and Tutsis were characterized as indigenous and alien, respectively (Mamdani 2001:76–102). Under the Rwandan Second Republic the distinction became ethnic, with the groups both being characterized as indigenous, but as separate. The Hutus and Tutsis were once again racialized with the rise of the Hutu Power movement in the early 1990s (Mamdani 2001:138, 190).

Accounts such as Mamdani's deemphasize the importance of eth-

nic divisions and long-standing ethnic conflict, but others deny their importance altogether. For political scientist Lee Ann Fujii, the main conflict in the Rwandan genocide was not between Hutus and Tutsis, but between elites of the same ethnicity—those committed to democratic reform and those opposed to it. "The story of genocide," she writes, "was thus not one of ethnic conflict—old or new—but an even older tale of power and politics" (Fujii 2009:47; compare Hintjens 1999:281; Longman 1995). Though these accounts point appropriately to the historically variable and sometimes complex nature of ethnicity in Rwanda and to the crucial role of political elites, ultimately they give a distorted view of ethnicity, ethnic conflict, and genocide. It is as if ethnicities are created out of whole cloth and then deconstructed and reconstructed multiple times within decades, as if major ethnic conflicts result in mass violence and then just disappear, and as if the grievances expressed by the perpetrators of genocide—both the organizers and the ground-level killers—can simply be discounted as a subterfuge. In fact Rwanda had long been an ethnically divided society, and its ethnic groups had been in conflict for years prior to the genocide.

Prior to the arrival of Europeans in Rwanda, Hutus and Tutsis had existed as ethnic groups for centuries (compare Mann 2005:432). Relations between the groups varied by region, and identities might sometimes be altered, but still, prior to the colonial era there was a pattern of hierarchical arrangements regarding land and access to cattle in which the cattle-owning Tutsis were normally dominant. The colonial powers—the Germans and later the Belgians—did not create these identities or the hierarchical group relations. What they did was to institutionalize these relationships where they did not exist and to simplify them where they did, thus sharpening ethnic divisions and exaggerating the dominance of Tutsis over Hutus (compare Newbury 1998). Beginning in the 1920s the Belgian rulers began altering the previously complex system of administration in which local rulers retained a great deal of power. The new system created chiefdoms and subchiefdoms of uniform size, with state officials ruling over previously autonomous areas. And unlike in the previous system, where Hutus often held local-level positions of power, Tutsis now held all ruling positions (Des Forges 1999:34–35; Gourevitch 1998:56; Mamdani 2001:90–91; Prunier 1995:26–27; Straus 2004:36). Hutus were also excluded from higher education. Finally, ethnic identity became less fluid in the 1930s when Belgians required Rwandans to register their identity and to carry identification cards indicating their ethnicity (Des Forges 1999:35–38; Gourevitch 1998:56–57; Mamdani 2001:98; Newbury 1998; Straus 2006:21).

It might be the case that political conflicts in late precolonial Rwanda took on an ethnic character (Longman 2004:31–32). This would mean that ethnic conflict in Rwanda has a longer history than most scholars have thought. Still, major interethnic violence seems to have been absent prior to the colonial period. The idea that Rwanda has a "centuries-old history of tribal warfare" is far off the mark. But neither was the conflict underpinning the 1994 genocide a new development or simply a ruse to divert attention from intraethnic conflicts. Rather, the grievances formulated and expressed by Hutu elites at that time were contemporary expressions of a decades-old ethnic conflict—a conflict handled previously with ethnic expulsion and flight, small-scale genocide, ethnic quotas, and various other acts of social control.

THE HUTU REVOLUTION

Following World War II European colonial powers were under international pressure to promote political reforms in their territories, and within Rwanda the Catholic Church had begun to promote the interests of Hutus. These pressures led the Belgian authorities to begin allowing the Hutus a limited amount of political power and increased participation in public life (Des Forges 1999:38; Lemarchand 2004:397; Straus 2004:331). Hutu elites then began to call for an end to Tutsi rule. In what became known as the Hutu Manifesto, a group of Hutu politicians and intellectuals warned against simply substituting European colonialism with Tutsi colonialism. Tutsi rule, they said, oppressed the Hutus, "who see themselves condemned forever to the role of subordinate manual workers" (quoted in Straus 2004:332; see also Mamdani 2001:116; Prunier 1995:45–46). Tutsi elites, on the other hand, favored independence from the colonial regime but strongly opposed majoritarian rule, which would shift power to the Hutus. In reaction to the Hutu Manifesto, a group of Tutsi elites defended Tutsi rule and proclaimed that ethnic relations in Rwanda were to be based on servitude (Straus 2004:333). Tutsis, they said, had a right to rule, as they had "conquered the land of the Hutu, killed their 'little' kings and thus subjugated the Hutu" (quoted in Mamdani 2001:118; see also Newbury 1998; Prunier 1995:47).

In 1959 this conflict became violent. After the sudden death of the king, Hutus called for an end to the monarchy while Tutsi elites quickly installed a successor without Belgian approval. At this time four political parties formed—two dominated by Hutus and calling for majoritarian rule, one dominated by Tutsis and supporting the monarchy, and a moderate party—also mostly Tutsi—which favored gradual change (Mamdani 2001:120–22; Straus 2004:334–36). During this period supporters of the Tutsi monarchist party began to attack Tutsi and Hutu opposition leaders, and in response Hutu crowds destroyed Tutsi property. The Belgians eventually backed the Hutu insurgency and installed a government that began putting Hutus into positions of power. The violence, normally consisting of attacks by Tutsis and then large-scale responses by Hutus, continued (Des Forges 1999:39; Hintjens 1999:255; Newbury 1998; Prunier 1995:48–54; Straus 2004:337–32). But the Hutu Revolution had been successful. The monarchy was abolished and the First Republic established.

EPISODES OF VIOLENCE AND PERIODS OF PEACE

Several serious episodes of violence occurred during the early years of the Hutu Revolution and the later years of the First Republic. The first was in 1962. Raids by the Tutsi party, which resulted in the deaths of Hutu police officers and civil servants, led to massive anti-Tutsi violence in which 1,000 to 2,000 civilians were killed (Mamdani 2001:129; Straus 2004:347). The second episode began in December 1963, when a group of Tutsi exiles invaded from Burundi. In response, self-defense committees organized by the government killed approximately 10,000 Tutsi civilians (Mamdani 2001:129–30; Prunier 1995:56; Straus 2004:350). After this violence was minimal until 1973, when groups of Hutu students began conducting purges of schools and colleges. While ethnic quotas officially limited Tutsis to proportionate representation in the government and education, about half of the teachers and students at the time were Tutsis. The Hutu students forcibly expelled Tutsis, often with the support of government and party officials. The violence then spread to other areas, targeting not just Tutsis but also Hutu officials associated with the current regime. At this time many Tutsis fled to neighboring countries (Straus 2004:355–57). Shortly after this the First Republic came to an end when Juvénal Habyarimana took power in a military coup. The formation of the Second Republic—a one-party dictatorship—shifted power from southern to northern Hutu elites. Interethnic violence subsided, but Tutsis were still shut out of positions of political power, and quotas restricted their numbers in schools and other areas of civic life. Also, Tutsis who had fled the country in 1973 and earlier were barred from returning (Lemarchand 2004:397–98; Straus 2004:357).

The period of peace during the Second Republic lasted almost two decades, but this was not because ethnic distinctions lost their salience or because Hutus had abandoned their grievances. In schools, for instance, Rwandan children learned that Tutsis were invaders from Ethiopia who had taken Rwanda from its inhabitants, that they were Hamites who shared no kinship with the Bantu Hutus, and that they were the natural enemies of Hutus (Fujii 2004:102). A Hutu man who was in school in the early 1980s says he was taught "that the Tutsi lived better than the Hutu and that the Tutsi had come to colonise them" (quoted in McDoom 2005:19). A Tutsi woman says that when studying Rwandan history in school, she learned "that the Tutsi were ruling with an iron hand. The students would then tease me because I was Tutsi" (quoted in McDoom 2005:19). Another Tutsi man says that Hutu schoolteachers would make Tutsi children stand "so they could humiliate us before the other students" (de Brouwer and Chu 2009:91–92). And another Tutsi woman tells of a Hutu teacher who "would beat us Tutsi without reason, call us snakes and ask us what Tutsi were doing among human beings" (de Brouwer and Chu 2009:105).

Hutus and Tutsis had not resolved the conflict that gave rise to the earlier violence. Ethnic divisions remained, as did the belief that the Tutsis were potential enemies who had oppressed the Hutus in the past. Hutus were now in control, however, and they believed that the gains of the 1959 Hutu Revolution were secure (Mamdani 2001:230; McDoom 2005:1). It was in this context that Hutu-Tutsi relations were peaceful—until Tutsis once again threatened Hutu dominance. The main threat began on October 1, 1990, with the invasion of Rwanda by the Rwandan Patriotic Front (RPF)—an army largely made up of Tutsi exiles. This, along with the internal challenges that preceded it, the signing of the Arusha Accords that followed, and finally the assassination of Rwanda's president, led to the genocide.

GENOCIDE IN NYAKIZU

At the time of the genocide, Rwanda was divided into eleven prefectures, each governed by a prefect, and the prefectures were divided into communes, each governed by a burgomaster. Here we focus on the killings in the commune of Nyakizu, located in the prefecture of Butare. The prefect of Butare, Jean-Baptiste Habyalimana, was a Tutsi who resisted orders to begin killings, and he worked to prevent genocide and to ensure that local authorities did so as well. In this he was mostly successful for the two weeks following the assassination of President Habyarimana, at which time the interim president, Théodore Sindikubwabo, removed him from his post. Sindikubwabo then gave a radio speech in which he called for the killing of RPF accomplices (in other words, Tutsis), and units of the Presidential Guard came from Butare to help start the massacres (African Rights 1995:336–37; Human Rights Watch 1994a:6; ICTR 1996:29; Lemarchand 2004:403; Mamdani 2001:218; Prunier 1995:244). Shortly thereafter genocide occurred throughout the prefecture.

Most of the burgomasters in Butare initially followed the lead of the prefect in resisting genocide. Maraba commune, for instance, was adjacent to the prefecture of Gikongoro, where attacks began early. Tutsis fleeing the violence in Gikongoro had gathered in the local parish, and outsiders attempted to pursue them. The burgomaster tried to keep the peace, but after a visit from the interim president and the removal of Habyalimana, he reversed his position, and genocide began almost immediately (McDoom 2005:4). A similar pattern occurred in Gishamvu commune, where genocide also began after Habyalimana was removed from office and after President Sindikubwabo visited the commune and met with the burgomaster (African Rights 2003). But in Nyakizu the burgomaster supported genocide from the outset, and killing began before the removal of the prefect.

The burgomaster of Nyakizu was Ladislas Ntaganzwa, who at the time of the genocide was a member of the Hutu Power faction of the main opposition party (called MDR-Power).[1] In 1991, with the legalization of rival political parties and prior to the split of the parties into the moderate and Hutu Power factions, Ntaganzwa had become MDR leader. Through a process called *kubohoza* (or "liberation"), he immediately began strengthening his party and weakening the president's ruling party (the MRND). This involved physical violence, property destruction, and other forms of intimidation to encourage "conversions" to his party. Supporters of the burgomaster's party would visit the homes of MRND members at night and have them relinquish their party cards, which they then impaled on poles. They would also engage in public acts of defiance, such as vandalizing communal property, withholding taxes, and boycotting administrative meetings. Eventually, in May 1993, Ntaganzwa became burgomaster in a run-off election carried out amid continued violence and threats on the part of Ntaganzwa's supporters (Wagner 1998).

Even after gaining control of the communal government, Ntaganzwa and his supporters continued using *kubohoza* to strengthen their power. Ntaganzwa also dismissed communal employees who were his personal or political opponents, and he began building an informal, parallel network of supporters who could wield power independently of the communal government. This consisted of Ntaganzwa's close associates and members of his party's youth wing. By early 1994 this group had begun to hold secret security meetings (Des Forges 1999:359; Wagner 1998).

Ntaganzwa also developed ties with the Burundian Hutu refugees who came to Nyakizu after the assassination of Burundi's president. Numbering about 15,000—one quarter of the population of the commune—most of the Burundians lived in a refugee camp near the communal office. Ntaganzwa appointed a member of his inner circle, Francois Bazaramba, to be chief of the refugee camp. Bazaramba was an earlier Burundian refugee—from the 1972 massacres—as well as the owner of a local bar and the youth director at the Baptist church. In his position over the camp, Bazaramba acted as a link between the communal government and the refugees, and the Burundians became some of the strongest supporters of the burgomaster. According to some accounts, the burgomaster sold the Burundians arms he acquired from the Rwandan authorities, and the Burundians received military training from former soldiers (Des Forges 1999:360–65; Nieminen 2007a, 2007b).

Ntaganzwa also had strong ties with officials outside the commune—such as Jean Kambanda, from the commune adjacent to Nyakizu and a member of the same political party, who would become the prime minister of the interim government (Des Forges 1999:361). With a network of supporters inside and outside the commune, Ntaganzwa was able to bypass the prefect and begin the genocide in Nyakizu soon after the president's assassination.

THE BORDER KILLINGS

The first massacres of Tutsis in Nyakizu occurred in the southern part of the commune along the border with Burundi. Genocide had already begun in Gikongoro, which borders Nyakizu, and many Tutsis had fled to Nyakizu for refuge. There they were directed to the Cyahinda Church, but many attempted to make it to Burundi. At this time the burgomaster and his supporters organized civilian patrols in each sector. Originally both Hutus and Tutsis took part in the patrols, which were supposed to deal with RPF infiltrators said to be among the refugees, and with Hutu troublemakers from outside the commune. Tutsis eventually stopped participating, though, when they realized that the purpose of the patrols was to keep track of the refugees. Burundian Hutus on the other side of the border also formed patrols to prevent Tutsis from entering Burundi. On Wednesday, April 13, one of these patrols stopped a group of Tutsis and brought them back into Rwanda. The Burundians, along with Rwandans who had been waiting across the border, then killed the Tutsi refugees with machetes and other traditional weapons and threw the corpses into the river (Des Forges 1999:370–73).

In Nkakwa sector Albert Nzimbirinda, the sector's councilor, did little to stop the movement of the refugees. Because there were also patrols on the other side of the border that kept Tutsis from entering Burundi, by April 14 hundreds of Tutsis had gathered at the border. That evening Ntaganzwa arrived in Nkakwa and with a loudspeaker encouraged the people to prevent the Tutsis from fleeing. Once their families were safe in Burundi, he declared, the men would return to attack Rwanda. Ntaganzwa then went to Rutobwe, also a border sector, and gave a similar message. After he left, leaders from Ntaganzwa's party led Hutus in attacking the refugees with machetes and other weapons. Ntaganzwa returned to Nkakwa twice during the night, and the next morning he traveled throughout the commune to find supporters, who then came to the border to assist in the killings. With the assistance of Burundians across the border who continued to prevent the Tutsis from crossing, the assailants were able to trap and kill nearly all of the hundreds of refugees. Then the assailants set out to attack local Tutsis. In Nkakwa and Rutobwe they pillaged Tutsis' property, set fire to their homes, and killed those they could find (Des Forges 1999:376–79).

Less severe attacks occurred in other areas of the commune at this time. Cyanwa was a cell of Cyahinda sector in the western part of the commune. Here local patrols initially prevented the Hutu militia from Gikongoro commune from pursuing Tutsi refugees fleeing to Nyakizu. On April 13, however, Damien Biniga—a subprefect in Gikongoro and one of the leaders of the genocide there—began visiting Nyakizu and meeting with Ntaganzwa. Soon afterward Biniga began organizing the militias for an attack on Cyanwa. On the evening of April 14, Biniga arrived at the border along with a group of gendarmes, police officers, and civilians. The men then distributed machetes to militia members who had gathered there, and the militia members began taunting the people gathered on the Nyakizu side and threatening to kill them all if the Hutus would not abandon the Tutsis. They refused but then fled when the gendarmes began firing. The militia then crossed the border and looted the homes of local Tutsis. The next morning local Hutus joined with the militia members in attacking Tutsis and burning their homes (African Rights 1999:43–45).

THE CYAHINDA MASSACRE

The largest massacre in Nyakizu—and one of the largest of the Rwandan genocide—took place at the Cyahinda Catholic Church. Tutsis from Gikongoro and other communes began taking refuge in the church shortly after Habyarimana's assassination, and once the violence began in Nyakizu, local Tutsis joined them. By this time the church itself was full, and people crowded outside and in nearby buildings.

The first attack began on the morning of April 15, when a group of attackers previously involved in the killings at Nkakwa began firing into the crowd outside the church. On this occasion the Tutsis were able to fight off their attackers by throwing stones. At 2:00 p.m. Ntaganzwa arrived, along with gendarmes, police officers, members of the burgomaster's inner circle, two hundred Burundian refugees, and activists from the burgomaster's party. Damien Biniga arrived shortly afterward with gendarmes and militia members from Gikongoro. Ntaganzwa first demanded that the Tutsis put down their weapons—mostly sticks and stones they had collected to defend themselves—and that those not from Nyakizu leave immediately. The gendarmes then began shooting into the crowd and throwing grenades, while the Burundians and militia members attacked with machetes. The Tutsis again tried to defend themselves with rocks, and many fled to the nearby soccer field, where the surrounding buildings offered some degree of protection. But the attacks continued until early evening, and about 800 Tutsis were killed (African Rights 1995:339–41; 1999:45–46; Bonner 1994; Des Forges 1999:382–86; French 1998; Human Rights Watch 1994b:8; ICTR 1996:32; Scherrer 2002:114).

The next morning, reinforcements (probably more gendarmes) arrived from Butare, and Ntaganzwa worked to recruit and better organize locals. The assailants were stronger now, and they attacked simultaneously from several directions to prevent the Tutsis from scattering. They continued until 5:00 p.m., but they were still unable to get into the church. At 7:00 the next morning, Sunday, April 17, the killing resumed, but a visit from Prefect Habyalimana halted it temporarily. The prefect spoke to the Tutsis and promised to remove the gendarmes and send soldiers in to protect them. More killing occurred after his departure, and that evening the national radio announced that the prefect had been dismissed from his post (African Rights 1995:339; 1999:46–47; Des Forges 1999:390–91).

By Monday the 18th the attackers had become more numerous, and they were able to organize a more successful attack. One group surrounded the complex to prevent people from escaping, while armed attackers went systematically from one building to another firing into the crowds with machine guns. Again, those who had only machetes or other crude weapons would attack those fleeing and would follow behind the attackers who had firearms, killing those who were left. While the attacks continued, President Sindikubwabo visited the area and thanked the people for their work. He also promised to send them more help. In the aftermath of the main massacre, several busloads of gendarmes and militia members arrived from Butare to assist in killing Tutsis who remained in the parish and hunting down those who had fled. The next day a lieutenant and twelve soldiers arrived to assist the assailants in completing their work. At the communal office the soldiers set up a large gun, which they used to fire rounds at the church, and they sought out and killed those who were in hiding.[2] By the evening of April 19, the killing was finished. In all, at least 5,000 Tutsis—but probably closer to 20,000 and perhaps as many as 30,000—had been killed at Cyahinda parish (African Rights 1995:337–42; 1999:47–50; Bonner 1994; Des Forges 1999:392–96; French 1998; Human Rights Watch 1994a:4; 1994b:9; ICTR 1996:32; Melvern 2004:210–11; Scherrer 2002:114).

MASSACRES AT NYAKIZU AND GASASA HILLS

With the Cyahinda Church under attack, many Tutsis sought refuge on Nyakizu Hill, in the center of the commune. On Saturday, April 16, a group of Hutus led by one of Bazaramba's employees attacked the Tutsis on the hilltop. They used mainly traditional weapons, and the Tutsis were able to fend off the attack. The next day, though, the attackers, now led by Bazaramba, were more numerous and armed with guns. The attack continued all day, and many Tutsis fled to another hilltop called Gasasa. Twenty thousand refugees from Cyahinda later joined them, and many of the Tutsis gathered there then attempted to flee the commune. They divided into three groups heading in different directions, and Hutus in neighboring communes later attacked each group. Those who remained were killed on April 20 and 21. The burgomaster directed these massacres, and Hutus from Nyakizu, along with Burundian refugees, carried them out. The attackers surrounded the hill and then began climbing it and killing the Tutsis with guns and machetes. Afterward they searched for survivors and kicked the bodies to make sure no one was still alive (Des Forges 1999:396–401; ICTR 1996:32; Nieminen 2007c; Scherrer 2002:114).

KILLINGS IN THE AFTERMATH OF THE MAIN MASSACRES

By the time the massacres at Cyahinda and the hilltops were over, most of the commune's Tutsis had escaped or perished. Those still present were mainly very young children—usually spared during the massacres—and women who were married to Hutus or had been forced during the killings to cohabit with Hutu men. Other Tutsis were hiding in the homes of friends, relatives, or co-workers. The genocide continued, but it was on a smaller scale and more tightly organized. In late April, officials were no longer calling upon the commune's whole population to kill, and the burgomaster began a campaign of "normalization." Markets and schools reopened, and people were required to register their firearms. The burgomaster also set up a "self-defense" program, in which ten men were selected from each sector and trained by local police and former soldiers in the use of firearms and grenades. Shortly after this Ntaganzwa established security councils for the commune and for each sector. These replaced the existing communal council with the burgomaster's strongest supporters. Following these changes Ntaganzwa and his supporters began conducting searches for Tutsis still in hiding (Des Forges 1999:402–10).

In late May, after a visit from prefectural authorities, a new round of killings began. At this time the attackers killed the women previously forced into cohabitation with Hutus, as well as children found hiding in Hutus' homes. They also searched the homes of Hutus who had refused to participate in the massacres. Some killing occurred throughout the month of June, but by early July, as the RPF continued to advance, the burgomaster and his closest supporters fled Rwanda (Des Forges 1999:411–31).

SOCIAL TIME

Several social changes—political conflict, the civil war, the Arusha Accords, and the president's assassination—preceded the Rwandan genocide. Rwanda experienced social upheaval, a succession of large movements of social time. And Nyakizu, the one commune in Butare where genocide began early, experienced local-level social upheaval—the rise to power of Ntaganzwa and his supporters, the political violence against opposition parties, and the influx of 15,000 Burundian refugees. It may be that Nyakizu was more genocidal than other communes in part because of its turbulent social atmosphere. Social upheaval alone does not produce genocide, though, either nationally or locally, unless it occurs in the right context.

INSEPARABILITY

To understand particular cases of genocide we also need to look at the physical context. The social geometry may be conducive to genocide, but this is irrelevant if the potential targets are not accessible to the aggressors. And even accessible targets might be expelled rather than killed when the physical context makes it possible. In Rwanda, though, the targets were accessible, and alternatives to genocide were limited. Rwanda had an extremely high population density—the highest of any rural country in Africa (Prunier 1995:4; Uvin 2001:81). Also, Tutsis and Hutus were not geographically separated, but lived side by side throughout the country. As sociologist Michael Mann (2005:432) notes, this meant that options such as regional decentralization or confederation—which might otherwise be peaceful means of handling political conflicts between ethnic groups—were not feasible. These factors also meant that when the conflict became violent, Tutsis were readily accessible targets.

Previous episodes of anti-Tutsi violence involved expulsion or mass flight, but the civil war in the 1990s closed off the option of further expulsions. The invaders were mostly exiles who had been driven from Rwanda during the earlier conflicts. Further expulsions would have enabled the rebels to expand their ranks with new exiles. The earlier ethnic cleansings were also more limited—confined to certain areas and directed mainly at elites. In 1994, though, the Hutu aggressors targeted all Rwandan Tutsis throughout the country. The expulsion of so many people into neighboring countries would have been difficult if not impossible.

The physical aspects of the conflict also explain some of the variation within the genocide. Three of the prefectures had lower levels of killing. In two of these, Cyangugu and Kibuye, it was easier for Tutsis to flee. Both were in close proximity to Lake Kivu and to Ijwi Island in Zaire. It was more difficult to police Lake Kivu than other international border areas, and it appears that many Tutsis in Cyangugu and Kibuye were able to get to Zaire in this manner (Straus 2004:79). Similarly, the particular locations where genocide occurred were places where Tutsis could be trapped. The largest massacres were in places such as the Cyahinda church in Nyakizu, where Hutus surrounded large numbers of Tutsis after promising them protection. Throughout the country, then, schools, churches, and community centers were the primary locations of mass killing (Lemarchand 2004:408; Scherrer 2002:111; see also African Rights 1995). The largest single massacre of the genocide occurred at the parish of Karama in the Runyinya commune of Butare, where 35,000 Tutsis were killed (African Rights 1995:345–51; Scherrer 2002:114). Even in such locations, though, limited opportunities for flight reduced the genocide to a degree. As mentioned above, thousands of Tutsis were able to flee from Cyahinda parish to Gasasa Hill, and those who could then left the hill along with other Tutsis before the massacre began. Hutus eventually attacked those who fled and killed most of them, but those who fled fared better as a group than those left behind in the parish or on the hilltops (Des Forges 1999:397–400; Scherrer 2002:114).

SOCIAL DISTANCE

The social context of the conflict also mattered in this case. The social distance between Hutus and Tutsis was conducive to the occurrence of genocide, and genocide was greater where social distance was greater. People are socially close, you will recall, when they are intimate, when they cooperate with one another, and when they are culturally similar. In the past, long before the genocide, the Hutu and Tutsi ethnic groups were in some ways socially close. In both Rwanda and Burundi, precolonial relations between the dominant Tutsis and subordinate Hutus involved close patron-client ties between pastoralist Tutsi chiefs and Hutu agriculturalists. A German observer in Rwanda during this period described these cooperative relationships as a system of "intertwining fingers" (quoted in Prunier 2001:110). Under this system there was little or no ethnic violence. Warfare was frequent, but it involved Tutsis and Hutus fighting together against rival kingdoms (Prunier 1995:14–15). After colonial rule and independence, however, political and economic changes had made the traditional forms of clientship obsolete (Prunier 1995:42).

Even at the time of the 1994 genocide, the two groups were close in some ways. They spoke the same language, for example, and had the same religion.[3] Still, ethnic identity was sharp, rigid, and highly visible. Everyone received an ethnic identity at birth, traced through the male line, and this identity was readily identifiable, either by appearance or by means of identification cards all Rwandans had to carry (Gourevitch 1998:56–57; Hintjens 1999:249; Mann 2005:432–33; see also Hatzfeld 2005a:105). Because children shared the ethnic identity of their fathers, even intermarriage did little to blur ethnic boundaries (Mann 2005:432). And the rigidity of ethnic identity had increased over time. Up until the 1920s a person born Hutu might later become Tutsi, but by the end of the colonial era, ethnic identities had hardened (Hintjens 1999:250).

THE ONSET OF GENOCIDE

Within Rwanda, differences in the degree of social distance explain differences in genocide. In four of the prefectures, violence began in the first few days after President Habyarimana's assassination. In five others, genocide began early in parts of the prefectures, but later in other areas. Finally, in two of the prefectures, genocide was delayed for weeks in most areas (Straus 2004:80–88). In the two late-onset prefectures—Butare and Gitarama—intimacy between Hutus and Tutsis was greater. The amount of interethnic marriage was considerable, and ethnic relations were generally harmonious (Fletcher 2007:44n22; Jefremovas 1995:29). Butare may even have had the most intermarriage of any prefecture, and as noted above, it had the only Tutsi prefect, Jean-Baptiste Habyalimana (African Rights 1995:336; Des Forges 1999:353–54; ICTR 1996:28–29).[4] Hutus in the north sometimes said that Butare had no Hutus—that they were so integrated with Tutsis that they had lost their distinctiveness (Des Forges 1999:353). In Gitarama and Butare, then, the interim government had to send in outsiders to help begin the massacres (ICTR 1996:29; Jefremovas 1995:29). This was to some extent the case even in Nyakizu, where genocide began earlier than in other communes in Butare, and where local authorities acted in opposition to the prefect. But here social distance between Hutus and Tutsis was greater due the presence in Nyakizu of 15,000 Hutu refugees from Burundi.[5]

REFUGEES AS AGGRESSORS

The presence of Burundian refugees helps explain communal variation within Butare—why genocide began earlier and with more local support in Nyakizu.[6] The Burundian refugees in Nyakizu were also more involved than others in the killing.[7] They participated throughout the several days of attacks on Cyahinda parish, and they were especially prominent in the early stages, when they made up the bulk of the local civilian participants. In the first days of the attacks, local Hutus for the most part were not involved, and those who did participate tended to loot rather than kill. They looted the schools and health center at Cyahinda, for instance, and then fled with the stolen items (Des Forges 1999:387). Locals were so underrepresented in the killings at the start of the massacre, in fact, that after the first day the Burundians declared that they would not continue without more support (Des Forges 1999:387). After this Ntaganzwa was successful in increasing the participation of locals, but outsiders continued to have prominent roles. From the outset, along with the refugees and other close supporters of the burgomaster, the killings were led by militia members from Gikongoro and by national police officers. As the massacres went on, more outsiders joined the killing. National police officers and militia members from Butare were bused in on more than one occasion, and on the final day of the massacre a group of soldiers arrived to assist in finishing the operation (African Rights 1995:337–45; 1999:45–50; Des Forges 1999:387–95).

The same pattern is evident in the other killings in Nyakizu. Burundians were involved in the first massacres, those that took place near the Burundian border, and the killings in Cyanwa were initiated by gendarmes, police officers, and militia members coming from Gikongoro (Des Forges 1999:376–79; African Rights 1999:43–45). In this latter attack local Hutus at first sided with the Tutsis and tried to prevent the outsiders from entering (African Rights 1999:45). Outsiders were also disproportionately the targets of the early massacres. At the border of Burundi, for instance, where locals—along with Burundians—were involved from the outset, the first killings were of Tutsi refugees from outside the commune, though the killers later attacked local Tutsis (Des Forges 1999:376–77).

CONTRADICTORY BEHAVIOR

Even after attackers began to target local Tutsis, some Tutsis were spared. This mainly occurred where Hutus and Tutsis were bound by marriage, friendship, clientship, or other ties (Des Forges 1999:378). For example, a Hutu worker at the Cyahinda parish was able to hide the Tutsi priest for some time, and one woman hid her eight grandchildren in her home until they were discovered and killed in late May (Des Forges 1999:410–13).

Some Hutus rescued Tutsis, just as others killed them, but as we have seen in previous chapters, killers and rescuers sometimes might be the same people. This strange behavior is important because it points to the difficulty of explaining killing or rescuing only with individual factors. Any general differences between killers and rescuers—differences in their childhood socialization, say—cannot account for the cases where the same person engages in both behaviors. But my theory can account for these cases. Explaining genocide with purely social rather than social-psychological or individual factors, it predicts that in cases of contradictory behavior people would kill those who are distant and save those who are close. This is what happened in Nyakizu. One woman, for example, recalls her encounter with gendarmes who found her hiding in the Cyahinda parish: "Many people fled from the church, but many others of us stayed there and hid. I hid behind some houses of the convent. There were some *militaires* [national police officers] who found me there. One of them wanted to kill me, but the others said to leave me alone. They knew my husband [a Hutu] and said that he was a good man" (quoted in Des Forges 1999:383–84).

As noted previously, even after the major massacres at Cyahinda parish and Gasasa Hill, a number of Tutsi women were still alive—mainly those who were married to Hutu men or who had agreed to cohabitate with them to avoid being killed (Des Forges 1999:409). These were among the final targets of the genocide (Des Forges 1999:412–13). In these cases ties of intimacy led the participants in genocide to save particular Tutsis.

INEQUALITY

Both Rwanda and Burundi have a minority Tutsi and majority Hutu population, and genocide occurred in both countries—in Rwanda against Tutsis and in Burundi against Hutus. As my theory predicts, though, both genocides had a downward direction; they were directed against a lower-status group. While historically Tutsis were dominant in both societies, in postcolonial Rwanda the Tutsis, already smaller in number, were excluded from the government and other key sectors of power, and by the time of the 1994 genocide, they had been the targets of many episodes of violence, discrimination, and propaganda. In Burundi, where Tutsis kept control of the government, Hutus retained their subordinate status. Still, as a group the Hutus were greater in number in Burundi, and the 1972 genocide there—where the targets were mainly Hutu elites—was less severe than the 1994 genocide of Tutsis in Rwanda.

THE ONSET OF GENOCIDE

Hutus and Tutsis were unequal, then, but the degree of inequality varied. In the south, where genocide was generally slowest to begin, Hutus and Tutsis were not just more intimate than elsewhere, they were also more equal. The proportion of Tutsis was greater, and these regions were outside the traditional center of Hutu power (Fletcher 2007:44n23). Butare, for instance, had a higher concentration of Tutsis than any other prefecture, and it was the center of the old Tutsi kingdom (Des Forges 1999:353; Jofremovas 1995:29). As noted previously, it was also the only prefecture governed by a Tutsi prefect, Habyalimana, a member of one of the opposition parties. The opposition parties were also stronger in Butare and Gitarama than elsewhere. In his study of prefectural variation, political scientist Scott Straus (2004:100) found that political party support was the strongest single predictor of the onset of genocide. This supports the theoretical relevance of inequality in that Hutus were more unified and the ruling party's power strongest in the early-onset prefectures.[8]

UNEQUAL SUPPORT

That genocide was associated with the strength of the ruling party also points to variation in another relevant type of inequality: unequal support. Opposition to the aggressors often prevented or delayed the genocide. Just as the prefect of Butare delayed the genocide within the prefecture, resistance by local authorities—such as the burgomasters of the communes—could achieve such a delay at the communal level. In the Giti commune of Byumba prefecture, for instance, the burgomaster refused to begin massacres, and he even arrested Hutu youths who killed cattle belonging to local Tutsis. Due to the actions of the burgomaster and other local authorities, Giti was the only commune where no Tutsis were killed. The RPF gained control of the commune on April 16, though, and the burgomaster later noted that he could not have prevented violence for much longer had the RPF not arrived (Janzen 2000; Straus 2004:123–27). In other places where burgomasters resisted the genocide, it was delayed but not prevented. In some of these cases the burgomasters reversed their previous positions after coercion from higher authorities. In others local extremists seized control and organized the genocide. In still others outside forces such as the military or the authorities of neighboring communes initiated the genocide (Fletcher 2007:35–36; McDoom 2005; Straus 2004:123).

In Nyakizu the burgomaster was not a member of the president's party, but he was part of the Hutu Power faction of the opposition and thus had become aligned with the president's party and with other extremists. And he had much support and little opposition as he began the genocide within the commune. This was in part because when he had earlier gained control of the local government, he had begun building a powerful, informal, and covert network of close associates and subordinates. As historian Michele Wagner notes, this was similar to the structure of the central government, which consisted of an informal network of elites alongside the formal administrative system: "Ntaganzwa's pattern of governing Nyakizu was in fact very much the pattern by which President Habyarimana governed Rwanda. Although he officially headed the governmental structure, Habyarimana nevertheless developed a parallel and informal MRND structure. In this way, he exerted direct control that reached from the highest level of the government down to the grassroots, unimpeded by checks and balances or intermediate levels" (Wagner 1998:34).

Through Ntaganzwa, the members of this network were linked to even higher-status officials and acted at their behest. This powerful group was also in a social location conducive to attracting further support from within the commune, given that people tend to support those who are socially close and high in status, as Donald Black's theory of partisanship predicts. Still, especially at first, some within the commune resisted the genocide. The most prominent of these resisters was Jean-Marie Vianney Gasingwa, the leader of another political party and the assistant burgomaster (Des Forges 1999:388). Separate from Ntaganzwa's circle, Gasingwa was nevertheless high enough in status to attract his own supporters. For example, on April 14, with the support of Gasingwa a temporary communal worker refused to implement the burgomaster's order to collect weapons from the Tutsis gathered at the church in Cyahinda (Des Forges 1999:375). The opposition of Hutu moderates such as Gasingwa can be explained by their social location—high in status and distant from the organizers of the genocide. Their presence also explains the reluctance of local Hutus to become involved in the killing. In the early stages the killers were mostly outsiders and those with connections to the burgomaster. But after the first day of the Cyahinda massacre, Gasingwa and other moderates were killed and participation increased.[9] The elimination of the burgomaster's political opposition left no one opposed to the genocide who could attract a large number of supporters.

THE RWANDAN GENOCIDE AS A MATTER OF DEGREE

The Rwandan Genocide was an extreme case—a hypergenocide more similar to the Holocaust than to the genocides in California, India, and Bosnia. It was especially extreme in its intensiveness, ethnic basis, and scale, though not in its one-sidedness.

INTENSIVENESS AND ETHNIC BASIS

In Rwanda the killing was more intensive, or more thorough, than in any case we have examined so far. For the most part killing was not combined with other strategies, and three-fourths of Tutsis were killed in only a few months. This kind of killing is more likely when physical separation is not an option. For the most part this was true in Rwanda, where Hutus could eliminate Tutsis only by extermination, not expulsion. And not only were most potential targets killed, all Tutsis were potential targets. The degree of polarization between the groups was extreme, and so was the extent to which the genocide was ethnically based. Most of the targets were killed simply for being Tutsis.

SCALE

Consistent with the high degree of organization on the part of those who planned and carried out the killing, the Rwandan genocide was also large in scale. As in the Bosnian case, the planners of the genocide were state elites—already organized and in an ideal social position to formulate collective grievances and to attract support. In Rwanda, moreover, the genocide was initially organized by a small group of no more than two dozen senior officials associated with the president's wife's clan (Valentino 2004:62). These officials formed "a small tight group, belonging to the regime's political, military, and economic elite who had decided . . . radically to resist political change they perceived as threatening" (Prunier 1995:241–42). So initiators of the killing were members of an especially high-status clique within the government. Upon taking power they could mobilize the military and paramilitary organizations throughout the country.

Certain features of Rwandan society also enabled them to obtain other supporters, and it appears that a greater percentage of civilians participated in the killing than in any other large-scale genocide. Rwandan authorities maintained a high degree of bureaucratic control over the population. They tightly controlled residential mobility and agricultural production, and they required Rwandans to perform one day of unpaid labor each week (Hintjens 1999:270–71). This system of communal work—known as *umuganda*—involved activities such as repairing roads, digging ditches, and building schools (Straus 2004:320–21). Structures connecting civilians to the state, then, were widespread.[10] The local-level leaders of genocide were thus able to recruit killers from the largely peasant population in much the same way as they mobilized them for other tasks. Those who joined the violence often described it as identical, or at least similar, to ordinary communal work. For instance, they frequently referred to the killing as "our work" (Taylor 2002:169). One participant noted that "everybody had to show up blade in hand and pitch in for a decent stretch of work" (quoted in Hatzfeld 2005b:13). "We had work to do," said another, "and we were doing our best" (quoted in Hatzfeld 2005b:15).

ONE-SIDEDNESS

The one feature of the Rwandan genocide that was not extreme was its one-sidedness. The violence by Hutus against Tutsis was to some extent connected to violence elsewhere by Tutsis against Hutus. In 1972 a genocide led by the Tutsi government of neighboring Burundi had resulted in 100,000 deaths, and in 1993, after Tutsi army officers assassinated Burundi's Hutu president, pogroms against Tutsis followed by army killings of Hutus resulted in 50,000 deaths (Prunier 1995:198–206). In 1990, as we have seen, an army of Tutsi exiles (the RPF) had invaded Rwanda, and Hutus blamed these Tutsi rebels for the 1994 assassination of Rwanda's president. After the president's death, the civil war between the Rwandan government and the Tutsi exiles resumed, and during its course the Tutsi exiles engaged not only in warfare, but also in civilian massacres resulting in 25,000 to 60,000 deaths (Des Forges 1999:16). Of course, the 1994 genocide of Rwandan Tutsis was larger than this or any previous massacre in either Burundi or Rwanda, and the Tutsis targeted were not involved in the civil war. Still, violence by Tutsis against Hutus was occurring at the same time, and Rwanda's Tutsis were attacked in part because of their ethnic similarity to Burundians who had killed Hutus and to Rwandan exiles leading an invading army.

The violence was thus mainly one-sided, but not completely so. The one-sidedness of genocide is associated with inequality, and consistent with this, violence by Tutsis against Hutus did not occur in the same places as the anti-Tutsi genocide, but in places where Tutsis were dominant. In Burundi, for example, Tutsis controlled the military, and the military power of Tutsi exiles in Uganda allowed them to invade Rwanda and later to inflict violence against Hutus in areas they controlled. Here the reciprocal elements of the genocide were due to the inconsistency in Hutu-Tutsi relations: Hutus and Tutsis might be dominant or subordinate at one time and place but not in another.

This chapter has demonstrated the ability of the distinctive theory presented here to explain the violence during the Rwandan genocide at multiple levels. The genocide occurred when and where it did because the conflict—caused by the RPF invasion and other movements of social time—occurred in a context of inseparability, social distance, and inequality. An invading army composed largely of Tutsis previously expelled from the country meant that Hutus were unlikely to use expulsion again as an alternative to genocide. And political and social developments, especially since the 1959 Hutu Revolution, had subordinated Tutsis to Hutus and increased the social distance between the two groups.

But the violence in 1994 varied across Rwanda's eleven prefectures. In two of these, where Tutsis were better able to flee, the level of violence was lower. In two others, where Hutus and Tutsis were more equal (such as in political participation) and less distant (for example, through intermarriage) genocide was delayed for weeks in most areas. One of these late-onset prefectures was Butare, and Nyakizu commune, which we examined more closely, was the only commune in this prefecture where genocide began earlier. And significantly, inequality and social distance were greater here. The Hutu Power faction of one of the political parties controlled the communal government, and many of the Hutus in Nyakizu were recent refugees from Burundi. As we saw, the Burundians were disproportionately involved in killing, especially in the early stages, and within the commune more distant Tutsis were more likely to be killed. Hutus sometimes aided neighbors and others with whom they had ties, and among the last targets of the killing were women married to or cohabitating with Hutu men. We also saw that my theory explains why genocide took the form it did. Though the Rwandan genocide was mostly an extreme case, Hutu superiority was not a feature of Hutu-Tutsi relations everywhere, so the overall conflict was less one-sided.

One thing this case illustrates is that we find a great deal of variation within all genocides—even the most extreme. Not everyone from the aggressors' group participates, and not everyone who participates does so with the same intensity. Nor is everyone from the targeted group killed. And when genocide operates over a large territory, it operates differently in some places than it does in others. It is important, then, to look very closely at what actually happens during genocides. If we are to understand genocide, we need to understand variation in genocide—any kind of variation.

7 JEWS AND GENTILES IN EUROPE

On the night of June 25, 1941, Lithuanians attacked residents of the suburb of Vilijampole, which the Jews called Slobodka. This was the home of strict Jews, important rabbis, and rabbinical students. The attackers used machine guns to massacre many of the Jewish men, women, and children. Others they cut up and disfigured (Gordon 1992:37; Mishell 1988:20–21; Oshry 1995:2). A prominent rabbi was later found "bent over his blood-soaked books while his severed head looked on from another room" (Littman 1983:44; see also Oshry 1995:3). The attackers killed and mutilated entire families too, as one Kovno resident found when he went to the scene after the violence was over:

> I went into one house where the floor was covered with blood. Two cut-off legs lay in one room and in another there was a mutilated body. The severed head of the body was resting on the table in the kitchen with two needles in the eyes. In a second home, I found a family of five, all with their tongues protruding and blue; they had been choked to death. In a third house there was a family of six: a mother, a father, and four little children. They had been nailed to the table with large nails. Before they died . . . they had enough time to write in Yiddish, in their own blood, on the walls and the floor, "Any brothers or sisters who survive, take revenge for our spilled and innocent blood." (Gordon 1992:37–38)

THE HOLOCAUST

The genocide of European Jews during World War II, known as the Holocaust, is the most extreme case of genocide in history. It is also the best-known case. Nearly everyone is familiar with its basic facts: in the early twentieth century, the anti-Semitic Nazi government of Germany orchestrated the killing of nearly 6 million Jews. The Nazis and their allies rounded up Jews throughout Europe, transported them by trains to death camps in Eastern Europe, killed them in gas chambers, and then burned their corpses in crematories. This is the popular view of the Holocaust, and it is accurate as far as it goes. But other facts about the genocide may be less familiar.

For example, many people overlook the close connection between the Holocaust and Germany's war with the Soviet Union. As bizarre as it may seem, the Nazis blamed Jews for Germany's war with the Soviets—a war begun by Hitler himself (Herf 2005). In a 1939 speech Hitler had warned that "if the international Jewish financiers in and outside Europe should succeed in plunging the nations once more into a world war, then the result will not be the Bolshevizing of the earth, and thus the victory of Jewry, but the annihilation of the Jewish race in Europe!" (quoted in Goldhagen 1996:142). Hitler called this statement a prophecy and referred to it many times after the war began. The idea was that the Jews had disbelieved Hitler's prophecy and failed to heed his warning, that they had plunged the nations into war, and that for their crime they were now being annihilated. And so the Holocaust began with Germany's invasion of the Soviet Union in 1941. At first paramilitary forces followed behind the German army, killing Jewish men and suspected communists. The Jews who remained in the newly conquered territories were then confined to ghettoes. That same year the Nazis began deporting German Jews to Eastern Europe, and killing operations escalated as the ghettoes became more and more crowded (Snyder 2010:207). In 1942 the Nazis established the death camps, though mass shootings and the use of gas vans continued in the areas that had recently been under Soviet control. By the end of the year, most of the Jews were already dead (Snyder 2010:219). Since the Holocaust was connected with the war, most of the killing occurred in Eastern Europe, where the genocide began and to which the Nazis deported Jews from the West.

THE HOLOCAUST IN LITHUANIA

In this chapter I examine more closely one part of the Holocaust: the killings of Jews in Kovno, Lithuania. Two features of the genocide in Lithuania recommend it as a case for study. First, the Holocaust in Lithuania was extremely severe—almost total. It resulted in the deaths of more than 150,000 and perhaps more than 200,000 Jews, or between 90 and 95 percent of Lithuania's pre-war Jewish population (Eidintas 2003:16; Ginaite-Rubinson 2005:219; MacQueen 2004:1; Matthäus 1997:15; Neshamit 1977:329; Shochat 1974:301). Only the Jews of Latvia and Estonia had lower survival rates (Shochat 1974:301). Second, as noted above, the Holocaust began in Eastern Europe, specifically in Lithuania (Dieckmann 2000; Matthäus 1997:15; Porat 1996:159). It was in Lithuania that the Nazis first began to kill Jews indiscriminately and in mass numbers.

Though the Holocaust proceeded differently in each of the states under Nazi influence or control, the Lithuanian case serves as a useful microcosm of the genocide as a whole, not only because this was the area where Nazis first began exterminating European Jews, but also because many of the features that distinguish the Holocaust in general, such as the degree of mass killing, are particularly characteristic of the killing in Lithuania. But just as in Rwanda, the genocide varied even though it was extreme. Some Lithuanians participated in the genocide; others did not. Germans and their Lithuanian supporters killed some Jews immediately; others they allowed to live much longer. Variations such as these can be explained with my theory. For example, the Jews in the Kovno Ghetto who lived the longest were those whose labor the Germans depended on. Interdependence of this kind inhibits genocide. So do other forms of social closeness, and we shall see that ties of intimacy or cultural similarity led some Germans and Lithuanians to rescue or aid particular Jews. My theory explains many other aspects of the genocide as well, but before we examine these further, let us look more closely at the general features of the Holocaust in Lithuania and the events preceding it.

LITHUANIAN INDEPENDENCE

Lithuania became an independent state in 1918, in the aftermath of World War I. Prior to this it had been under Russian control since the eighteenth century. Jews had lived in Lithuania since the twelfth century, and at the time of independence approximately 150,000 Jews lived in Lithuania, about 7.5 percent of the population (Littman

1983:28). For most of Lithuania's history Lithuanians were relatively tolerant of Jews, but not always. In 1495, for instance, the king expelled all Jews from Lithuania, though he invited them back eight years later (Mishell 1988:4). Other expulsions of Jews, such as repeated expulsions from the city of Kovno, were more localized (Beinfeld 1997:25). Still, large-scale pogroms of the kind that occurred in Russia during the mid-seventeenth century were absent (Mishell 1988:4). During the czarist occupation Russian authorities oppressed both Jews and Lithuanians, and in 1915 they expelled the Jews of a number of Lithuanian cities into the Ukraine (Mishell 1988:4; Schoenburg and Schoenburg 1991:38). Those Jews returned upon the collapse of the czarist government, however, and many of them joined the fight for Lithuanian independence (Mishell 1988:4).

When Lithuania became independent, the new government granted Jews equal rights as citizens as well as a degree of political autonomy unknown in any other European country (Beinfeld 1997:26; Eidintas 2003:64; Oshry 1995:ix). The time during which this lasted was known as the "golden era" for Lithuanian Jews (Beinfeld 1997:27; Mishell 1988:4; Schoenburg and Schoenburg 1991:39). Beginning in 1922, however, after the Vilna region was incorporated into Poland, the golden era came to an end. Laws limited Jewish agricultural activity, newly formed Lithuanian cooperatives displaced Jews from their merchandizing positions, opposition to the use of Hebrew on signs of Jewish enterprises began to rise, and the Jewish autonomy structure began to be dissolved (Beinfeld 1997:27; Mishell 1988:5; Neshamit 1977:291; Schoenburg and Schoenburg 1991:39; Shochat 1974:301). In 1926, when military officers seized power to form a nationalist government, they removed Jews from government posts and effectively barred them from the courts (Mishell 1988:5). By this time the Jewish schools were all that remained of Jewish autonomy (Shochat 1974:302; Oshry 1995:ix).

SOVIETS AND NAZIS

Despite such measures Jews generally prospered under Lithuanian independence, and most were strong supporters of the Lithuanian state. Lithuanian independence increasingly came under threat, though, from both Germany and the Soviet Union. As World War II began, and as Germany and later the Soviet Union invaded Poland, Lithuania remained neutral (Beinfeld 1997:28). Meanwhile, Germany and the Soviet Union had agreed to divide Eastern Europe between them in the 1939 Molotov-Ribbentrop Pact, and they had subsequently agreed that Lithuania would be in the Soviet sphere of influence (Beinfeld 1997:29). In October 1939 the Lithuanian government agreed to allow the Soviets to station troops in Lithuania, in return for which Vilna—at the time under Polish control—would again be part of Lithuania (Budreckis 1968:3).[1] This turned out to be a preparation for Soviet rule. On June 15, 1940, the Soviets invaded Lithuania, at first installing a pro-Soviet government and soon thereafter annexing Lithuania as a Soviet republic (Beinfeld 1997:29; Littman 1983:29).

The ethnic Lithuanian population widely and intensely opposed the Soviet invasion and the oppressive policies that followed it. The reaction of Jews was different. Most Jews opposed communism and supported Lithuanian independence, but as it became clear that Lithuania would fall under either Soviet or German control, many welcomed the Soviet invasion as an option preferable to rule by Nazi Germany (Beinfeld 1997:29; Budreckis 1968:18; Eidintas 2003:158; Mann 2005:282; Shochat 1974:304). One Jewish resident described the reaction of Jews in Kovno upon learning that the invaders were Russians rather than Germans: "Suddenly our mood changed. Instead of panic, we felt an unnatural joy. Everyone started hugging and kissing each other, family and neighbors, as if the Messiah had just arrived. . . . Those who had been hiding ran out of their houses and began throwing bouquets of flowers at the approaching army" (Gordon 1992:9–10).

Ethnic Lithuanians, on the other hand, saw Nazi rule as preferable and resisted the Soviet annexation (Mann 2005:282). So when the Nazis invaded in June 1941, Lithuanians greeted them with the same level of enthusiasm that many Jews had extended previously to the invading communists (Budreckis 1968:60; Littman 1983:40). Meanwhile Jews attempted to flee with the departing Russian troops into the Soviet Union—though only about 6,000 were successful (Budreckis 1968:58; Eidintas 2003:174; Elkes 1999:15; Gordon 1992:22; Littman 1983:39–40; Mishell 1988:12). Organized groups of Lithuanian partisans welcomed the Nazis in an eventually failed effort to reestablish an independent Lithuanian state. Hoping that the Nazis would recognize an anticommunist and pro-Nazi Lithuanian state, these small military bands acted quickly throughout the country to drive out the Soviets, take control of the country, and declare a provisional government prior to the Nazi arrival (Budreckis 1968:34–35). In the first days of the war, many of these partisans attacked and arrested Jews, and when the Nazis arrived the partisans aided them in anti-Jewish violence. Later, when the Nazis dissolved the provisional government and the partisan bands, many of the partisans became part of German-led battalions that helped carry out the genocide during the remainder of the Nazi occupation (Mishell 1988:16–26; Neshamit 1977:293–95; Piotrowski 1998:164; Porat 1996:162–63).

The genocide of Jews in Lithuania proceeded in several stages. At first the targets were mainly Jewish men and communists. The first attack was on June 24, 1941, in the Lithuanian border town of Garsden, where a division of the *Einsatzgruppen*—the SS paramilitary death squads—shot 201 persons, mostly Jewish men (Dieckmann 2000:240; Goldhagen 1996:150). Similar killings followed in other areas, as the *Einsatzgruppen* would follow the German army to secure territory and eliminate potential enemies. During this time the Nazis also orchestrated pogroms and other killings in the cities with the help of Lithuanian collaborators (Dieckmann 2000:249). In this stage, which occurred from the beginning of the war until August 1941, 10,000 to 12,000 persons were killed (Dieckmann 2000:241).

The second phase of the genocide occurred from mid-August to November 1941, when German and Lithuanian units killed Jewish men, women, and children in the rural areas and confined those in the cities to ghettos. Then a series of killing operations lasting until the end of November 1941 drastically reduced the numbers of Jews in the ghettos. By the end of this period, at least 120,000 Jews had been killed (Dieckmann 2000:251; Porat 1996:167). The third stage occurred in 1943 and 1944, when the Nazis liquidated the ghettos. At this time they killed nearly all ghetto residents or deported them to German concentration camps.

"A HATCHING GROUND OF JEWS"

Like other genocides, the Holocaust occurred in response to grievances against the targeted group. Many Germans believed that the Jews were "clannish, aloof, and distant," as well as clever, greedy, dishonest, and striving for power and success (Adam 1996:43; compare Bonacich 1973:591). They were parasites who lived off the labor of others (Friedländer 1997:96; Goldhagen 1996:412; Weitz 2003:108). Jews were disloyal to the nation and responsible for Germany's defeat in World War I (Staub 1989:100; Friedländer 1997:73–74). Jewish doctors harmed their non-Jewish patients, and Jews molested and murdered children (Friedländer 1997:104; Staub 1989:104). Jews were aesthetically repulsive genetic misfits (Lerner 1992:66–67), sexual predators (Weitz 2003:106), and a threat to racial purity (Lerner 1992:35; Staub 1989:104). They had taken over German culture (Johnson 1987:477–81; Friedländer 1997:107), and they were the source of all the modern ills—capitalism, communism, liberalism, democracy, and urbanism—that threatened the German way of life (Cohn 1969:170). They formed "a conspiratorial body set on ruining and then dominating the rest of mankind" (Cohn 1969:16), and they were" wicked creatures" who belonged to an "anti-race" outside of the hierarchy of human races (Goldhagen 1996:411). The Nazis' grievances were against Jews broadly—against German Jews as well as against those in Lithuania and elsewhere in Eastern Europe, where most of the killings occurred. In fact, they believed Eastern European Jews to be especially threatening, since the East, they said, was a "hatching ground of Jews" (Eidintas 2003:175).

But the Lithuanians also had numerous grievances against Jews—both long-standing and more recent. During the period of Russian control before Lithuanian independence, Lithuanians said that Jewish merchants used inaccurate weights and measures, that Jews were not suited for hard work, that they were "bootlickers" of Russian officials, that they had the power to bewitch children and animals, that they knew magic spells, and that they killed Christian children for rituals (Eidintas 2003:26–52). Many Lithuanians blamed Jews collectively for Christ's crucifixion, and some said that when a Jew prays the devil carries off his prayers, or that when Jews are on their deathbeds their relatives choke them with pillows to keep them from uttering the name of Jesus (Eidintas 2003:43–44). Lithuanians also blamed Jews for various misfortunes and failures: "When a farmer got drunk—his excuse to his family would be that the Jewish shopkeeper was to blame. When he got deep into debt—it was the money-lending Jew, who was to blame, because the debt had to be repaid with an added percentage" (Eidintas 2003:39).

Many of these grievances continued into the era of independence, when Lithuanians accused Jews of dishonest sales practices, of kidnapping women and children, and of not engaging in physical labor (Eidintas 2003:75–82). They blamed Jews collectively for the rare crimes committed by Jews, and they objected when Jews spoke languages other than Lithuanian (Eidintas 2003:82–89). At the university in Kovno, for instance, Lithuanians assaulted Jewish students who spoke Yiddish to one another and ridiculed those who spoke Lithuanian with an accent (Mishell 1988:6). Economic grievances also intensified, especially after the rise of Lithuanian nationalism, and groups such as the Lithuanian Merchants' Union accused Jews of trying to achieve world domination (Ginaite-Rubinson 2005:26). But the most immediate grievances had to do with the association of Jews with communism and with the hated Soviet regime.

"HITLER WILL COME SOON AND THEN WE WILL GIVE YOU YOUR DUE"

Both the Lithuanian partisans and many ordinary Lithuanians blamed Jews for Soviet rule. One of the proclamations of the Lithuanian underground identified the Jewish population as the enemy of Lithuanians: "Lithuanian brothers and sisters, the fateful and final hour has come to settle our account with the Jews. The right of asylum given to Jews in the time of Vytautas the Great is hereby cancelled in all respects" (quoted in Shochat 1974:310). Likewise, when the Lithuanian partisans seized control of the media during the first days of the Nazi invasion, a program was aired called *What the Activists Are Fighting For*. It claimed that Jews had been responsible for the downfall of the Lithuanian state and that communism was a Jewish ideology (Ginaite-Rubinson 2005:27). Over the radio Jurgis Bobelis, the commander of the partisan forces, claimed that Jew-Bolshevik guerrillas were firing at the German army and warned that his troops would execute a hundred Jews for every German life lost (Littman 1983:42).

Ordinary citizens made similar statements. During Soviet rule Lithuanians would insult Jews by saying things such as "Jews *ka-*

put," "Hitler will come soon and then we will give you your due," and "Hey, you! Jew! You think Stalin is your Daddy? You think you are in heaven? It isn't going to last!" (Neshamit 1977:289–90; Gordon 1992:16). One Jewish resident of Kovno recounts going to the office where he worked shortly after the invasion. He soon found out that all of the Russians who worked there had gone, as well as most of the Jews. One of the Lithuanians there told him, "Your buddies are gone. They packed up yesterday and left town and didn't even leave a forwarding address" (quoted in Mishell 1988:12). Such sentiments fit well with the Nazi conception of a Jewish-Bolshevik conspiracy, and upon their entry into the country, the Germans further propagated the notion that the Jews were allied with the Soviets and accused Jews of having resisted their advance (Kwiet 1998:5, 13).

As noted above, many Jews did prefer Soviet to Nazi rule, and many were relieved when the Soviets invaded. There was little truth, though, in the notion that the Jewish population as a whole, or any substantial part of it, were communists or Soviet collaborators. Religious Jews and Zionists—who together made up the overwhelming majority of Jews—were especially hostile to communism, and they disapproved of collaboration with the Soviets (Eidintas 2003:158). Jews were, however, more likely than Lithuanians to be involved in the Communist Party. In some locations they were even dominant—such as in Kovno, where before the Soviet invasion 70 percent of the members of the Communist Party were of Jewish descent (Eidintas 2003:126). The Soviets treated Jews as equal citizens, and while that sometimes meant they equally oppressed them, it also meant that Jews could now teach at the universities, serve in the government, and work in government institutions (Mishell 1988:8). Their numbers in these institutions were small. In the central committee of the Communist Party, for instance, there were only two Jews but forty to fifty Lithuanians (Mishell 1988:8–9). But the presence of even a few Jews in high political positions where none were before led Lithuanians to characterize the regime as Jewish in character (Eidintas 2003:154; Mishell 1988:8).

Neither the Lithuanians nor the Nazis, then, distinguished between the few Jews who were communists or Soviet collaborators and the bulk of the Jewish population (Eidintas 2003:158). They held all

Jews responsible. The charge of Soviet collaboration and other grievances formed the basis of the subsequent genocide. This and the other grievances resulted from movements of social time, and they occurred within a social context conducive to genocide. Before examining how these factors explain the genocide, though, let us look more closely at the killing in Kovno.

THE HOLOCAUST IN KOVNO

At the time of the Nazi invasion on June 22, 1941, Kovno (called Kaunas by Lithuanians) had a population of about 120,000, which included about 35,000 Jews (Mishell 1988:15). As the invasion began, thousands of Jews fled the city, but most returned when they failed to make it into the Soviet Union. Even those who made it as far as the border were usually turned away. As was the case elsewhere in Lithuania, Lithuanian partisans called White Armbanders, moved quickly to seize control of the city. By June 23, before the Germans arrived, the Soviets were already gone and the partisans in control (Beinfeld 1997:31). No mass killings of Jews occurred during the first few days, only a few shoot-outs with single victims (Eidintas 2003:178; Kwiet 1998:14). At this time the partisans began harassing and arresting Jews, particularly those with connections to the Soviet regime and those attempting to flee (Beinfeld 1997:31; Eidintas 2003:202). German troops arrived on June 24, and the next day genocide in Kovno began—first in the form of pogroms and later with mass arrests and killings.

THE EARLY KILLINGS

It was at this time that Lithuanians attacked Slobodka and killed between 600 and 1,500 Jews, including nearly all of the area's seminary students (Beinfeld 1997:31; Budreckis 1968:63; Eidintas 2003:178; Ginaite-Rubinson 2005:35–36; Gordon 1992:38; Mishell 1988:20–21; Oshry 1995:1–4; Tory 1990:23). Shortly after the Slobodka pogrom, Lithuanian partisans killed between seventeen and fifty Jewish men in a massacre at the Lietukis garage.[2] First they forced a group of Jews to clean horse manure off the floor of the garage. Then they took the Jews to the water hoses to wash up, and there they beat them with rifles, wrenches, crowbars, and various other tools. They revived those who were knocked unconscious and then beat them until they died. In some cases they forced the high-pressure hoses into the men's mouths and gorged them with water until their stomachs burst. German soldiers looked on and took pictures, and nearby civilians watched and cheered the slaughter. One of the killers began playing Lithuania's anthem on an accordion while the killing continued. When the killings were over, another group of Jews had to clean up the blood and the bodies (Eidintas 2003:185; Kwiet 1998:14; Littman 1983:44; Matthäus 2004:18; Mishell 1988:25; Tory 1990:23).

At the same time, partisans began arresting Jews who attempted to flee the city. They also conducted house arrests in which they rounded up Jews they accused of shooting at German troops. Eventually they took most of these Jewish prisoners, along with some Lithuanians, Russians, and Poles, to the Seventh Fort—one of a number of forts built far outside the city under czarist rule. Due to the expansion of Kovno the forts were now just outside the city and, being of no use in modern warfare, were used mainly for storage (Beinfeld 1997:31; Mishell 1988:37–38). These became prisons and sites of executions under Nazi rule.

At the Seventh Fort the partisans put women and children into the cells and corridors of what was formerly an underground barracks. These became so overcrowded the prisoners were stacked on top of one another. For days the prisoners stayed in the unheated and damp cells with no food or water, and periodically the Lithuanian guards would beat them and take their jewelry and other valuables. They would also force women to undress and dance, and sometimes they raped and killed them (Littman 1983:45; Mishell 1988:43–44; Tory 1990:23–24). Meanwhile the Lithuanians took the men to the valley that formed the center of the compound. The men were in the open air, also without food and water, and the guards told them not to move or talk—that they would open fire if the men disobeyed. The partisans would regularly select groups of men, ostensibly for work, and take them outside the fort and shoot them. They would select others to bury the bodies and then shoot them as well. Some men attempted to attack the guards and were immediately gunned down. Others were shot when they begged for water. As more and more men asked for water, the guards finally took a group out to the well and shot them (Littman 1983:45; Mishell 1988:38–39). Eventually the guards took the women and children out of the barracks and opened fire on them as they approached the gate. The shooting stopped quickly, though, and the guards released the women and children who were still alive. Next they released men who had fought as volunteers for Lithuanian independence. On July 6 the partisans opened fire on those who were left. The killing continued all day and into the night, and by July 7 everyone was dead (Ginaite-Rubinson 2005:21–23; Mishell 1988:39–44). Altogether, at least 3,000 and perhaps as many as 7,000 Jews were killed at the Seventh Fort during the first few weeks of the war (Beinfeld 1997:31; Ginaite-Rubinson 2005:22–23; Mishell 1988:391; Tory 1990:23–24).

Mass killings in Kovno then subsided for a while, though sporadic killings and arrests continued. During this period the Nazis made plans to isolate and control the Jewish population by confining them to a Jewish ghetto in Slobodka, where it was announced that all of Kovno's Jews would have to relocate by mid-August. In the meantime Jews could not have newspapers, radios, cameras, typewriters, or bicycles. They could not walk on sidewalks, sell property, use public transportation, employ non-Jewish help, or receive treatment from non-Jewish doctors. Jewish doctors could not treat non-Jewish patients. Jews also had to wear a yellow Star of David on their clothing, and they could shop only during certain hours (Elkes 1999:19–27; Littman 1983:59; Mishell 1988:48, 56). On August 7, as Jews were moving into the ghetto before the deadline, Lithuanian partisans began a final wave of arrests. They took more than 1,000 Jews to the Fourth Fort and killed them the next day. This was known as the "Black Thursday Massacre" (Mishell 1988:59; see also Elkes 1999:28; Littman 1983:61).

THE GHETTO ACTIONS

Slobodka, the site of the Jewish ghetto, was one of the poorest areas of the city, where residents lived in small wooden houses without indoor plumbing. An area only two kilometers in length and one kilometer in width, previously home to no more than 8,000 people, was now to house all 30,000 of Kovno's Jews (Beinfeld 1997:31; Ginaite-Rubinson 2005:48; United States Holocaust Memorial Museum 2007). The ghetto consisted of two sections. A street divided the smaller section, known as the Small Ghetto, from the Large Ghetto, and a bridge over the street connected them (Beinfeld 1997:31; United States Holocaust Memorial Museum 2007). During the transition period Jews sought to obtain property in the ghetto from the departing Lithuanian residents, often trading large homes and other valuables for small dwellings where they crowded in with friends and family members. A Jewish committee, which later became the Jewish Council in the ghetto, was established to help with the transfers. By August 15 all of the city's Jews had moved into the ghetto, and they could leave only in work brigades under armed escort. They were then subjected to a series of "actions," or operations, which consisted of confiscations of Jewish property and the removal of groups of Jews to other areas for work or immediate death. By the end of 1941, nearly half of the residents had been killed.

The first action, known as the Intellectuals Action, took place just days after the sealing of the ghetto. The German administration informed the Jewish Council that five hundred "intellectuals" were needed to help put the municipality archives in order. The Council posted notices and drew up a list of candidates. On August 18 a number of professionals lined up for work, but many became suspicious when they saw that the Gestapo and Lithuanian auxiliaries were involved. Because they were two hundred people short of the quota, the troops began dragging men off the street and from their homes. Eventually the quota was met, and the troops took 534 men to deeply excavated holes at the Fourth Fort, where members of the Lithuanian guard shot them all (Beinfeld 1997:32; Elkes 1999:29; Goldstein-Golden 1985:50–51; Littman 1983:63–67; Matthäus 1997:22; Mishell 1988:65–67).

The Gold Action, or Valuables Action, followed right away. Beginning on August 19 German soldiers began searching from house to house and taking gold, silver, clothing, furniture, art collections, and appliances—anything of value—and they severely beat anyone who complained or was otherwise uncooperative. A second phase followed to uncover valuables hidden before. If they found anything that should have been turned over previously, the Germans shot the men in the house. During this phase of the action, the Germans would also force women to undress and then, claiming to be looking for hidden gold, perform gynecological investigations on them. In early September many of the valuables were still hidden, and the Nazis ordered the

Jewish Council to demand that all residents turn over their valuables to the Council the next day. Moreover, the searches would continue, and whenever anything was found, the whole household along with a hundred Jews living nearby would be shot. The Jewish police went from house to house encouraging people to hand things over voluntarily, and they collected tens of millions of dollars worth of jewelry (Gordon 1992:46–49; Littman 1983:69–70; Mishell 1988:67–72).

In mid-September, in what appeared to many of the ghetto residents as preparation for another action, Fritz Jordan, the Jewish Affairs Specialist for Kovno's German civil administration, gave the Jewish Council five hundred cards to be distributed to artisans and trade specialists. Each person receiving a card could add three family members to the card. The cards were known as "Jordan passes" or "life certificates" because it was suspected that those with the cards would be spared in future actions (Beinfeld 1997:32; Littman 1983:71; Mishell 1988:75–76). This proved true when on September 17 German and Lithuanian troops surrounded the Small Ghetto and began to chase the residents out of their homes and into the public square. A selection followed dividing those with Jordan passes from those without. Those without passes were loaded into trucks and driven toward the Ninth Fort. At this time, however, no one was killed. A messenger came and handed the Gestapo officer a piece of paper, and the officer then called off the action and dispersed the residents. Those on their way to the Ninth Fort were brought back (Littman 1983:71; Matthäus 1997:22; Mishell 1988:76–77). But this was soon followed on September 26 by the Kozlowski Action. Kozlowski, a Lithuanian policeman, claimed that snipers had targeted him as he walked down a ghetto street, and the Gestapo demanded that the Jewish Council find the culprit by the next day. When the Council was unable to do this, German and Lithuanian troops surrounded the area of the ghetto where the shooting was said to have occurred, forced the residents from their homes, beat them, and took those without Jordan passes to the Ninth Fort. There they shot more than 1,000 men, women, and children after forcing them to take off their clothes and line up in front of an open trench (Littman 1983:72–73; Matthäus 1997:22; Mishell 1988:81).

On October 4, in the Small Ghetto Action, German and Lithuanian troops surrounded and then liquidated the Small Ghetto. This followed the pattern of previous actions. First the troops chased people from their homes and forced them to assemble in the plaza. Again they made a selection, and they usually sent Jordan pass holders to the "good" side. When the selection was over, the troops took those on the other side—including the 180 orphans who lived in the Small Ghetto—to the Ninth Fort and killed them. Those remaining they forced to move into the already crowded Large Ghetto. The same day the attackers nailed shut the doors and windows of the Infectious Diseases Hospital. They then set the hospital on fire, and the patients, doctors, and nurses inside burned to death. That day about half of the Jews in the Small Ghetto—more than 1,800 persons—were killed (Beinfeld 1997:32; Elkes 1999:30–31; Matthäus 1997:22; Mishell 1988:85; Oshry 1995:48–50; United States Holocaust Memorial Museum 2007).

Next was the Great Action, the last genocidal operation to occur for some time and the largest single mass killing in Lithuania. Toward the end of October, the Nazis ordered the Jewish Council to post a proclamation stating that everyone was to assemble in Demokratu Plaza on the morning of October 28. The Council posted the proclamation, making clear that the orders were from the Nazis. On the 28th about 26,000 persons gathered in the plaza, where they were told to pass by Helmut Rauca, the local Jewish Affairs Specialist for the Gestapo, who then directed them to the right or left. This time Jordan passes did not matter, and Rauca made the selections on the basis of appearance. At first those sent to the right[3] were mostly old people, sick people, pregnant women, single women, and families with a number of children—those regarded as "useless eaters." But as the selections continued, they seemed to observers to become more indiscriminate. Rauca directed many workers to the right, for instance, especially those who looked dirty or unkempt, including one group of five hundred nightshift workers who had just returned from their jobs. Attempting to save as many as possible, Elkhanan Elkes, the chair of the Jewish Council, tried to intervene with Rauca to spare certain groups, but Rauca said, "You will be grateful to me, Elkes, for ridding you of this pile of manure." At the end of the day those on the right side numbered nearly 10,000, and they were taken to the now-vacant Small Ghetto (Beinfeld 1997:33; Ginaite-Rubinson 2005:64–66; Gordon 1992:65–67; Littman

1983:75–79; Matthäus 1997:22; Mishell 1988:90–92; Oshry 1995:62–64; Tory 1990:43–55).

The following day all of those selected were divided into groups of a hundred, marched to the Ninth Fort, and held in the barracks. There, one group at a time, the prisoners were taken out of the barracks, stripped, and told to lie down in trenches that had been prepared by Russian prisoners of war. Those who resisted were beaten and forced into the trenches or immediately shot. Members of a Lithuanian police battalion then fired into the trenches with machine guns that had been positioned there in advance. They would then repeat the process with each subsequent group, forcing each new group to lie on top of the corpses. The shootings went on all day. About 9,200 Jews were killed, including nearly 3,000 women about 4,200 children. Only about 17,000 Jews now remained in the ghetto (Beinfeld 1997:33; Ginaite-Rubinson 2005:66; Gordon 1992:68; Littman 1983:81; Matthäus 1997:22; Mishell 1988:93–94; Tory 1990:58).

After the Great Action the Nazis halted the mass killings of ghetto inmates for the next two years, though they still brought tens of thousands of Jews from outside of Lithuania to the Ninth Fort and executed them. The one large killing during this time was the Stalingrad Action. On February 2, 1943, the Germans surrendered to the Soviets in Stalingrad, and the next day the Gestapo began arresting Jews found away from their job sites. Others they arrested for bringing food into the ghetto and for various other offenses. Later they took the prisoners, numbering more than fifty, to the Ninth Fort and executed them (Elkes 1999:83; Mishell 1988:146–147; Oshry 1995:99–100). Throughout 1942 and 1943 the Nazis killed numerous other Jews for various individual infractions—for smuggling in food, for example, or for attempting to escape, or simply for failing to take off their hats as they approached the guards. Others died from overwork, malnourishment, or lack of medical care. And in several new actions the Nazis deported more Jews, confiscated more of their possessions, and continued to restrict their freedoms. In February and October 1942, for example, they deported several hundred Jews to Riga for slave labor. Also during this period the Nazis closed the ghetto's schools and synagogues, and they decreed that Jews in the ghetto must turn in their furs and their books and end all pregnancies (Elkes 1999:82; Matthäus 1997; Mishell 1988:392–93).

For some time the SA and SS had disagreed about how to deal with Kovno's Jews. The SA administrators favored a continuation of the current arrangements, in which the Jews of the ghetto lived with their families while their labor was exploited during the day for the benefit of the Reich. The SS, on the other hand, wanted to dissolve the ghetto, separate families, and confine the productive workers to smaller concentration camps (Elkes 1999:84; Matthäus 1997:24; Mishell 1988:162). Beginning on September 15, 1943, SS-Obersturmbannfuehrer Wilhelm Goecke was in charge of the ghetto (Beinfeld 1997:38; Elkes 1999:84; Matthäus 1997:23; Mishell 1988:162). With SS control, a new series of actions began. On October 26, in the Estonian Action, the Nazis deported 3,000 laborers for work in Estonia at the concentration camps of Vaivora and Klooga, and they took workers' children to Auschwitz and gassed them (Beinfeld 1997:38; Ginaite-Rubinson 2005:118; Mishell 1988:170–72; United States Holocaust Memorial Museum 2007).

Next, in November 1943, Goecke began transforming the ghetto into a concentration camp. He reduced the territory of the ghetto itself, so just 7,000 to 8,000 Jews were left. He divided the others into small work brigades and placed them in camps near their places of work. There the men and women lived separately in barracks under the supervision of SS guards (Beinfeld 1997:28; Elkes 1999:85; Ginaite-Rubinson 2005:118; Mishell 1988:164–80). In early 1944 the SS moved to destroy the Jewish underground, remove those unfit for work, and dissolve the ghetto completely. On March 27, in the Children's Action, they first arrested the 130 members of the ghetto police, who had been involved in underground activities and had extensive contacts with anti-Nazi partisans outside the ghetto. They then tortured the police officers, mostly unsuccessfully, trying to force them to reveal hiding places in the ghetto and information regarding the partisan movement. The same day they executed thirty-six of the police officers at the Ninth Fort (Beinfeld 1997:40; Ginaite-Rubinson 2005:204; Gordon 1992:126–27; Littman 1983:104; Mishell 1988:208–209; Oshry 1995:124).

The Germans also began removing children, the elderly, and the sick from homes in the ghetto and from the hospital. They forced many of the detainees into buses with painted windows, where they gassed them, and they drove others away to be killed later (Gordon 1992:127; Mishell 1988:209). The next day the action continued, and the SS policemen used axes, picks, and grenades to break into the bunkers of Jews who were in hiding. Nearly 2,000 Jews were killed in this action, including more than 1,000 children (Beinfeld 1997:40; Elkes 1999:95; Ginaite-Rubinson 2005:204; Gordon 1992:127–29; Littman 1983:104; Matthäus 1997:23; Mishell 1988:208–217; Oshry 1995:122–25). In the camps outside the ghetto, where the action also took place, not a single child survived (Mishell 1988:211; Oshry 1995:125). In the ghetto itself there were now officially no children, though many remained who had hidden in undiscovered bunkers. After this the Jewish Council and Jewish Police were dissolved, and the ghetto was renamed Concentration Camp Kauen.

The final action began on July 8, 1944. The Soviet armies were approaching, and the SS decided to liquidate the camps and evacuate the few thousand remaining inmates. The 2,000 prisoners who volunteered or were detained at this time were deported to concentration camps inside the Reich—the women to Stutthof and the men to Dachau. Others hid in bunkers and other hiding places, hoping to survive until the Soviets took control of Kovno. For the next few days the SS searched the houses, looking for bunkers (Beinfeld 1997:40; Littman 1983:105; Matthäus 1997:23; 2004:25; Mishell 1988:243–49). Then came the *Einsatzgruppen,* who for days methodically destroyed every building with fire or dynamite and shot Jews who ran from the burning or collapsing buildings. By July 16 the ghetto was destroyed, and almost none of the remaining Jews survived. As many as 2,000 Jews were killed during the liquidation (Mishell 1988:358–359; United States Holocaust Memorial Museum 2007). Most of those who had been deported for work also died—from overwork, disease, or starvation in the concentration camps or on the subsequent death marches. Some of the residents had escaped the ghetto and joined with the resistance movement. Others—especially children—had hidden in the homes of Lithuanians. But most of Kovno's Jews, along with nearly the entire Jewish population of Lithuania, were gone. No more than 7,000 Lithuanian Jews were still alive after the war (Ginaite-Rubinson 2005:219).

SOCIAL TIME

Major movements of social time intensified conflict between Germans and Jews. Germany's defeat in World War I, and later its prolonged war with the Soviet Union, were changes in and threats to status, the kinds of events that may lead to ethnic conflict, including conflicts involving false accusations, as in this case. Other movements of social time contributed, too, such as Germany's economic depression in the 1920s and 1930s and Jewish success during the late-nineteenth and early-twentieth centuries (Black 2011:68–70). It was their success, it would seem, that made Jews in particular—more than any other group—the targets of the Nazis' wrath. Their upward mobility exceeded that of any group in Germany, and their success was especially noticeable in business, academics, and the arts (Black 2011:68).

Lithuania, like Germany, had been racked by movements of social time—most notably the Soviet invasion and the loss of Lithuanian independence. This is especially noteworthy given the high rate of Lithuanian collaboration with the Nazis in killing Jews. To some extent Lithuanians collaborated because they had their own grievances against Jews, many of them associated with the Soviet invasion and accusations of Jewish treachery. As we saw above, many Lithuanians also held traditional beliefs about Jews—including the false belief that Jews killed Christian children for use in rituals. Many Christians throughout Europe shared such beliefs, which had been caused in part by long-ago movements of social time—the crucifixion of Jesus, for example, and the first-century persecutions of Christians recounted in the New Testament.

INSEPARABILITY

In both Germany and Lithuania, cataclysmic social change caused conflict and then genocide. But genocide was the response to the conflict only because features of the physical and social environments facilitated it. In previous chapters we have seen that genocide is more likely where exit and expulsion are more difficult. The same pattern occurred in Lithuania, where the large-scale mass killings of women and children began only after the first few months of the war. As noted above, there was genocide from the beginning, as the *Einsatzgruppen* massacred Jews in the border regions, and as the Nazis and Lithuanian partisans orchestrated the pogroms in Kovno and the killings at the Seventh Fort. But the killings of arrested Jews in the cities and by the *Einsatzgruppen* in the countryside were mainly directed against Jewish men and communists, and the pogroms were relatively small-scale operations. It was not until August 1941 that the Nazis began killing Jewish women and children throughout Lithuania, and this was only after a change of plans (Dieckmann 2000:241; Matthäus 2004:20).

At the start of the war, the plan was to deport Jews to the northern regions of the Soviet Union. But as the war dragged on, it quickly became clear to the Nazis that they now had control over a large population of Jews from conquered Soviet territories, with no possibility of deporting them to the East. This, along with other considerations, such as food shortages in the conquered areas, soon led to a change in policy with regard to the Jews. Thus in mid-August a second wave of killings began. These were more indiscriminate and on a greater scale than the killings in the first wave, immediately after the invasion. In the rural areas the Nazis exterminated Jews immediately, while in the cities, where the Jewish populations were large and concentrated, they would first confine them to ghettos. Most of Lithuania's Jews died during this phase of the genocide. By the end of November 1941, the various actions in the ghettos had resulted in the deaths of large portions of the Jewish populations of the cities, and the *Einsatzgruppen* had killed nearly all the Jews in the countryside. By this point at least 120,000 Lithuanian Jews had been killed (Dieckmann 2000).

SOCIAL DISTANCE

Consistent with my theory, genocide in Lithuania also occurred across considerable social distances. Broadly speaking, Jews were neither intimate with nor culturally similar either to the Nazis or to ethnic Lithuanians. Lithuanian Jews were the center of a larger community of Jews known as Litvaks. Having developed in a context where the non-Jewish population was mostly poor and backward, the Litvak communities had made little effort to integrate with their neighbors and were thus more "inward and Jewish" than other European Jews (Schoenburg and Schoenburg 1991:41). As historian Solon Beinfeld notes, "No major European Jewish community seemed so immune to assimilation" (1997:28; see also Eidintas 2003:19). The culture was firmly rooted in Orthodox Judaism, and even modernizing movements such as Zionism maintained a strong Jewish identity (Beinfeld 1997:28). Nearly all of Lithuania's Jews spoke Yiddish as their first language, and many also spoke Hebrew and Russian (Beinfeld 1997:28; Eidintas 2003:67). Lithuanian and Jewish practices differed in many other ways, too:

> A good Catholic took his hat off, going to church; a Jew wore his hat even in the synagogue. Catholics christen their infants with holy water; Jews don't have any of it. Jews circumcised their boys. . . . People were buried in caskets; Jews were only brought to the cemetery in a casket, but buried without it. The holy day for Jews is only the last, the seventh day—the *sabas* or Shabbat in Hebrew. Lithuanians celebrate the resurrection of Christ; Jews don't recognize Christ at all. Jews don't count the years from the birth of Christ; they have no Holy Christmas or Easter. Differences in dress were extreme, particularly when Jewish men went to the synagogue. (Eidintas 2003:60)

Such cultural differences existed along with barriers to interaction. Lithuanians and Jews celebrated holidays and weddings separately, and the observance of kosher dietary practices prevented religious Jews from being guests in the homes of Lithuanians, even when they were invited, and led vacationing Jews to stay in separate hotels (Eidintas 2003:59; Ginaite-Rubinson 2005:11). Even Jews who did not keep kosher had little interaction with Lithuanians. Holocaust survivor Sara Ginaite-Rubinson, for example, notes that her family would stay in Lithuanian hotels while on vacation, and that although they never felt hostility from the guests, "we never socialized with them either and certainly made no friends with the Lithuanians summering beside us" (2005:11). Lithuanians and Jews also lived in separate areas. Kovno was "in practice fairly rigidly segregated and Jewish areas were quite easily identified" (Mishell 1988:15). Altogether, relations between Lithuanians and Jews were characterized by a high degree of cultural and relational distance. The two groups lived "a separate, though parallel, cultural and social existence" (Ginaite-Rubinson 2005:10).

Despite this social distance, historically the two groups had been somewhat interdependent—though this was much less the case by the time of the genocide. Prior to the twentieth century, there was virtually no Lithuanian middle class, and Lithuanians relied on the services of Jewish artisans, merchants, and tavern owners. As Bishop Motiejus Valančius noted in a tract mostly hostile toward Jews, "Jews are wealthy, and merchants; truthfully speaking, they are beneficial and necessary for the country.... There would be no one else to buy our flax with our grains were it not for the Jews" (quoted in Eidintas 2003:26). By the 1890s, however, Lithuanians were engaging in business and trade, and with interdependence decreasing the Lithuanian population became more hostile to the Jewish merchants (Eidintas 2003:31). Later, during the period of Lithuanian independence, there was another expansion of the Lithuanian middle class. During this time, hostility toward Jews again increased. The Lithuanian merchants and artisans organized into cooperatives, and they urged ethnic Lithuanians not to do business with Jews. Also at this time the nationalist government instituted policies designed to favor Lithuanian businesses and to oust Jews from their favorable economic positions (Beinfeld 1997:27; Eidintas 2003:69; Ginaite-Rubinson 2005:26; Shochat 1974:302). These policies further reduced the interdependence between Jews and Lithuanians.

OUTSIDERS AS AGGRESSORS

While much social distance separated Jews and Lithuanians, an even greater amount separated the Jews and the occupying Germans, and it was the Germans who instigated the genocide. It is not the case, as some have reported, that the Lithuanian partisans began mass killings of Jews prior to the German arrival, or that they acted on their own shortly afterward. Many of the accounts of the genocide have been confused about this, probably because the Germans orchestrated the pogroms precisely so they would appear to be the spontaneous actions of the Lithuanian population. For example, Franz Stahlecker, the commander of the *Einsatzgruppen* unit assigned to Lithuania, wrote that "everything has to publicly appear as though local residents have done everything at their own initiative, reacting naturally to the previous communist terror and pressure from Jews, which they have suffered for long decades" (quoted in Eidintas 2003:178). From such reports we now know that each of these "spontaneous" mass killings occurred after the arrival and under the direction of Germans. Nowhere did neighbors simply turn on and murder the Jews living alongside them (Eidintas 2003:20).

Many of the armed partisans even resisted participating in pogroms. In Kovno, for example, the partisans had control of the city for days before the Nazis' arrival, and they began making arrests and harassing Jews, but no large pogroms took place. When Stahlecker arrived on June 25, though, he immediately sought out local partisans to organize massacres. This proved more difficult than expected, but he was able to enlist Algirdas Klimaitis and a group of partisans to conduct the Slobodka pogrom "in such a way that neither the directives we provided nor our initiative came to light" (quoted in Eidintas 2003:178–82). When leaders of the Lithuanian partisans in Kovno later found out about the massacre, they asked Klimaitis to resign and leave the city (Ginaite-Rubinson 2005:36). The Nazis also inspired the massacre at the Lietukis garage, which they even documented by taking photographs (Eidintas 2003:185–86).[4] While social conditions in Lithuania were conducive to genocide, and many Lithuanians participated in it, the more socially distant Nazis took the leading roles.

JEWS AS SLAVE LABORERS

The principle that genocide increases with social distance can also explain other aspects of the genocide within Lithuania. As noted above, in Lithuania the genocide increased as it became clear there would not be space available in the East for resettlement. But after the killings from August through November eliminated 80 percent of Lithuania's Jews, the genocide slowed down considerably for the next two years. This occurred along with an increase in interdependence, as the Jews in the ghetto became slave laborers and as the Nazis suddenly became more dependent on them. After the large actions in the ghettos in 1941, Hinrich Lohse, the Commissar for the Ostland, ordered a halt to the killings. Other sources of labor had dried up. Soviet prisoners of war had already died in large numbers, and Lithuanians had proved resistant to forced labor (Matthäus 1997:20; 2004:22–24; Mishell 1988:109; Porat 1996:166–67).

Even prior to this, Lohse's initial orders for the ghettos had envisioned keeping the inmates alive to exploit their labor, but after Stahlecker complained that the guidelines interfered with the ongoing killings, Lohse had amended the orders to allow for "further measures" to be taken by the Security Police (Matthäus 1997:21). The killing operations thus continued for the next four months, but as should be evident from the description of the actions in the Kovno ghetto, each of the genocidal operations (with the exception of the Intellectuals Action) disproportionately targeted the least productive residents of the ghetto—such as those without "Jordan passes," the sick, the elderly, and children. The same was true of the wave of actions following the SS takeover of the ghetto. Interdependence is thus the key factor in explaining the variation in genocide within the ghetto. Additionally, it explains why the Jews in the countryside, who were not performing slave labor, were eliminated completely during the same time period. The less interdependence, the more genocide.

This did not go unnoticed by the Jewish Council in the Kovno ghetto, who sought to obtain employment for as many residents as possible. To this end the Council came up with the idea of creating workshops inside the ghetto—which would not only increase the size of the labor force but also provide work for those who were unable to perform hard manual labor (Mishell 1988:100; Oshry 1995:95–97). Eventually more than 6,000 Jews were employed in workshops making children's toys, shoes, clothing, candles, and many other items (Elkes 1999:43; Oshry 1995:97; United States Holocaust Memorial Museum 2007). The ghetto became extremely profitable, and it was valuable not just to the German war effort, but particularly to those involved in administering the ghetto. For one thing, they took many of the goods for themselves, sending boxes of expensive items to their families back in Germany. When the German administrator left Kovno in July 1944, he took with him a railway car full of goods (Matthäus 2004:24).

Also, as long as Jews were alive and employed, it justified the jobs of the Germans in charge of the ghetto and kept them from being sent to the front lines (Elkes 1999:80). German supervisors would even create pointless tasks for Jews to complete—such as moving furniture back and forth—and then report to their superiors that the Jews under their command were employed and still needed supervision (Gordon 1992:116). These relations of interdependence account for the aforementioned conflict between the SA-run civil administration, which wanted the current situation to continue, and the SS, which wanted to begin liquidating the ghetto. This conflict persisted for some time, and it was evident in disputes about particular actions as well as those about overall policy. In many cases, for instance, the administrators were able to prevent or delay killing by "arguing that the Jewish workers were needed to finish a contract, to guarantee delivery of the shipment, or to provide warm underclothing for freezing German soldiers" (Littman 1983:102). Thus the civil administrators, interdependent with the ghetto Jews, were instrumental in curbing genocide in the ghetto before the SS finally took complete control.

ALTRUISM TOWARD JEWS

Throughout the conflict many Germans and Lithuanians spared the lives of individual Jews who were in some way socially closer to them than the others. William Mishell, for example, was arrested in Kovno during the first days of the war, along with many others who were later taken to the Seventh Fort and killed. The next day he was released by the same partisan who arrested him. "You speak Lithuanian very well," the partisan told him, "rather unusual for a Jew; you also volunteered for work yesterday, didn't you?" When Mishell replied that he had, the partisan said, "You Jews are parasites, you know, none of you want to work, but you seem to be different. You are free, you can go home" (quoted in Mishell 1988:23). Here it seems that Mishell's volunteering for work, along with his social closeness to the Lithuanian—he spoke Lithuanian fluently—led to his release. In another case a woman whose husband was arrested and taken to the Seventh Fort received aid from a co-worker who was a close friend of the commander of the partisans in Kovno, Colonel Jurgis Bobelis. The co-worker arranged for the woman to meet with Bobelis, and after the meeting her husband was released (Ginaite-Rubinson 2005:20). During the same period Jacob Goldberg, who had previously fought for Lithuanian independence and had been imprisoned during the Soviet occupation, was arrested by Lithuanian partisans who accused him of being a communist. Upon arrival at the Kovno prison, however, he quickly recognized the warden—they had graduated from the same military academy—and asked for his help. He was released within minutes (Littman 1983:46).

Social closeness was also a factor in the rescues of Jews by ordinary Lithuanian citizens.[5] During the first year of the genocide, no organized groups aided the Jews, but some individuals brought food to Jews in the ghetto, hid Jews in their homes, or helped them escape. Nearly all of these people were socially close to the Jews they aided. They were "individual friends and acquaintances—co-workers, neighbors, business partners, workers in Jewish factories, maids in Jewish homes, etc." (Neshamit 1977:301). Later on, beginning in 1943, nationalist and anti-Fascist groups and members of the Catholic clergy conducted more organized rescues. Social closeness also played a part in these activities. For example, many priests had actively aided the killers or remained silent, but later on priests began to organize rescues, particularly of Jewish children. Often these children were subsequently baptized, and in at least one monastery, the priests required Jews to convert to Christianity as a condition of their rescue (Neshamit 1977:312–15). In such cases, Jews were aided only after reducing their cultural distance from their potential rescuers. While the more organized rescues of Jews began, many Jews also fled the ghetto to join the anti-Nazi partisans in the forests. Though the partisans were hesitant at first, they eventually began to allow Jews into their ranks. But here interdependence was crucial. The partisans did not actively engage in rescues,[6] and they normally accepted only those who were young enough and physically able to fight—those who could contribute to the resistance (Neshamit 1977:324–26). In at least one case potential partisans were also required to have their own rifles (Ginaite-Rubinson 2005:138).

CONTRADICTORY BEHAVIOR

Even Germans and Lithuanians aiding the killers or participating in the killing might act to save Jews whom they were acquainted with or who worked for them. One resident of the Kovno Ghetto, civil engineer Chaim Lipman, was one day summoned to fix the furnace at the headquarters of the Third Lithuanian Police Company. There he met the commander of the company, Captain Alfred Tornbaum, who was pleased with Lipman's work and recruited him to organize a permanent maintenance crew to work for Tornbaum. Later, on the day of the Great Action, Tornbaum saw that Lipman had been selected for removal, and he quickly acted to help Lipman and his family by directing them to go to a house that had previously been searched (Littman 1983:85–87).

Likewise, after the SS gained control of the ghetto, Leah Elstein, a secretary for the Jewish Council, would frequently be asked to deliver documents to Goecke's headquarters. There she became acquainted with SS Unterscharfuhrer Pilgram, and she was asked occasionally to work for him. Shortly before the Children's Action, Pilgram ordered Elstein to report to him at once to perform a few seemingly unimportant tasks. He also ordered her to come to his office the next day, the second day of the action. This kept her from being harmed during the action, and thereafter she continued to work for Pilgram until the ghetto was finally liquidated (Littman 1983:106–8).

And in another case, even Helmut Rauca, who directed the selections during the Great Action, acted on the basis of a personal tie to allow a Jewish woman to live outside the ghetto. Edwin Geist was a German composer who lived in the ghetto. While in Germany he had fallen in love with Lida Bagriansky, a Lithuanian Jew, and then followed her back to Lithuania. He later moved with her into the Kovno Ghetto, but since he was not Jewish he was able to go into the city whenever he wanted. At the German club in Kovno, he met Rauca, who became interested in his music. Geist later appealed to Rauca for Bagriansky's release from the ghetto. Rauca agreed, but he stipulated that the two must not live together. When he later found out Bagriansky was again living with Geist, he demanded that she be sterilized or return to the ghetto. When Geist angrily confronted Rauca, Rauca had him sent to the Ninth Fort, where he was later shot. Upon learning of Geist's death, Bagriansky committed suicide (Littman 1983:94–97).

INEQUALITY

The genocide in Lithuania also had a downward direction in social space. In Lithuania Jews were a minority of the population, and Lithuanians had long treated them as second-class citizens (Ginaite-Rubinson 2005:Prologue). While many Jews had prospered economically, they were always underrepresented in the government, and after nationalists came to power in 1926, they were almost totally excluded. At this time the Jewish autonomy structure, which had allowed the Jews considerable control over their own community, was dissolved, and the few Jewish officers in the army were discharged (Beinfeld 1997:27; Mishell 1988:5; Neshamit 1977:291). Jews were excluded or underrepresented in many other areas as well. There were no Jewish police officers or bankers, no Jewish teachers in Lithuanian schools, and (with one exception) no Jewish professors at the university (Mishell 1988:5).

Support for each side was also unequal. The aggressors, but not the targets, attracted supporters from the Lithuanian population. As soon as the Nazis seized control, Lithuanians cooperated with the Germans, who co-opted bands of Lithuanian partisans to carry out pogroms in Kovno and other areas. Later some Lithuanians became part of German-led auxiliary units, which helped carry out more organized killings. Support for Jews was much weaker. Particularly in the first stages of the genocide, those who did not actively cooperate mostly remained uninvolved. Some individuals helped Jews, but not many, and not a single Lithuanian institution—neither the Catholic Church nor the provisional government nor any other institution—publicly protested the killings (Ginaite-Rubinson 2005:42).

THE HOLOCAUST AS A MATTER OF DEGREE

The Holocaust was a hypergenocide—a genocide extreme in all its features. As table 4 illustrates, it was the most extreme of all the cases we have discussed.[7] It was also the most extreme case in history. The killing in Lithuania was extremely intensive, resulting in the deaths of more than 90 percent of the Jewish population. It was large in scale, occurring throughout Lithuania and beyond. It was extremely one-sided, directed against an ethnic group not at war with Lithuanians or the Nazis. And most of it was indiscriminate, based on ethnicity alone. As my theory of the degree of genocide would predict, the Holocaust was a response to continuous deviant behavior on the part of members of a low-status ethnic group against extremely organized, and well-connected members of a high-status ethnic group in a situation where these ethnic groups were socially distant, unequal, and difficult to separate.

Table 4. Comparing cases of genocide

	Protogenocide				Hypergenocide
	CALIFORNIA	GUJARAT	BOSNIA	RWANDA	HOLOCAUST
Intensiveness	Low	Low	Low	High	High
Scale	Low	Low	High	High	High
One-sidedness	Low	Low	Low	Low	High
Ethnic basis	Low	High	Low	High	High

The Holocaust was the most extreme case of genocide in history. But what is it that distinguishes the Holocaust? What distinguishes it, for instance, from the Rwandan genocide, another extreme case? In part it is that the Holocaust has high values on every dimension, whereas in Rwanda the degree of one-sidedness was lower. But it is more than that. The scale of the Rwandan genocide was nowhere close to that of the Holocaust, though Rwanda was also a large-scale genocide. The scale of the Holocaust would be comparable to that of the Rwandan genocide—or the Bosnian genocide, the other large-scale case we have examined—if it had occurred, say, only in Lithuania. But it occurred throughout Europe in most of the areas under Nazi control. It was almost a continent-wide genocide, something not seen before or since. It is the scale of the Holocaust that most distinguishes it from other cases. So let us look more closely at the features that account for the large scale of the Holocaust in general and in Lithuania and Kovno in particular.

In previous chapters we have seen that for a large-scale genocide to occur, the aggressors must be highly organized. And indeed, the Holocaust was more organized than genocides like the one in Rwanda. Those who planned and carried out the killing were the leaders and agents of a technologically advanced and totalitarian state. They controlled the military, paramilitaries, communication and transportation networks, and numerous bureaucracies that could all be employed to carry out large-scale actions. And through warfare they had expanded the state's borders and brought other states under their control. The Nazis controlled an international organization that could operate on an international scale.

In Lithuania, as we have seen, the Nazis were able to increase their organizational capacity further by attracting Lithuanian support. Though Germans instigated the killing, most of it was carried out by Lithuanians. But why did Lithuanians side with the invading Nazis against local Jews? Recall that according to Black's theory of partisanship, one-sided, strong support arises where third parties are inferior to the aggressors and superior to the targets and where they are close to the aggressors and distant from the targets. Each of these conditions was present in Lithuania. First, Nazi Germany and its agents were superior to the ethnic Lithuanians, while the Jews were inferior. From the outset Lithuanians approached the Nazi invaders from a position of inferiority. Though the anticommunist partisans and the provisional government they set up resisted the Nazis as they tried to establish Lithuanian independence (Budreckis 1968:138), the independent Lithuanian state they hoped for was to be allied with the Nazis. The partisans always sought to cooperate with the Nazis, not to oppose them. Partisans were instructed to greet the German invaders enthusiastically, and they moved against those said to be resisting the German advance (Littman 1983:42; Piotrowski 1998:163). The high-status Germans, then, attracted considerable support, and when they sought help in killing Jews, numerous Lithuanians readily participated.

German-Lithuanian relations were also characterized by social closeness. Prior to the Soviet invasion, the Lithuanian government, isolated from its neighbors, maintained close ties only with Germany (Schoenburg and Schoenburg 1991:36). They signed a nonaggression agreement, which stipulated that neither would give aid to a nation attacking the other, and the two countries also signed various economic agreements (Shochat 1974:302–3). During the Soviet occupation anti-Soviet partisans also developed extensive ties with the Nazis. Former government officials, officers, civic leaders, and members of the Lithuanian Security Police took refuge in Germany, where they cooperated with the Nazis and joined with Colonel Kazys Škirpa, the former Lithuanian ambassador to Germany, to form the Lithuanian Activist Front (LAF) (Budreckis 1968:12–27; Kwiet 1998:12; Mann 2005:282–83; Matthäus 2004:18; Piotrowski 1998:163). The members of the LAF had various political views and were united around the main goal of restoring Lithuanian independence, but Škirpa's Berlin staff was dominated by the Voldemarists—a group of pro-Fascist Lithuanians whose ties to the Nazis were even closer (Budreckis 1968:28). The resistance movement in Lithuania soon acknowledged the leadership of the Berlin group, and the two groups cooperated to organize bands of armed partisans throughout Lithuania who would take action during the coming Nazi invasion to drive out the Soviets and install an independent government (Budreckis 1968:27, 34). When the invasion occurred, the partisans grew quickly in numbers, as Lithuanians enthusiastically joined their ranks (Budreckis 1968:69).

These bands of Lithuanian partisans were inferior to the Germans and socially close to a degree. It was from their ranks that the Germans found collaborators to carry out massacres. Still, many were reluctant, and the Nazis eventually ordered the disarming of the activists and incorporated those deemed trustworthy into units of auxiliary police led by Germans (Kwiet 1998:14). Those who joined the auxiliary units were now directly subordinate to Germans and socially closer, and they were much more willing to kill (Eidintas 2003:174). It was only after the formation of these auxiliary units that massive Lithuanian involvement in the genocide began.

Major social changes in Germany and Lithuania led to conflict with Jews. The Nazis saw Jews as parasitical and dangerous, while the Lithuanians associated Jews with the Soviet regime that had ruled Lithuania prior to the Nazi invasion. But as in other cases the genocide was also predatory. The Nazis and their Lithuanian collaborators confiscated Jewish property, sexually exploited Jewish women, and forced Jews to labor. We also saw that my theory explains patterns in the killing. The genocide occurred in a context where expulsion was difficult. War with the Soviet Union had put large numbers of Jews under Nazi control, and then as it dragged on, left nowhere to deport them. It occurred under conditions of great social distance between Jews and ethnic Lithuanians—different religions, languages, cultural practices, and social networks, as well as recently decreasing interdependence. And the genocide was downward, toward an ethnic group excluded from government and other areas of civic life and unable to attract supporters. Participation also varied, as my theory predicts, with the more socially distant Germans acting as instigators of the killing. So did the targeting, with ties of interdependence through slave labor saving many Jews or at least delaying their deaths. And we saw that my theory also explains the rescuing that occurred—even in cases of contradictory behavior, where the rescuers were also killers. Finally, we saw that my theory explains the features of the Holocaust in comparison with other genocides. It explains why this case was so extreme. Its scale, in particular, was extreme due to the Nazis' high degree of organization and their ability to draw support from the local populations in places such as Lithuania.

Some scholars (for example, Heinsohn 2000; Katz 1994; 2001; Rosenberg 1987; Rubenstein 2001) view the Holocaust as unique in some sense, but we have seen here, the Holocaust had the same kinds of causes and occurred in the same kind of social environment as other genocides. It differs only in that it is the most extreme case. Different from other cases in degree but not kind, the Holocaust is not unique, and neither is genocide. Genocide has variable features, none unique or mysterious. Like warfare, genocide involves mass killing. Like lynching, it is one-sided violence. Like ethnic cleansing, it targets people on the basis of their ethnicity. As these features vary they distinguish genocides from one another, and they distinguish genocide from other ways of handling conflict.

CONCLUSION

Genocide arises out of ethnic conflict caused by overdiversity and understratification. Overdiversity in this context means that a society is ethnically divided or that previously separated ethnic groups have come into contact. Understratification means that a high-status ethnic group experiences a decline in or threat to its status or that a low-status ethnic group rises or attempts to rise in status. Together these social changes—movements of social time—produce intense ethnic conflict, but for genocide to occur, the conflict's location in social space must be right. Genocide is more likely when the aggressors and targets are socially distant (lacking in cultural similarity, interdependence, and intimacy) and when they are unequal, with the aggressors higher in status (wealthier, more numerous, better supported, and better organized) than the targets. That is the core of my theory of genocide, and it is very different from all other theories of the subject.

My theory employs pure sociology, a type of sociological theory originally developed by Donald Black to explain legal behavior, but which he intended as a new and more powerful way to explain all human behavior. Here I have drawn from pure sociological theories of conflict and social control, theories that apply to all clashes of right and wrong. These theories explain both the origin of conflict and the handling of conflict with purely social features—with patterns of diversity, stratification, and intimacy. They make no reference to psychology, and my theory of genocide likewise does not explain genocide with the participants' goals or any other psychological states—or with the individual characteristics of the participants at all. And because it is rooted in a general theory of conflict and social control, it classifies genocide alongside an array of other moralistic phenomena.

These aspects of the theory give it particular strengths. The nature of the strategy allows us to explain many different kinds of variation—why genocide occurs, for example, and why some people but not others participate in it. As we have seen, it even allows us to explain cases of contradictory behavior, in which the same people act as both killers and rescuers. The other strength of the theory is that as a theory of conflict and social control, it allows us to see how similar genocide is to certain behaviors we might otherwise think are very different. For example, the same kind of theory that explains genocide can also explain reactions to genocide, including when people condemn genocide or punish it. In this concluding chapter let us look at each of these issues in more depth.

CONTRADICTORY BEHAVIOR DURING GENOCIDES

It is a remarkable fact about genocides that behaviors such as killing and rescuing occur closely together—in the same setting. But in each of the five case studies, we have seen the even more remarkable fact that on some occasions the very same individuals may engage in both behaviors. In the Round Valley a rancher who had participated in killing expeditions against the nearby Indians intervened to save Indians who worked for him. In Bosnia a Serb concentration camp guard gave food to a Muslim man he had known before the violence began. In Rwanda a group of Hutu killers spared a Tutsi woman because they knew her husband. And so on. Cases such as these present a special challenge to the sociology of genocide, but as we have already begun to see, the pure sociology of genocide can explain them. Let us now look more at the nature of the problem and how pure sociology overcomes it.

THE PROBLEM OF CONTRADICTORY BEHAVIOR

Those who take notice of contradictory behavior often express bewilderment. For example, political scientist Mahmood Mamdani, considering such behavior during the Rwandan genocide, asks, "How could the same person risk his or her own life to save another at one time and place, and yet take life another time in another place?" (2001: 221). Similarly, ethicist David P. Gushee, reflecting on an incident of contradictory behavior during the Holocaust, says it "illuminates the limits of any typology" and "reveals the complexity of human behavior" (2003:77–78). Political scientist Janine Natalya Clark, after discussing several cases of contradictory behavior during the Bosnian genocide, likewise notes the problem with prior typologies of perpetrators' behavior. In cases of contradictory behavior, she says, it is hard to classify someone as having reached a particular position along a "continuum of destruction"—a concept developed by psychologist Ervin Staub (1989)—because what we see is fluctuation "between the two ends of this continuum" (Clark 2009:437).

Contradictory behavior is an anomaly that cannot be explained with any of the existing theories of genocide—or, for that matter, theories of anything else. The reason is that most theories of genocide, like most theories of violence in general, are either collectivistic (often called macrosociological) or individualistic (often called microsociological). Collectivistic theories of violence seek to explain why some societies, cities, cultures, or other large social units are more violent than others (for example, Beeghley 2003; Blau and Blau 1982; Messner and Rosenfeld 2007; Wolfgang and Ferracuti 1967). But no society, city, or culture is uniformly violent. The degree of violence differs from place to place and from person to person, and collectivistic theories cannot account for these kinds of differences. Such theories overcollectivize violence (Black 2004b:147).

Collectivistic theories of genocide are likewise unable to explain the occurrence of rescuing—even by different individuals. If genocide results from the characteristics of whole societies or from some other macrosociological phenomenon, what accounts for the presence of altruism within genocidal settings? Collectivistic theories cannot explain this kind of variation.

Theories of violence may also be individualistic (see, for example, Akers and Silverman 2004; Berkowitz 1962; Dollard et al. 1939). Such theories explain why some individuals within a society are violent. But just as large social units are not uniformly violent, neither are individuals. Individualistic theories are thus unable to explain why individuals are violent on one occasion rather than another. Instead of overcollectivizing violence, they overindividualize it (Black 2004b:147).

Individualistic theories of genocide address the variation that occurs within social units by explaining why individuals take on a particular role—why some people but not others act as killers or rescuers. A number of theorists argue, for example, that killers or rescuers differ from others in some fundamental way—such as in their personality or moral outlook (Adorno et al. 1950; Baum 2008; Block and Drucker 1992; Fogelman 1994; Midlarsky, Jones, and Corley 2005; Monroe, Barton, and Klingemann 1990; Oliner and Oliner 1988; Staub 1993; Steiner 1980; Tec 1986). Others seek to identify factors that transform people into killers or enable them to kill (Alvarez 2001:115–28; Bauman 1989:151–68; Browning 1998; Kelman 1973; Kressel 2002; Lifton 1986; Waller 2002). But as we have seen, the same individuals may both kill and rescue. What this illustrates is that persons as such are neither genocidal nor altruistic. Something other than the properties of individuals must explain participation in genocide.

Unlike other theories, pure sociology does not explain human behavior with the characteristics of collectivities and individuals, but instead with its social geometry—its position in social space. This unique approach differs even from other theories that deemphasize the importance of individual personalities. One idea within genocide studies, for example, is that the killers are "ordinary men" (Browning 1998; see also Bauman 1989; Charny 1999; Waller 2002). Much of the discussion around this idea has an anti-individualistic bent, but the theories themselves still cannot explain contradictory behavior. Let us more closely examine two of these approaches to see why this is so.

"ORDINARY MEN" AND CONTRADICTORY BEHAVIOR

Sociologist Zygmunt Bauman notes that when the killers of the Holocaust took off their uniforms, they ceased to act in any way that would distinguish them from others: "They behaved much like all of us. They had wives they loved, children they cosseted, friends they helped and comforted in case of distress" (1989:151). These were ordinary people, according to Bauman, not people with diseased personalities or faulty socialization (Bauman 1989:152). Likewise, historian Christopher Browning (1998) describes one group of killers—the men of Reserve Police Battalion 101—as "ordinary men." They were not specially selected to kill Jews on the basis of their suitability for the task; rather, they were simply the people who were available at that point in the war (Browning 1998:164–65). For both Bauman and

Browning, the ordinariness of the killers means that their participation cannot be explained by individual factors. It is instead the situation that leads to killing. They are pointing in the right direction, but the explanations they give, explanations that focus on how ordinary people come to commit genocide, do not go far enough in rejecting individualism, and they are unable to account for the range of contradictory behavior we see in genocides.

Bauman assumes that killers find it difficult to kill, and his explanation of participation in genocide[1] is that certain social situations make killing easier.[2] Reflecting mainly on the findings of Stanley Milgram's (1969) well-known study, which examined conditions under which subjects would agree to administer electric shocks to someone they believed was the subject of a learning experiment, Bauman proposes that it becomes easier to harm others as "physical and psychical" proximity to the victims decreases, as the actions leading to killing are split into specialized tasks, as the action becomes more collective, as the action proceeds through incremental steps, as the action becomes more technically remote from its effects, as responsibility for the actions is given to an authority, and as that authority is more monopolistic (Bauman 1989:154–65). Each factor is important because of its psychological effect on potential perpetrators. For example, proximity to the victims matters because "it is quite easy to be cruel towards a person we neither see nor hear" (Bauman 1989:155). And when actions proceed through incremental steps, the first steps do not seem morally consequential, and later people are unable to break from the sequence without acknowledging that their past behavior was wrong (Bauman 1989:157–58).

Browning also wants to understand how ordinary people become genocidal killers, but he focuses on a particular group of killers. He thus rejects many of the factors proposed by Bauman and others that do not apply to the killings by the men of Reserve Police Battalion 101. For example, these men killed their victims at point-blank range, a task that did not involve segmentation, physical distance, or incremental actions (Browning 1998:162). Browning instead focuses on two factors also discussed by Bauman: authority and conformity. The authority was represented by the commander of the battalion and the more distant authority he invoked, but conformity to the group, according to

Browning, was even more important. Though no one forced the men to kill, those who refused would be leaving the work to other members of the battalion, which would be "an asocial act vis-à-vis one's comrades" (Browning 1998:185). The battalion was a close-knit group stationed abroad, and the men had few social contacts with anyone else. Most of the men were thus unwilling to let down their fellow group members, and even fewer were willing to morally reproach them, even implicitly. Those who declined to participate said they were simply "too weak" to kill (Browning 1998:185).

For both Bauman and Browning, then, the characteristics of social situations may motivate otherwise nonviolent people to kill. Ordinary men and women are thus able to commit extraordinary evil (Bauman 1989:151). But what we see in contradictory behavior is more dramatic. Not only do the killers also engage in ordinary behaviors, they may even engage in rescuing—an extraordinary behavior. Extending the logic of Bauman's and Browning's approaches, we might say that ordinary people may engage in extraordinary good as well as extraordinary evil. In this view neither behavior would result from personality characteristics, and the same individuals might find themselves motivated to kill in one situation and motivated to rescue in another.[3]

But the individualistic nature of these theories inhibits an explanation of many of the cases. True, killing and rescuing might be expected when the same individuals are in different situations. Different environments would have different psychological effects, one motivating killing and another rescuing. But even if we were to supplement these theories of killing with a similar theory of rescuing, we still could not explain cases in which an individual in the same situation engages in both behaviors.[4] In many instances of contradictory behavior, killing and rescuing occur simultaneously. For example, though the men studied by Browning engaged in genocide, sometimes they refused to kill particular Jews or even helped them escape to safety (1998:153–154).

Although Bauman and Browning argue for the importance of social factors in explaining genocidal killing, their explanations are largely psychological. Pure sociology, on the other hand, eliminates not merely the mind and personality of human beings from its explanations; it eliminates the individuals themselves. The personal characteristics, the socialization, or the motivations of killers or rescuers are not what account for their behavior, but rather the relationships of those involved. Thus my theory can explain cases where the same individuals engage in both killing and rescuing behaviors. It predicts that in cases of contradictory behavior, people will be more distant from those they kill and closer to those they help.

CASES OF CONTRADICTORY BEHAVIOR

The scant attention given to the issue of contradictory behavior has come almost exclusively from scholars of the Rwandan genocide (for example, Fujii 2009; 2011; Gourevitch 1998:130–31; Jefremovas 1995:28; Mamdani 2001:221). And certainly numerous such cases occurred in Rwanda. Several days after the Rwandan genocide began, the Hutu president of Catholic Workers Youth warned a young Tutsi woman named Mectilde that she was on the list of those to be killed the next day. Mectilde, who lived in Kigali at a youth hostel for Catholic women workers, decided to flee to Gitarama along with two friends, and the president agreed to accompany them and to help the Tutsi woman through the roadblocks (Mamdani 2001:222). Without his help Hutus would likely have killed Mectilde. Yet this same man later joined in the killing of Tutsis in Butare. As Mectilde put it, "A Hutu can help you in Kigali, but in Butare he can begin to kill Tutsis" (quoted in Mamdani 2001:224).

Other Rwandans behaved similarly. One Tutsi man attributes his survival to a Hutu man who was one of the killers, a friend and militia member, who came to tell him the militia was coming (Fujii 2009:93). Another Tutsi man, Richard, was at the edge of a mass grave, preparing himself for death at the hands of Hutu killers, when one of the killers, a former friend, saw him and spared his life (Alvarez 2001:112). In another case a Hutu named Michel assisted in killing a Tutsi man who stopped at his home to ask for directions, but he and his siblings also hid four Tutsi neighbors in their homes (Fujii 2009:144–47; 2011:153–55). Likewise, another Hutu, Laurent, hid two Tutsi friends in his home, but killed others. Here is how one of the Tutsis, the only one to survive, describes it: "He saved us by hiding us, but it was agony to be alive. Laurent would wake us to say good morning every day, then go out and spend hours hunting Tutsis with the people who killed my family.... Our lives were in his hands, so I couldn't say anything. I don't understand how people can do good and evil at the same time" (quoted in Ilibagiza 2007:144).

Groups might also engage in both killing and rescuing. Members of one Hutu militia group, for example, allowed their friend Eugene, a Tutsi, to join their group. These Hutus spared a Tutsi in their midst as they went out killing other Tutsis (Fujii 2009:141–44). Leaders of the genocide might also act to save some Tutsis. We see this in the context of a dramatic act of rescue, later depicted in the film *Hotel Rwanda* (George 2004), in which hotel manager Paul Rusesabagina, a Hutu, helped more than 1,000 Tutsis take refuge at the *Hôtel des Mille Collines* in Kigali (Gourevitch 1998). In many cases men affiliated with the regime not only knew about Rusesabagina's actions, they even enlisted him to help save particular Tutsis, such as their wives and other family members (Gourevitch 1998:140). Father Wenceslas Munyeshyaka, who was later convicted in absentia by a Rwandan court for his role in the genocide, brought his Tutsi mother to the hotel for protection. According to Rusesabagina, when Father Wenceslas arrived with his mother, he pleaded for her protection using an anti-Tutsi slur: "Paul, I bring you my cockroach" (quoted in Gourevitch 1998:141).

It might be that contradictory behavior occurred more often in the Rwandan genocide than in other cases, but as we have already seen in previous chapters, it is not unknown in other settings. Consider the Holocaust. In chapter 7 we saw that several incidents of contradictory behavior occurred in the Kovno Ghetto, but they occurred elsewhere too. Sociologist Nechama Tec describes how a young Jewish woman in the Lublin Ghetto was helped by a German guard—a man who was a "known murderer, who killed with ease" (quoted in Tec 1986:28). After the liquidation of the ghetto, while the Nazis were trying to round up the remaining Jews, the guard discovered the woman in hiding:

> Suddenly when he noticed me he became furious and screamed: "What are you doing here?"... He began to act like a maniac, repeating again and again: "What will I do? What will I do with you?" I told him: "Do what you want." I was already fed up. I had had enough. He said: "No, I want you to leave the ghetto." But how could I get out?... I shook my head. He said: "Come early

to meet me near the gate. I will take you out." I told him that I would go only with my husband. . . . My husband was reluctant to come with me, but in the morning he came. The German was already waiting. . . . He told me, "I want to save you." I told him that I did not believe him. He kept saying, "I do not want to kill you, you are too beautiful to die." He then took us to the gate. The Ukrainian guards did not want to let us out. When, in anger, the German took out his gun and pointed at the Ukrainians, they opened the gate. He came with us through the gate and said: "I am leaving you here." I was afraid to turn. But I did. He stood there and said, "God be with you." (quoted in Tec 1986:28–29)

Also, just as we saw in the Rwandan case, rescuers during the Holocaust—even those hiding Jews in their homes—sometimes helped to kill others. One Polish farmer helped hide eight-year-old Dana Szapira and her mother, but while these two Jews were living in his cowshed, he aided in the killing of two others. A Jewish man had come to his door asking him to find a doctor for his teenage son. They had been hiding in the woods, and the boy had gangrene. But instead of finding a doctor, the farmer reported them to the Gestapo. The two Jews were shot, and the farmer received two kilograms of sugar as a reward for his information (Gilbert 1985:492; see also Gushee 2003:77–78).

Contradictory behavior also occurred in the 1915 Armenian genocide. Here the killing was carried out in large part under the direction of Turkish soldiers who escorted caravans of deported Armenians. The deportations themselves were genocidal, as those leading the caravans commonly denied the Armenians food and even water. Other killings, such as the shootings of Armenian men prior to the deportations, were quicker and more direct. Also, the soldiers allowed Kurds and others along the way to attack the remaining women and children. Consider the experience of Vahram, an Armenian child living in a village in eastern Turkey. First Vahram's father was arrested and killed along with other Armenian men of the village. Next Turkish soldiers announced that all the Armenians in the village would be deported. Several days into the journey, Ibosh, the gendarme in charge of the caravan, told the Armenians to leave all their possessions behind in order to avoid being attacked by Kurds. Once they did this the Kurds attacked anyway, and Vahram's grandfather and uncle were among the Armenians killed (Miller and Miller 1993:9–12).

This attack was orchestrated by the same Turkish gendarme who told them to leave behind their belongings, the man who was ostensibly in charge of protecting the caravan. And yet this man, Ibosh, later acted to save the lives of Vahram and his sister. Because Ibosh wanted to marry Vahram's older sister, Siroun, he began giving preferential treatment to her family. Such treatment may have enabled their survival, as many of the other deportees were dying due to the lack of food, water, and medical care. Later on Ibosh's altruism toward the family intensified. After turning over control of the caravan, he took Vahram and Siroun with him to his father's home. After he arrived in his hometown, a local official told him they should deal with Vahram as they had dealt with other Armenian boys coming through the area. But Ibosh appealed to a higher official, who gave him permission to take Vahram as a servant. Vahram and Siroun then joined Ibosh's father's household, where they lived for the next two years (Miller and Miller 1993:12–15).

Each of these incidents, like the incidents discussed in the previous chapters, conforms to the predicted pattern—at least where the relevant information is known. That is, genocide varies directly and rescue inversely with social distance. In the first case from Rwanda, Mectilde had an interdependent relationship with the man who aided her—the president of Catholic Workers Youth—who went on to kill more distant Tutsis in Butare (Mamdani 2001:222–24). In the case of the Hutu militia member who warned a Tutsi, there was a relational tie between the killer and the man he rescued—a fact recognized as crucial by the Tutsi survivor, who, when asked why a Hutu would help him, responded that it was "because the man had been his friend" (Fujii 2009:93). Likewise, Richard was spared by "an old school friend" who was among the killers (Alvarez 2001:112). In the fourth case, Michel hid his Tutsi neighbors, but aided in the killing of a Tutsi stranger (Fujii 2009:144–47; 2011:153–55). In the fifth case, Laurent hid his friends while going out to kill others; and in the sixth case, a Tutsi joined a militia group consisting of his Hutu friends, who targeted those who were less close to them (Fujii 2009:141–44; Ilibagiza 2007:144).

The same was true of the Hutu perpetrators who brought Tutsi family members to the *Hôtel des Mille Collines*. Those they aided were intimates, such as wives, or in Father Wenceslas's case, a parent (Gourevitch 1998:140–41). The German guard and the woman he helped in the Lublin ghetto also had a tie—albeit a weak one. The woman said that in the past he "had paid a lot of attention to me" (quoted in Tec 1986:28). In the case of the Polish farmer who hid two Jews but turned over two others to be killed, the relationships are unclear (Gilbert 1985:492; see also Gushee 2003:77–78). Those he turned in were certainly strangers, however, and it is possible that he had some tie to the women he helped. In the Armenian case, as the caravan traveled, the Turkish gendarme developed a relationship with the two Armenians he later saved.

In each case—except possibly one, in which the information was unavailable—those engaging in contradictory behavior were more socially distant from those they killed and closer to those they rescued. In some cases the differences were slight—such as when killers aided those with whom they had only recently become acquainted—yet the pattern was the same in multiple contexts. Where a person both kills and rescues, it is social distance that varies from one incident to the next. The person is the same, and so, in many cases, is the social situation. But killing and rescuing—the behaviors themselves—have different social geometries.

VICTIMS AS VICTIMIZERS

Most of the focus here and in the earlier chapters has been on the behavior of members of the aggressor group. But just as members of the aggressor group are not limited to one role—perpetrators, bystanders, or rescuers—neither are members of the target group limited to the role of victim. They too may act as rescuers, killers, or both. Because social closeness makes rescue more likely, members of target groups most frequently act as rescuers of their fellow targets, even when we do not recognize them as such (compare Tec 2011:109–12). In one notable case, portrayed recently in the film *Defiance* (Zwick 2008), a group of Jewish partisans in Belarus saved more than 1,200 Jews—mostly women, children, and the elderly—by accepting them into their ranks (Tec 2011:110). But nearly all targets of genocide act as rescuers to some degree, as they try to help intimates—friends and family members—as well as themselves. At the same time they may aid the killers—often hoping to spare themselves or their loved ones—so they are both killers and rescuers. What shocks us in these cases is not the contradictory behavior as such, but the fact that the victims act as victimizers—that any member of the target group would aid the killers.

But they do, as we have already seen in the case of Eugene, a Tutsi who joined one of the Hutu militias. His friends who allowed him to join engaged in contradictory behavior, but so did he. Even while aiding in the killing of some of his fellow Tutsis, he tried to save his Tutsi uncle by providing food for him while he was in hiding. And he aided himself, of course (Fujii 2009:141–44). Similarly a Tutsi who played for a local football team denounced his neighbors in order to "save himself by the grace of his footballing colleagues," though he was killed in the end (Hatzfeld 2005a:74). During the Holocaust some Jews aided in the killing of other Jews. In the Netherlands Friedrich Weinreb told the Nazis about a woman hiding twenty-five Jews in order to save himself and his family. By assisting the Nazis in other ways as well, he ultimately betrayed about 150 Jewish families (Moore 2010:352–53). Also in the Netherlands, Bernard Joseph, a Jewish refugee from Germany who thought of himself as German, helped the Nazis find Jews in hiding, thus saving himself as well as his father and sister, who also helped hunt Jews (Moore 2010:350). Other Jews who aided the Nazis include Icek Glogowski, who helped the Gestapo find Jews in Brussels and who bragged that he could "'smell' Jews at a distance"; Ans van Dijk, who began by helping Jews find hiding places but later helped run a false safe house to trap Jews looking for refuge; a Turkish Jew living in Belgium who helped find other Jews so his parents would be spared; and several Jewish stool pigeons who extracted information from arrested Jews who believed them to be fellow prisoners (Moore 2010:346–50).

Hoping ultimately to save Jewish lives, Jewish Councils in the ghettoes also cooperated with the Nazis to varying degrees. This was less the case in the Kovno Ghetto than it was elsewhere. In Kovno the Jewish Council and Jewish police were more autonomous, and they repeatedly attempted to save lives by resisting Nazi demands, withholding information, helping Jews to escape or hide, and cooperating with the resistance movement outside the ghetto. They deliberated and debated among themselves about their cooperation with the Nazis, and they justified it on the grounds that they were trying to save as many lives as possible. But regardless of their motivations or how their actions should be evaluated, we have seen that they cooperated in numerous ways. The Council drew up lists of people they chose for deportation, posted orders for the residents to assemble for genocidal actions, assigned people to slave labor (often under life-threatening conditions), and ordered people to turn over their valuables. The Jewish Police enforced the Council's decrees, and this involved dragging people from their homes for work or deportation, confiscating Jewish property to turn over to the Nazis, and beating and arresting those who did not comply (Ginaite-Rubinson 2005:50–51; Goldstein-Golden 1985:55–56; Gordon 1992:44–45, 74).

In other ghettos cooperation was greater. In chapter 1 I mentioned Mordechai Chaim Rumkowski, leader of the Lodz Ghetto in Poland, who said, "If I can save a hundred Jews in the ghetto, everything will have been worthwhile" (quoted in Midlarsky 2005:290). "Despite the horrible responsibility," he said after being ordered to deport 20,000 Jews, "we have to accept the evil order. I have to perform this bloody operation myself; I simply must cut off the limbs to save the body!" (quoted in Fein 1979:139). Jacob Gens, head of the Jewish Council in the Vilna Ghetto in Lithuania, similarly defended his own cooperation: "I could have told them that I do not wish to smear my hands and send my police to do the filthy work, but I said, 'Yes, it is my duty to foul my hands.' After five million have been slaughtered, it is our duty to save the strong and the young and not let sentiment overcome us" (quoted in Fein 1979:139). Beyond aiding in the selections, Jews in the ghettoes sometimes participated directly in anti-Jewish violence, such as on one occasion in the Vilna Ghetto when the Jewish police shot 406 Jews under the direction of the Nazis (Eidintas 2003:270). Some Jewish police officers even seemed to embrace their roles. One Holocaust survivor tells of seeing a Jewish officer she knew in Poland's Warsaw Ghetto catch a Jewish laborer trying to smuggle in groceries. When the man begged for mercy and pulled a bank note from his pocket, the policeman "gripped his truncheon, and with all his strength began beating the frail old man about the head, about the face. Next he knocked him down to the cobblestones and kicked his helpless body with his heavy boots" (Bauman 1986:92).

Thus the targets of genocide, like the aggressors, may engage in contradictory behavior. These cases differ in some ways. Targeted persons often agree to kill only so they can rescue others, and sometimes they rescue no one but themselves. Still, these cases involve similar behaviors, if not motives, and they exhibit the same geometrical pattern. When people kill some of their fellow targets and aid others, they kill those who are more socially distant while aiding those who are socially closer. Where social distance is great, the targets of genocide are not safe, even from their fellow targets. It is dangerous to be a stranger.

PURE SOCIOLOGY AND CONTRADICTORY BEHAVIOR

Contradictory behavior by individuals during genocides may seem shocking and incomprehensible, especially since we tend to view these behaviors as representing opposite moral extremes. "Of all the varieties of violence of which our sorry species is capable," writes psychologist Steven Pinker, "genocide stands apart, not only as the most heinous but as the hardest to comprehend" (2011:320). Others likewise see genocide as standing apart in some way even from other evils. Social psychologist James Waller, for example, views genocide as "extraordinary human evil" (2002:9–22). Sociologist Peter Berger calls the Holocaust an "icon of evil" (2004:145, 157). Irene Gut Opdyke, a Polish woman who during the Holocaust observed the killings of Jews—including a baby who was flung up and shot in the air as if it were a bird—described what she saw as a "miracle of evil" and "the worst thing man can do" (Opdyke and Armstrong 1999:117–18). And survivors of the Rwandan genocide have described what happened in Rwanda as "more than wickedness ... more than barbarity" and as "the supernatural doings of ordinary people" (quoted in Hatzfeld 2005a:27, 50).

Conversely, people often see altruism toward the targets of genocide as representing an extreme—and possibly mysterious or supernatural—type of goodness (see, for example, Bauman 1989:168; Block and Drucker 1992:5, 10; Flescher 2003:127–48; Paldiel 1986). If morality resides solely within individuals—if bad people do evil things, and good people do praiseworthy things—then contradictory behavior is indeed hard to understand. But another common view would see it as unsurprising that individuals are capable of both kinds of behavior. The Russian writer and gulag survivor Aleksandr Solzhenitsyn said, "The line dividing good and evil cuts through the heart of every human being" (1985:75). In this view our hearts are divided, and morality is volatile. Individuals may engage in both good and evil as their morality fluctuates: "During the life of any heart this line keeps changing place" (Solzhenitsyn 1985:75).[5]

The perspective offered here is different, however, even from Solzhenitsyn's. Pure sociology focuses on the social geometry of the human condition—its location in social space and time. The individual plays no part in its explanations, so contradictory behavior during genocide—even by the same individuals—is neither surprising nor inexplicable. Persons move about the social world, from encounter to encounter, and the social spaces they inhabit have different geometries. Some geometries are violent—even genocidal. Others are nonviolent—even altruistic. So some individuals are both genocidal and altruistic—killing some people and rescuing others. This contradictory behavior results not from the division of their hearts, but from the division of their locations in social space.

THE SOCIAL CONTROL OF GENOCIDE

It is not just the explanatory strategy, but also the subject matter that distinguishes my theory of genocide from others. The subject is genocide, obviously, but genocide is only one way of handling conflict. And my theory of genocide is just one part of a body of work addressing this broader subject: the occurrence and handling of conflict. We need not view genocide in isolation. We can consider how its causes and social context compare to forms of social control as diverse as gossip (Black 1995:855n129), law (Black 1976), suicide (Manning 2012; 2015), and lynching (Senechal de la Roche 1997). No aspect of moral life is alien to the theory. It can even address behaviors that seem to be moral opposites: genocide and rescuing, as above, or genocide and the punishment of genocide, which I now consider.

Genocide, we have seen, responds to movements of social time, usually increases in diversity and decreases in stratification. But genocide is itself a movement of social time, a social change. It decreases diversity and increases stratification, so according to Black's theory of moral time, it too causes conflict. The targets of genocide condemn their killers, and when they are able, they may punish them. For example, in 1921 Soghomon Tehlirian, an Armenian, assassinated former Turkish interior minister Talaat Pasha, one of the architects of the Armenian genocide. Likewise, in 1960 Israeli operatives captured Adolf Eichmann in Argentina and took him to Israel, where he was tried, found guilty, and hanged for his role in the Holocaust. Outsiders too may involve themselves in genocidal conflicts and attempt to punish or prevent genocide. Or they may simply condemn it. So even though genocide is social control, a response to deviant behavior by the targets, it is also a deviant behavior—extremely deviant, or evil—and its perpetrators may be subject to social control by others.

GENOCIDE AS DEVIANT BEHAVIOR

It may seem obvious that genocide is deviant behavior.[6] But the deviant nature of genocide is a variable, not a constant. The targets condemn the genocides against them, but the aggressors often, if not always, see their own actions as praiseworthy. And though some outsiders to the conflicts might condemn genocides or even try to prevent them, others might not care. Apathy was especially common in the distant past, when genocide was hardly deviant at all. "The shocking truth," says Steven Pinker, "is that until recently most people didn't think there was anything particularly wrong with genocide—as long as it didn't happen to them" (2011:334; compare Chalk and Jonassohn 1990:8; Evans 2008:13; Payne 2004:44–51). Because few people in the premodern world viewed genocide as wrong—much less evil—people boasted of the genocides they committed, and they might falsely claim to have committed other genocides, exaggerating their brutality in order to frighten their enemies or impress their subjects (Chalk and Jonassohn 1990:59–60; Freeman 1995a:214–20). They might even praise genocide and condemn restraint, as when Moses, in the Old Testament, chastises the Israelite army for allowing defeated Midianite women and children to live (Numbers 31:14–17). But in modern societies genocide has become more deviant. It is roundly condemned, and instead of boasting, those who commit genocide and those who defend them now engage in what is called genocide denial (Freeman 1991:195; Payne 2004:57; Pinker 2011:335).

The move from boasting to denial occurred as genocide became increasingly deviant—an object of moral condemnation. Even the coining of the word *genocide* is an example of this process. After Winston Churchill described the Nazis' destruction of nations as a "crime without a name," jurist Raphael Lemkin determined to name it and to get it recognized as a crime under international law (Power 2002:29–45). He succeeded, and in 1948 the United Nations passed the *Convention on the Prevention and Punishment of the Crime of Genocide.* This has not always led to the willingness of outsiders to stop genocide. Governments are often reluctant even to label an ongoing mass killing a genocide, for fear that it might require military intervention (Miles 2006:255–56; Power 2002). But intervention has not been completely absent, and it appears to be increasing. The International Criminal Tribunal for the Former Yugoslavia (ICTY) and the International Criminal Tribunal for Rwanda (ICTR), established by the United Nations after the Bosnian and Rwandan genocides, respectively, have convicted more than a hundred persons of genocide and other international crimes (Hola, Smeulers, and Bijleveld 2011:412). And governments and intergovernmental organizations sometimes use military force to try to prevent or halt genocides and other mass killings. Examples include the 1994 United Nations Assistance Mission for Rwanda (UNAMIR), a small operation that saved thousands of Tutsis, though it was unable to stop the genocide; the 1995 and 1999 NATO air strikes against Bosnia and Yugoslavia, respectively; and the 2011 air strikes against Libya by the United States and several other nations. The UN Security Council resolution authorizing the intervention in Libya's civil war referred to a 2005 UN document that identified an emerging norm known as the "responsibility to protect." Governments, according to the document, have a responsibility to protect their civilian populations from genocide, war crimes, ethnic cleansing, and crimes against humanity, and when they cannot or will not do so, this becomes the international community's responsibility (Evans 2008:48–49).

We have moved from a world where most people cared little about the genocides committed by others—perhaps not even disapproving of them—to a world where genocide is a crime, where international courts convict and imprison government officials for killing their fellow citizens, where nations intervene in civil wars to prevent the killing of civilians, where humanitarian groups document and publicize what they consider human rights violations all over the world, and where academics from numerous disciplines fill bookshelves with discussions of the evil of genocide and ways to prevent it. Why this change? Why is genocide—once ignored or even praised—now thought of as an incomprehensible evil? Why is genocide so deviant? Why does it attract so much social control?

Genocide has become more deviant, first of all, because it is a reduction in and even destruction of diversity—a movement of social time that Black calls underdiversity—and underdiversity has become more deviant in the modern world. Black theorizes that underdiversity is more serious in diverse settings, while overdiversity is more serious in homogenous settings (Black 2011:139).[7] And his theory seems to be right: with modern communication and transportation technologies have come drastic increases in the diversity in people's lives—increases, for example, in their knowledge of and participation in other cultures and their interaction with cultural outsiders (Cowen 2002:79–80). International organizations like the United Nations and multicultural societies like that of the United States are especially diverse, and those associated with them are especially likely to condemn political censorship, religious persecution, and other assaults on diversity.

Genocide is more deviant now than in the premodern world also because it involves a greater movement of social time. If the Israelites slaughtered the Midianites, the effects were mostly localized, but in an interconnected world with dispersed populations, the effects of genocide might be felt all over the world. Hitler's slaughter of European Jews, for example, altered the lives of Jews everywhere—and the lives of those connected to them. Lemkin pointed to the possible effects of genocide on the culture of people other than the targets:

> We can best understand this when we realize how impoverished our culture would be if the peoples doomed by Germany, such

as the Jews, had not been permitted to create the Bible, or to give birth to an Einstein, a Spinoza; if the Poles had not had the opportunity to give to the world a Copernicus, a Chopin, a Curie; the Czechs, a Huss, a Dvorak; the Greeks, a Plato and a Socrates; the Russians, a Tolstoy and a Shostakovich. (quoted in Power 2002:53)

THE FUTURE OF GENOCIDE

As genocide becomes more deviant, intervention to prevent or punish genocide becomes more likely. And intervention makes genocide less likely for two reasons. First, it may directly prevent or stop the killing. Though not all interventions are successful, those that involve direct challenges to the aggressors or support for the targets do tend to reduce the severity of genocide (Krain 2005).[8] Second, remember that genocide occurs in a context of inequality, where the aggressors are superior to the targets—normally in size, political authority, and military strength. But as intervention becomes expected, conflicts are equalized. Outside opposition to the aggressors decreases their status, and support for the targets increases theirs.

For the same reason, genocide declines with the proliferation of liberal democracies. Genocides are more likely in totalitarian and authoritarian states, where political elites have extraordinary power relative to the populations they rule, than in democratic states, where political power is more diffuse (Rummel 1994; 1995; see also Cooney 1997b). Currently more than half of the world's population lives in a democracy (up from just over 12 percent in 1900), and the democratic form of government continues to spread (Modelski and Perry 2002:365).[9]

Remember also that genocide is more likely in a context of ethnic diversity—where there is cultural distance between ethnic groups—and that increasing diversity is one of the common causes of genocide. But increasingly, communication and transportation technologies allow for social closeness despite physical distance. While this increases the diversity in people's lives by bringing diverse peoples into contact with one another, it reduces the distances between them. They become culturally closer, more intimate, and more interdependent

(Black 2004a:24; Cowen 2002:79). Ultimately globalization destroys the social distances conducive to genocide. There is no genocide in a global village.[10]

Already we see a decline in the kinds of situations that lead to serious ethnic conflicts, and fewer of these conflicts means less genocide. Many of the large movements of social time that commonly lead to genocidal conflicts—colonial wars, interstate wars, civil wars, and revolutions—are much less common. Colonial wars have ended, and since the end of the Cold War interstate wars have "become few in number, mostly brief, and relatively low in battle deaths" (Pinker 2011:302). The number of civil wars peaked in the 1990s but has declined since then. The decline in the number of deaths caused by civil wars is even greater (Pinker 2011:303–5). Revolutions have likewise become less frequent, and when they occur, they are less violent (Payne 2004:100–115).

The causes of genocide and the conditions associated with it are declining, and the people of the world have become more hostile to it. But is genocide really any scarcer? All the attention given to genocide recently may leave the impression that it is not, but the evidence suggests otherwise. Since the end of World War II and the mass killings associated with it, the world has not again seen such a high level of genocide. The killings in Bosnia, Rwanda, and Darfur were severe, but they were "spikes in a trend that is unmistakably downward. . . . The first decade of the new millennium is the most genocide-free of the past fifty years" (Pinker 2011:340).

Ending genocide, of course, is the goal of many genocide scholars, whose work, as sociologist Thomas Cushman puts it, is "characterized by a strong ideological belief that genocide is preventable and that knowledge about genocide will help bring about prevention" (Cushman 2003:524). Information about genocide cannot prevent genocide, though, if no one wishes to prevent it—if people wish instead to exterminate their ethnic enemies or to stay out of others' conflicts. Genocide is caused not by lack of knowledge but by particular kinds of social changes occurring in particular social contexts. When the social conditions conducive to genocide are strongest, the conditions conducive to genocide prevention are weakest. Better knowledge about genocide earlier on would not have done much to prevent it, and perfect knowledge about genocide is not required now for its prevention.

Recent social trends have led to the decline of genocide and to an increase in efforts to stop it when it occurs. This is likely to continue regardless of how much our theories of genocide advance. Fewer international and civil wars mean fewer of the conflicts that lead to genocide. New transportation and communication technologies mean that diversity in the form of intercultural contact is increasing, and diverse peoples are becoming more similar to one another and more involved in one another's lives. They treat attacks on other cultures more seriously, and they are less likely to handle their own ethnic conflicts with violence. The proliferation of liberal democracies means fewer ethnic conflicts involve extreme inequality between the disputants, and governments are less likely to try to exterminate ethnic minorities. Some of these trends may be temporary, so we cannot know for certain how the arc of the moral universe will bend. But should these trends continue, my theory makes this prediction: genocide is destined for annihilation.

NOTES

1 GENOCIDE AS SOCIAL CONTROL

1. My stipulation that genocide is one-sided corresponds to other definitions of genocide that either use this term (Chalk and Jonassohn 1990:23–24) or otherwise clearly distinguish genocide from warfare (Charny 1994:75; Fein 1993b:24; Midlarsky 2005:22). Even though warfare is not genocide, genocide frequently occurs alongside war (Krain 1997:346–51; Melson 1992:19–20). For instance, during a civil war people may be killed because of their ethnic similarity to members of a rebel group, though they are not citizens of enemy nations or residents of rebel-occupied territory. Also, genocide may occur in the aftermath of warfare when mass killings continue after the outcome of a battle or war has been decided (compare Chalk and Jonassohn 1990:24; Horowitz 2002:37–39). Genocide is also similar in many ways to warfare, especially to so-called total war (Bartrop 2002; Markusen 1987:101; 1996:81; Traverso 2003:77–99). Total war involves a "high degree of societal mobilization for war and an extremely high level of death and destruction" (Markusen 1987:102). Like genocide it may target noncombatants, including women and children. But unlike genocide, total warfare is reciprocal. In its pure form both groups of combatants indiscriminately target citizens of the enemy nation as well as its civilian infrastructure.

2. I use *ethnicity* in a broad sense to refer to cultural groups characterized by a notion of common descent (compare Horowitz 2000 [1985]:55–57; 2001:48–49; Jaret 1995:71–74; Mann 2005:11; van den Berghe 1981:27; Weber 1978:385–98). Among the groups included as ethnic groups, then, are tribes, castes, nationalities, language groups, and many groups marked by race or religion. These differ from other cultural groups in that identity normally is ascribed at birth and is relatively unchangeable. Like political scientists Barbara Harff and Ted Gurr (1988:360), I distinguish genocides, which target ethnic groups, from politicides, which target political groups. Many other definitions are similar (for example, Bauer:1999:35; Midlarsky 2005:22; United Nations 1948). Other scholars, though, prefer to broaden the scope of genocide to include groups such as classes or political groups (for example, Chalk and Jonassohn 1990:23; Fein 1993b:24; Hinton 2002:4–6; Huttenbach 1988:295; Katz 1994:128–31; Melson 1992:26; Porter 1982:12; Rummel 1997:341; Staub 1989:8).

3. This differs from both the original definition of genocide offered by Polish jurist Raphael Lemkin and from the United Nations definition, as well as several others (for example, Barta 1987; Dadrian 1975; Huttenbach 1988; Porter 1982:12; see Moses 2002:22–28; 2004:26–28 for a discussion of such conceptions). But here I follow many other definitions in limiting genocide to mass killing (for example, Charny 1994:75;

Chalk and Jonassohn 1990:23; Melson 1992:36; Midlarsky 2005:22). Now it is common for scholars of genocide and ethnic conflict to use terms such as *cultural genocide* (Burton 1991:519–20; Katz 1991:220), *ethnocide* (Chalk and Jonassohn 1990:23), or *culturecide* (Huttenbach 1988:292) to distinguish the suppression of a culture from genocide. Similarly, many use the term *ethnic cleansing* to distinguish deportations (Bell-Fialkoff 1996:3, 53–54; Naimark 2001). Ethnic cleansing, distinct from genocide, often takes place in conjunction with genocide, however, and in many cases such deportations are genocidal—such as when the Hereros of South-West Africa were driven into the Omaheke desert (Drechsler 1980 [1966]:155–56) and when Armenian women, children, and elderly people were deported to the Syrian desert (Balakian 2003:175–80; Mazian 1990:78–82; Melson 1992:143–47).

4. This does not mean other definitions are wrong. Social scientists do not formulate real definitions—at least not in the sense of determining the essential nature or essential attributes of some phenomenon (Hempel 1952:6). Definitions of genocide cannot justifiably be described as correct or incorrect, as if genocide is somehow out there awaiting the proper definition (compare Gibbs 1989:329; Senechal de la Roche 2004:1n1). This is sometimes misunderstood in discussions of definitions of genocide. For instance, historian Frank Chalk and sociologist Kurt Jonassohn say they found it "necessary" to define genocide as perpetrated by "a state or other authority" in order "to deal with some cases in which the perpetrator was a local authority other than the state" (1990:26). This implies that certain cases are genocides independently of any definition and that a definition must be formulated to include them. But no particular definition of genocide is necessary, and no cases are inherently genocidal; they are genocides if they are defined as such.

5. Many previous definitions of genocide are difficult to apply to actual cases, as they specify certain motives or goals on the part of the perpetrators that are difficult or impossible to observe (compare Senechal de la Roche 2004:2). For instance, Chalk and Jonassohn's (1990) definition requires the intention to destroy an entire group. So does philosopher Steven T. Katz's (1994), but while Chalk and Jonassohn classify numerous cases as genocide, Katz argues that only one case, the Holocaust, fits his definition. The UN definition of genocide is likewise difficult to apply. It requires an intent to destroy, and because of this and other elements of the definition—such as its ambiguity about what actions constitute genocide—those applying it often disagree considerably. Sociologists John Hagan and Joshua Kaiser (2011a, 2011b), for example, argue that forced displacements, such as those recently occurring in Darfur, are genocidal according to the UN definition of genocide, but development anthropologist Tim Allen (2011) and sociologist Martin Shaw (2011) disagree. In both cases, the inherent difficulty in observing an intention makes it easy for authors with very similar definitions to include different cases. After all, how would we determine whether the intent to destroy an entire group existed? Would all participants need to have this intention, or only the high-level organizers of the killing? Even if it is the latter, clear statements of intention may not exist, and where they do, they may be contradictory, as some leaders at some times speak of total annihilation while others do not. And even when we observe stated intentions to annihilate an entire group, do we really know the speakers' purposes? Such statements might be hyperbole or political rhetoric, or they might be intended as a threat to the targeted group. We cannot know. In contrast, we

can usually observe whether mass killing has occurred, whether it is one-sided, and whether it is ethnically based.

6. Similarly, other scholars see genocide as some other kind of deviant behavior—as "madness" (Aronson 1987) or as a crime that can be explained with a theory of criminality (Alvarez 2001:1–9; Hagan, Rymond-Richmond, and Parker 2005; Maier-Katkin, Mears, and Bernard 2009; Nyseth Brehm 2013; Olusanya 2013; Savelsberg 2010:49–85).

7. It is a distraction because it adds nothing to the explanation. An explanation of genocide does not depend on how anyone evaluates genocide. Sociologically speaking, evil is not a type of human behavior; nor is madness or crime. These are evaluations—labels (Becker 1963:1–18; Durkheim 1933:70–82; Horwitz 1982; Scheff 1984 [1966]). Acts labeled evil, insane, or criminal may have little in common with one another. They may be different forms of social life requiring completely different explanations (Black 1983:42; 2004b:146; Cooney and Phillips 2002; Cooney 2006:53–55).

8. To assume that the killers see their own behavior as immoral misses this completely. For example, social psychologist Herbert C. Kelman (1973) approaches genocide as a type of "violence without moral restraint" and seeks to explain the factors that lead perpetrators to disregard moral decision making. It is clear in a sense that some kinds of moral restraints are indeed absent during genocidal violence. But do the perpetrators really disregard moral decision making? They disregard the condemnations of outsiders. They disregard the wishes of the targets as well as any ethical codes forbidding such killing. But moral evaluations are not absent. They are in fact present and applied by the perpetrators to the targets. Genocide itself is the product of moral decision making, a way of dealing with wrongdoing.

9. For example, scholars have used Black's strategy to examine forms of social control such as law (Baumgartner 1992a; Black 1976; Cooney 1994; Silberman 1985), gossip (Black 1995:855n129), complaint (Campbell and Manning 2014), apology (Cooney and Phillips 2013), therapy (Horwitz 1982:121–85; Tucker 1999), negotiation (Black 1998 [1993]:83–85), employee theft (Tucker 1989), corporal punishment (Tucker and Ross 2005), feuding (Black 1995:855n130; 2004b:153–154; Cooney 1998:73–82), lynching (Senechal de la Roche 1997; 2001), honor killings (Cooney 2014; forthcoming), terrorism (Black 2004a; Hawdon and Ryan 2009; Senechal de la Roche 1996), collective violence (Hawdon 2014; Senechal de la Roche 1996, 2001), interpersonal violence (Baumgartner 1992b; 1993; Cooney 1998; 2003; Jacques and Wright 2008; Michalski 2004; Phillips 2003; Phillips and Cooney 2005), and suicide (Manning 2012; 2014; 2015; forthcoming). They have examined the social control of particular forms of behavior, such as sexual intimacy (Barlow 2013), mental illness (Horwitz 1982), medical malpractice (Mullis 1995), and homicide (Cooney 2009b). And they have examined social control by particular actors, such as suburbanites (Baumgartner 1988), children (Baumgartner 1992b), corporate executives (Morrill 1989; 1995; Tucker 1999), Alcoholics Anonymous members (Hoffmann 2006), reality show participants (Godard 2003), institutional review boards (Jacques and Wright 2010), members of minority ethnic groups (Baumgartner 1998, Cooney 2009a), and nation-states (Borg 1992).

10. Although all cultural conflict is collective in logic, and although all interethnic conflict may potentially collectivize, other features of conflicts help determine whether collectivization occurs (Senechal de la Roche 2001).

11. One Tutsi survivor, for example, tells of false accusations against her father, who was said to have aided the RPF. After learning of these accusations, the Hutu man who was hiding this woman in his home told her, "Your father was a very bad Tutsi." When he said the authorities had found six hundred guns in her father's home and a death list of Hutu names, she became furious: "If my father had so many guns, why didn't he pass them out to the thousands of Tutsis who came to us asking for protection. . . . Why didn't he use the guns to protect his wife and daughter from killers and rapists?" (Ilibagiza 2007:95–97).

12. This theory draws from various pure sociological theories of social control—in particular historian Roberta Senechal de la Roche's theory of collective violence. According to Senechal de la Roche (1996; 2001), unilateral collective violence varies directly with multiple forms of social distance: relational distance, cultural distance, functional independence, and inequality (Senechal de la Roche 1996). Collective violence is variable, though, and her theory also explains this. For example, collective violence characterized by individual liability—where alleged wrongdoers are targeted—occurs at lower levels of social polarization, while collective violence characterized by collective liability—where people are targeted on the basis of their social characteristics—varies directly with the degree of social polarization, or the degree of relational and cultural distance, functional independence, and inequality (Senechal de la Roche 1996:116–17). In genocides, the aggressors target people on the basis of ethnicity. Genocide thus employs a logic of collective liability—specifically, ethnic liability—and it arises from conflicts between members of highly polarized ethnic groups.

13. Sociologist Leo Kuper describes this as "an infra-structural restraint on genocidal attacks on the subordinate group by reason of the dependence on its labor" (1981:207).

14. Another example of a situation where cooperative ties seem to have inhibited genocide is in the relations between Muslims and Jews in Morocco. There Jews were subordinated to Muslims, but massacres of Jews on the scale of those that occurred at various times in Europe were largely absent. And in Morocco Jews were bound more closely economically to the dominant group than elsewhere. Patron-client relationships "were marked by dyadic contracts between an individual Jew and his family on the one hand, and a powerful Muslim and his family on the other" (Zenner 1987:264).

15. Organization refers broadly to the capacity for collective action, and it is present to some degree in any group (Black 1976:85). Groups are more organized, however, where there are administrative officers, where decision making is centralized and continuous, and where collective action itself is greater (Black 1976:85).

16. Just as the natives' low level of complexity throughout the continent led to more genocide in Australia than in North America, it also led to more genocide in Australia than New Zealand. K. R. Howe notes that relations between British settlers and natives were strikingly different in New Zealand than they were in Australia, and he attributes this largely to the relative size and military strength of the indigenous societies (1977:vi, 1–10, 84–85). The hunter-gatherer Aborigines of Australia had a low population density and little political or cultural cohesion. The horticulturalist Maoris of New Zealand, in contrast, were more numerous overall and more settled. They lived in larger groups, spoke a common language, and were more politically and militarily organized (Howe 1977:3–6). Accordingly, Maori resistance was met with

conventional warfare and attempts at the "amalgamation" of Maoris into the colonial society rather than with genocide (Howe 1977:39–42).

17. Genocide was also widespread and severe in the northwestern mining region, where Indians also outnumbered whites. Here though, they were less intimate and interdependent with whites than the Indians in the southern and central districts (Hurtado 1988:117–24).

18. According to a 1938 Italian census, in 43.7 percent of marriages involving Jews, one of the partners was not Jewish (Brustein 2003:91, 172). This was about three times higher than the rate in Germany just before the Nazis came to power (Brustein 2003:162, 172).

19. We would expect, then, that where other conditions favorable to genocide also occur—such as ethnic division and the exclusion of an ethnic group from governing—state power would increase the likelihood and scale of genocide. And this is the pattern we see; as with other forms of violence, democracies are less genocidal than authoritarian states, and authoritarian states less so than totalitarian states. Political scientist R. J. Rummel (1995) found genocide to be strongly associated with government power, as did sociologist Helen Fein (1993a:92–93) and political scientist Barbara Harff (2003:62–63).

20. The Native Police Force consisted of Aborigines, and the fact that they engaged in genocide against other Aborigines may at first seem inconsistent with the theory. But the Aborigines who served in the Native Police were actually socially closer to their officers and to whites in general than to the Aborigines they killed. This was due to the social characteristics of Aboriginal societies and to the manner in which the Native Police were recruited. Aborigines were socially close only to their kin and near neighbors. They had no concept corresponding to "Aborigine" or even "Australia," and distant Aborigines—especially those who spoke incomprehensible languages—were normally treated as enemies responsible for diseases and natural disasters (Reynolds 1990:80). The police officers were recruited from areas far away from the frontier precisely so they would have no sympathy for local clans (Reynolds 1990:83). Any Aborigines they encountered on the frontier were complete strangers differing in language and other cultural practices. At the same time they were socially closer to whites because the Native Police were recruited from among the Aborigines living on the fringes of white society, where the men often worked for whites as unpaid laborers and stockmen, and where the women often served as domestic servants or concubines (Reynolds 1990:74).

21. Violence in general may be one-sided or reciprocal, but this is a matter of degree. When one-sidedness is extreme, only one side of a conflict uses violence, such as would usually be the case when a parent spanks a disobedient child. But one-sidedness varies, and there may be some violence flowing from the other direction even when violence is mainly one-sided. This occurs when reciprocal violence gives way to one-sided violence during the course of a conflict—such as when a victorious fighter continues pummeling a defeated and incapacitated enemy. One-sided violence may also occur in response to previous violence, such as when a child is spanked for slapping her mother, or it may provoke violence, such as when a child being spanked tries to fight back. These are not pure cases of one-sidedness, but the violence is asymmetrical enough to distinguish these cases from reciprocal violence, where the adversaries behave similarly toward one another. We saw earlier that the one-sidedness

of genocide distinguishes it from warfare and other reciprocal forms of violence. But since the degree of one-sidedness is variable, genocides may be distinguished from one another along this same dimension. Like a fistfight, a war may become one-sided with the defeat of one side, such as when soldiers engage in mass killing after battles (Collins 2008:94–99; Freeman 1995a:218–21) or after standoffs initially consisting of low-level reciprocal violence (Klusemann 2010). Genocide is also less one-sided when it provokes a violent response or when it is itself a response to previous violence, as in many of the Australian killings.

22. Because genocide involves targeting people on the basis of ethnicity, it is distinguished not only from lynchings, state executions, and other forms of violence that punish only an alleged offender, but also from violence that targets people on the basis of political affiliation, sex, occupation, social class, or some other nonethnic social category. But the extent to which genocide is based on ethnicity is a matter of degree. Many genocides involve the targeting of only certain segments of an ethnic group. For instance, it may be that only male members of fighting age are killed; men of "battle age" have been disproportionately the targets of most genocides (Jones 2004). Also ethnicity itself is variable. Historian Norman Naimark notes that political groups or classes may be "ethnicized" (2010:5). In such cases, they begin to be treated as ethnic groups, as "invented nations" (Naimark 2010:29). For example, the *kulaks,* wealthy peasants in the Soviet Union, were depicted by Soviet propaganda as genetically inferior, and thus their relatives and children were also treated as *kulaks* (Naimark 2010:58–59).

23. Similarly, *Village Voice* theater critic Michael Feingold wrote in 2004 that Republicans' "chosen work" is to "destroy the human race and the planet," and that they "should be exterminated before they cause any more harm" (quoted in Haidt 2012:287–88). This is a call for politicide rather than genocide—politically based rather than ethnically based mass killing—but as with Kambon's exhortation to exterminate whites, it has no chance of being carried out. The social geometry is not conducive to mass killing.

2 GENOCIDE AS PREDATION

1. Often, for example, the target of a robbery fights back. In such cases, as sociologists Mark Cooney and Scott Phillips note, "the robber's violence is predatory, but the would-be victim's violent response is moralistic" (2002:94).

2. For example, Donald Black (1983:37) tells of a case in which a man robbed his girlfriend's sister to collect a debt for a baby carriage he had bought her. And criminologists Richard Wright and Scott Decker (1997:69) found that on the rare occasions when armed robbers targeted someone they knew well, the targets were people they disliked or had fallen out with.

3. Social control is in a sense the opposite of deviance. It is not the "intentional violation of a prohibition," but a reaction to wrongdoing by others (Black 1983:34). Predation, on the other hand, may be deviant even from the perspective of the predator. This is not always the case, though, and certain forms of predation, such as slavery or taxation, may be widely regarded as legitimate (Payne 2004:188–89, 200–1).

4. It is also consistent with Black's (1998 [1993]:91; 2004a:21) principle of isomorphism, which predicts an affinity between the forms of moral and economic life. For example, negotiation, a form of social control where the parties to a dispute work

out an agreement among themselves, occurs in what Black calls tangled networks, social fields characterized by equality, cross-linkages, organization, homogeneity, and accessibility (Black 1998 [1993]:83–85). And as Black points out, people in tangled networks "continually bargain over their conditions of life as well as their conflicts" (1998 [1993]:91). These moralistic and economic behaviors—negotiation and exchange—resemble one another and have the same geometry. Other behaviors that closely resemble one another—toleration and sharing, genocide and plunder—also occur in the same social environments.

5. Prior to that, Rath's death had led to the massive anti-Jewish pogrom known as Kristallnacht, or the Night of Broken Glass, which resulted in the death of about one hundred Jews and the destruction of thousands of businesses (Melson 1992:226). As is clear in the case of the atonement payment, there was a moralistic element to much of the looting and taxation.

6. Rape occurred in both circumstances during the Armenian genocide as well. During the deportations of Armenian women and children, guards and others sometimes raped girls and women, as they did in one incident where "8 to 10-year-old girls were raped in front of the other deportees and subsequently shot since they could not walk as a consequence of the abuse" (Bjørnlund 2009:25). But Armenian girls and women might be spared from death after being forced to become the wives or concubines of Muslim men (Bjørnlund 2009:38).

7. At Auschwitz and elsewhere, male guards sometimes also raped Jewish boys and men (Flaschka 2010:86–88). Most rapes, though, were of women and girls by men.

8. We saw in chapter 1 that Nazis spared the lives of most German Jews married to non-Jews, even though Nazi ideology condemned intermarriage. And here we see that Jewish women were victims of rape even though Nazi ideology condemned the rape of Jews along with other sexual contact with them. In both cases the aggressors' behavior is consistent with the theory even though it contradicts their own beliefs. We should not overemphasize the importance of ideology.

9. We also see universalistic morality whenever morality is identified with empathy. Journalist Robert Wright, for example, speaks of the "moral imagination" as "our capacity to put ourselves in the shoes of another person" (2009:418). One problem with speaking of this as the "moral imagination" is that moral imaginations differ. In some social contexts empathy toward enemies may be condemned, and the tack of the "moral imagination" is then to see enemies as different from other human beings. Consider, for example, the advice Aristotle gave to Alexander the Great: "to have regard for the Greeks as for friends and kindred, but to conduct himself toward other peoples as though they were plants or animals" (quoted in Wright 2000:208).

3 INDIANS AND WHITES IN CALIFORNIA

1. A number of other books on genocide use case studies to illustrate and test theories, but the following accounts differ from most of these in one important respect: they examine genocide up close. Other theoretical studies of genocide focus on society-wide killings. In *Why Genocide?*, for instance, sociologist Florence Mazian (1990) reworks sociologist Neil Smelser's theory of collective behavior to apply to genocide, then focuses in detail on the Armenian genocide and the Holocaust to illustrate the plausibility of her theory. In *Revolution and Genocide* political scientist Robert Melson (1992) applies his theory to these same two cases. Political scientist

Benjamin Valentino (2004), in *Final Solutions,* applies his theory of ethnic mass killings to these cases and to Rwanda. In *The Roots of Evil* psychologist Ervin Staub (1989) examines the Holocaust, the Armenian genocide, the mass killing in Cambodia under the Khmer Rouge, and killings conducted by the Argentine military in the late 1970s. Other studies of genocide offer up-close descriptions, but these works are mainly atheoretical: they tell us about particular cases rather than about genocide more generally. Examples include historian Christopher Browning's (1998) study of the killing operations of Germany's Reserve Police Battalion 101, historian Jan Gross's (2001) study of the massacre of Jews in Jedwabne, Poland, and political scientist Scott Straus's (2004; 2006) study of the dynamics of genocide in five Rwandan communes.

2. Genocide involves mass killing on the basis of ethnicity, so targeting people on the basis of their individual wrongdoing is not genocide. Some of the massacres in the Round Valley may not have been genocides, then, if the settlers were targeting a number of individual wrongdoers simultaneously rather than targeting people on the basis of their ethnicity or their association with the offenders. It is not always clear whether this is the case, but in most of the accounts, even when the whites targeted a specific group of Indians, it seems they then held them all responsible for the offense.

3. The settlers' opinions about the Yuki were much like those of whites about California Indians more generally. The Indians were said to be ugly, filthy, stupid, indolent, disgusting, effeminate, undiscriminating in what they ate, one of the lowest races of humankind (or perhaps the lowest), and more like beasts than people (Rawls 1984:186–201; see also Stannard 1992:145). One settler said that touching an Indian woman would cause a "feeling of repulsion just as if I had put my hand on a toad, tortoise, or huge lizard" (quoted in Rawls 1984:198).

4. As was the case here, the victims of genocide normally do not have guns, and many genocides are "preceded by a very careful government program that disarms the future victims" (Kopel, Gallant, and Eisen 2006:1321). The disparity in weapons is one form of inequality between aggressors and targets, as many of the African targets of Arab militias in the recent genocide in Darfur pointed out. "None of us had arms and we were not able to resist the attack," said one of the victims. "I tried to take my spear to protect my family," said another, "but they threatened me with a gun, so I stopped. The six Arabs then raped my daughter in front of me, my wife and my other children" (quoted in Kopel, Gallant, and Eisen 2006:1317).

5. Other newspapers supported the killings enthusiastically. The *Humboldt Times* of Eureka, for example, encouraged the settlers to "go to work seriously with the determination to make the present the last Indian war that we are to be troubled with" (quoted in Carranco and Beard 1981:62).

6. They would also have failed to attract support due to their lack of strong ties to other settlers in the area.

7. Something very similar occurred in Queensland, Australia, where at first small groups of settlers would organize voluntarily in response to an offense, engage in low levels of mass killing, and then disband until another grievance arose. But as the organization of the killing increased, so did the scale. The organization increased with the formation of Native Police units intended to protect whites in frontier areas (Palmer 2000:49–50). Made up of Aborigines led by white officers, the Native Police would attack Aborigines in response to various offenses, or they would attack gatherings of Aborigines without provocation. Though extremely small in number—consisting of

groups of six to twelve troopers and one officer and never numbering more than 206 men total (Moses 2000:102)—these forces were more permanent and formal than the small bands of settlers. As in California, organization increased along with changes that led to stronger support for the settlers. The original commandant of the Native Police, Frederick Walker, intended the force to protect both whites and Aborigines, but settlers who demanded a more aggressive policy toward blacks succeeded in having Walker replaced in 1855 (Moses 2000:100; Palmer 2000:50). They also had control of the Native Police transferred from Sydney to local magistrates, who were socially closer to the aggrieved settlers and sympathetic to their concerns (Moses 2000:100). The Native Police were now in a social location suited to stronger support of the settlers, and they began regularly engaging in genocidal acts.

8. Collective liability of all types increases with social polarization (Senechal de la Roche 1996:116). Collective liability occurs when people are punished or otherwise held liable for an offense because of their social characteristics rather than their individual wrongdoing. Genocide involves ethnic liability, a type of collective liability in which people are held liable based on their ethnic identity.

9. In Australia, similarly, Aborigines attacked white settlers when circumstances temporarily reduced the settlers' organizational and technological superiority, such as when they found white settlers alone. Even European technology could be overcome once the Aborigines learned its limitations. The muskets used in the early part of the nineteenth century took minutes to reload, for example, and Aboriginal clans sometimes would surround an isolated settler and try to provoke him into firing his gun, after which they could attack a temporarily unarmed man. In the second half of the century, however, whites were armed with revolvers and repeating rifles, and the one-sidedness of the killing increased as Aboriginal attacks became more difficult (Reynolds 2006:101–107).

4 MUSLIMS AND HINDUS IN INDIA

1. Law professor Donald Horowitz defines a "deadly ethnic riot" as "an intense, sudden, though not necessarily wholly unplanned, lethal attack by civilian members of one ethnic group on civilian members of another ethnic group, the victims chosen because of their group membership" (2001:1).

2. Even though this violence was more extreme, many of the prior riots that seemed to be the spontaneous reactions of unorganized crowds may have involved a fairly high degree of hidden planning and cooperation on the part of the aggressors. Political scientist Paul Brass contends that little is spontaneous about Hindu-Muslim riots, which generally take the form of massacres of Muslims by Hindus. Rather, they are "dramatic productions in which what is spontaneous can occur only because the scene has been prepared with numerous rehearsals marked by tension, rumors, and provocations, in which the signals that an outbreak is about to occur and that the time for participation has arrived have been made clear" (Brass 2003:378). Anti-Muslim violence, says Brass, is produced deliberately by political actors who have created "institutionalized riot systems" that they can activate when such violence would be politically advantageous (Brass 2003; 2004).

3. Some Hindutva activists have been involved in the "rescue" of Hindu girls from relationships with Muslims. For instance, Babu Bajrangi, a low-level Hindutva leader who was also involved in the massacre of Muslims at Naroda Patiya, headed a group

called the Navchetan Trust, which makes such rescues a priority. Bajrangi explained the group's purpose as follows: "These girls go to college, make friends with some *lafanga* [loafer], roam with them on their bikes, fall in love, and then run off and get married.... We bring them back and convince them that they are ruining their future." Asked how they convince the women, Bajrangi said, "We do whatever it takes and somehow bring them. If it's a Musalman, we definitely use force even if the girl doesn't want to leave. Musalmans don't have a right to live in our country. How dare they marry our girls?" (quoted in Bunsha 2006).

4. The Hindu nationalists also see the practice of polygyny as connected to what they consider Muslim privileges. One example they give of the appeasement of Muslims by political leaders is that Muslims are allowed four wives by law while Hindus are allowed only one. Hindutva leaders see this as indicating that the secularism advocated by their political opponents is only a "pseudo-secularism" used to obtain Muslim votes (Engineer 2003:10–11).

5. These bull sacrifices are legal in Gujarat, but only a small number are allowed. Since the quota is so small, any particular sacrifice can be treated as illegal (Ghassem-Fachandi 2006:531).

6. The information in this section about the events in the Gulberg Society comes mainly from Chenoy, Shukla, Subramanian, and Vanaik 2002; Concerned Citizens Tribunal 2002a:26–35; "Genocide—Gujarat 2002" 2002; Ghassem-Fachandi 2006:124–35; and Human Rights Watch 2002:18–20. These accounts are mostly in agreement, though they differ slightly on the exact timing and order of some of the events. I have therefore tried to present the most plausible sequence of events, taking all of the sources into consideration.

7. The information in this section comes mainly from Chenoy, Nagar, Bose, and Krishnan 2002; Concerned Citizens Tribunal 2002a:36–42; "Genocide—Gujarat 2002" 2002; Ghista 2006:64–65; Human Rights Watch 2002:15–18; and Sharma and Pandey 2002.

8. The information in this section comes mainly from Chenoy, Shukla, Subramanian, and Vanaik 2002 and Concerned Citizens Tribunal 2002a:52–61.

9. There were also as many or more incidents of deaths caused by civilian shootings (Concerned Citizens Tribunal 2002a:57).

10. This has not always been the case everywhere in Gujarat, however. For example, prior to the 1992 riots following the destruction of the Babri mosque, Hindus and Muslims in Pandarwada celebrated their religious festivals together at the central *chowk* in the their village. After 1992 the *chowk* was named the Ayodhya Chowk, and Muslims stopped going there (People's Union for Democratic Rights 2002:64–65).

11. Despite the initial violence in Godhra that ended in the deaths of fifty-eight Hindus, there were not any retaliatory killings in this area, only property damage. Journalist Jyoti Punwani (2002) attributes this to the growing interdependence between the two sections of Hindus and Muslims—the Sindhis and Ghanchis, respectively—who were involved in earlier riots. Following previous riots the Sindhis had managed to rebuild and to prosper economically, and according to Punwani, "they are not interested in becoming cannon fodder for the VHP. Already the destruction of Bohra shops in the villages has meant massive losses for them as wholesale suppliers" (2002). When the 2002 violence put a strain on Muslim-Hindu relations, the Sindhis even invited Muslim traders into the area and gave them a guarantee of safety (2002).

12. The report by the Concerned Citizens Tribunal seems to refute this, noting that "neighbors attacked neighbors even though outsiders were called in to make up the numbers" (Concerned Citizens Tribunal 2002b:25). The same report, however, notes later that "in as many instances, victims categorically stated that the violence was the work of outsiders" (2002b:32). Also it seems that if the attackers were neighbors in the sense of persons who lived close to and regularly interacted with the targets, there would have been little need for the attackers to be bused in or to rely on lists of Muslim establishments. The Gulberg Society had only one Hindu family, and they were not involved in the attacks. It seems that the authors of the report are referring to people from nearby areas as neighbors, rather than to people living in the same neighborhood. Thus there was not any significant social closeness.

13. This is true even of those scholars who have focused on other factors. Israeli judge Moshe Bejski (1977:635), for example, sees personal acquaintance and friendship as an important (but not dominant) motive in many rescues. Likewise, Holocaust scholar Mordecai Paldiel (1986:92) and sociologist Samuel P. Oliner (1982:12) see friendships as the cause of a particular cluster of rescues. Many rescuers also had other intimate ties, such as through marriage, or functional ties, such as through work or political party affiliation, with those they saved (Block and Drucker 1992:8; Fogelman 1994:181–202; Friedman 1980:411; Henry 1984:102, 105; Moore 2003:299). Often those who ended up aiding strangers started by rescuing intimates and then extended their rescuing activities (Oliner and Oliner 1988:89; Paldiel 1986:92; Staub 1993:334; Tec 1986:135–36). Additionally, rescuers had more ties with Jews in general than nonrescuers did. Oliner and Oliner (1988:114–15) found that more rescuers lived among Jews, worked with them, and had Jewish friends than nonrescuers prior to the war. And sociologist Nechama Tec (1986:130) found that more than half of the altruistic Polish rescuers she studied—but none of those who aided Jews in exchange for payment—had close ties to Jews before the war. Cultural closeness was also a factor in rescue. For instance, much of the aid was to fellow Christians—Jews who had converted to Christianity but were still classified as Jews by the Nazis (Milton 1983:284; see also Gushee 2003:136).

14. Few studies exist of rescues in genocides other than the Holocaust, but the evidence suggests similar patterns. For example, in interviews with survivors of the Armenian genocide, historian Richard G. Hovannisian found that in about a quarter of the reported cases, rescuers had a prior acquaintance with those they helped (1992:288). And in almost half (43.8 percent) of the cases, he says an economic motive was dominant (Hovannisian 1992:292). Some of these involved direct payment, but the most common type of rescue in this category involved Turks taking in Armenians who could help with herding, field labor, and other tasks (Hovannisian 1992:294). Many Armenians were also rescued as a result of their willingness to convert to Islam (Hovannisian 1992:290, 295–297; see also Tevosyan 2011; Üngör 2011). And in many of the other cases, Armenians likewise provided labor for their rescuers and accepted their religion, even if this was not considered the dominant motive for the rescue (Hovannissian 1992:290). Rescue during nongenocidal mass killings can also be explained with social closeness. For example, beginning in 1976 Argentina's military government kidnapped, tortured, and killed tens of thousands of suspected political opponents. This was not genocide, but it provided opportunities for altruism amid mass killing, and many Argentineans aided the targets in various ways. As sociologist

Jessica Casiro (2006:439) argues, the rescuers' social networks were much more important than their personal characteristics in explaining their actions. One-time rescuers aided either family members, friends, acquaintances, or those referred to them by their friends. Repeat rescuers did help strangers, but these were almost always people who shared their political ideology (Casiro 2006:443). One repeat rescuer stated this explicitly: "I wouldn't have helped just anybody. Not a right wing person. I helped people who shared with me an ideology, a way of seeing the world" (quoted in Casiro 2006:443). Nearly all rescuers in this case, then, were either relationally or culturally close to those they aided.

15. Both men were later given punitive reassignments due to their actions on behalf of Muslims.

5 MUSLIMS AND SERBS IN BOSNIA

1. At this time ethnic identification followed political alliances. In the Yugoslav parliament of 1924, for instance, nearly all of the Bosnian Muslim deputies identified as Croats (Malcolm 1994:165–66).

2. In Bosnia as a whole the population was 31 percent Serbian, 44 percent Muslim, and 17 percent Croatian (Cigar 1995:5).

3. In the 1990 elections voting divided along ethnic lines. But a number of Serbs supported a rival Serb party, led by Ante Markovic, rather than the SDS. For instance, 90 percent of Serbs who lived in mixed families—12 percent of the population—voted for Markovic's party. The SDS received only 28 percent of the votes in Prijedor, even though 42.5 percent of the population was Serb (Greve 1994:44; Wesselingh and Vaulerin 2005:38).

4. Most of the prisoners at Omarska were men, but between thirty and forty women were also held there. Though they were not killed, the women were subjected nightly to beatings and rapes (Greve 1994:67; Gutman 1993:144–149; ICTY 1995; 2000; 2001b).

5. Differences in intermarriage explain regional variations in the violence in Yugoslavia. Botev (1994:475) notes that Vojvodina—which, along with Kosovo, was one of Serbia's two autonomous provinces—had high rates of ethnic intermarriage, and, as my theory predicts, this province remained relatively peaceful throughout the conflict.

6. The CIA estimated that Serbs carried out 90 percent of the acts of ethnic cleansing in Bosnia (Maass 1996:32). And though the conflict was a civil war of sorts, there was very little actual warfare in the sense of confrontations between armed groups of adversaries. The Serb military and paramilitary operations in Bosnia were for the most part directed against an unarmed population—against towns and villages with no military defenses. For example, prior to the assault on the tiny Muslim village of Kevljani in the Prijedor district, the village was surrounded on all sides by more than a thousand soldiers. As one resident described it, "We were like a group of Bushmen confronted by a battalion of the French Foreign Legion" (Pervanic 1999:30). And whenever there was any defense at all, the Serbs would simply shell the defenders until they surrendered, then enter the town and begin rounding up and killing civilians (Maass 1996:33; Sells 1996:117).

7. For example, according to General Lewis MacKenzie, the first U.N. commander in Sarajevo, the various actors were simply irrational people who, obsessed with past

grievances, refused to get along. "Dealing with Bosnia is a little bit like dealing with three serial killers," he remarked at one point (quoted in Maass 1996:33; see also Gutman 1993:168–73).

8. Journalist Peter Maass chides the American media for referring to "ethnic rivalries" in Bosnia. He says that the conflict had nothing to do with the "complexities of ethnicity" because all the combatants were Slavic and therefore members of the same ethnic group (Maass 1996:69). Others, without denying the existence of ethnicity in Bosnia, have denied that the conflict was primarily ethnic. Political scientist V. P. Gagnon, for example, sees the violence as resulting from the dynamics of within-group conflict. In this view political elites within Serbia created the conflict as a strategy to deal with intraethnic challenges to their power (Gagnon 1994–1995; see also Cigar 1995:6; Doubt 2000:15–24; Pervanic 1999:xvi).

6 TUTSIS AND HUTUS IN RWANDA

1. Ntaganzwa's indictment (ICTR 1996) by the International Criminal Tribunal for Rwanda says that he was an MRND member. This is apparently an error, however, as it is contradicted by many other sources and does not seem at all plausible in light of the events described in those sources.

2. There is a discrepancy in the sources as to when the soldiers arrived. According to African Rights (1999), the soldiers were there on the 18th and set up the gun at the communal office at this time. Human Rights Watch (1994b) says they arrived on the 20th. I have followed Des Forges (1999), whose account is more detailed, in placing this event—and the last day of the killings—on the 19th.

3. Cultural differences also existed, even if many observers have downplayed them. As Jean Hatzfeld notes, "Country people love nothing better than resembling the stereotypes strangers have of them. . . . The Tutsi cattle-farmer is no exception to this rule. You will never see a Hutu farmer walking along holding a long stick, a felt hat on his head; but you will often see his Tutsi counterpart wearing those cattle-breeders' accessories and, in the evening or at the weekend, you shouldn't be too surprised to see this or that school principal, bureau chief, this or that shopkeeper or doctor walking into the café holding his staff, sporting a hat—signs that he owns a cow in a herd" (2005a:41). Some Rwandans also say that Tutsis, unlike Hutus, like cows, and they say that Tutsis have softer expressions, stiffer postures, and different ways of dressing (Hatzfeld 2005a:105, 146–47).

4. There is scant documentation of differences in intermarriage rates, but a comparison of two cells in Butare with two cells in the northern prefecture of Ruhengeri found considerable differences. In the two Butare cells, 21 percent and 12 percent of Tutsis had married Hutus. In contrast, only three percent of Tutsis had married Hutus in one of the Ruhengeri cells and none in the other (McDoom 2005:15). The same study also found that after the 1990 RPF invasion, interethnic marriage declined in the northern cells but not in the southern cells (McDoom 2005:16).

5. Burundian refugees were also present elsewhere in Rwanda. Prior to the 1994 genocide in Rwanda, about 200,000 Hutu refugees had entered Rwanda after fleeing from the violence in Burundi that followed the 1993 assassination of that country's first Hutu president. These refugees—socially distant from local Tutsis—had leading roles in starting massacres in south-central Rwanda, and they were known for practicing the most extreme means of torture (Mamdani 2001:205). Rwandan Hutu refugees

from the civil war may also have been disproportionately involved in the genocide (Mann 2005:465).

6. Straus (2004:99) found no correlation between the presence of refugees and the onset of violence, but this concerns only the difference in onset between prefectures. The presence of refugees seems to have been more important at the local level.

7. People who were socially distant in other ways were also likely to participate more intensely. For instance, though a sample of perpetrators of the Rwandan genocide showed that nearly 70 percent had a Tutsi family member, the lack of a Tutsi family member was strongly correlated with the degree of participation (Straus 2004:214–15; 2006:128–29).

8. Straus also found that the onset of genocide was earlier where there were fewer Tutsis, which supports the theory and is in agreement with the other sources that note the high concentration of Tutsis in the south. But the correlation is weak when one looks at all the prefectures, as some of the early-onset regions also had high concentrations of Tutsis (Straus 2004:98).

9. The elimination of opposition leaders also took place on the national level. Shortly after Habyarimana's death, for example, Prime Minister Agathe Uwilingiyimana and other opponents of the regime were killed (Scherrer 2002:109). Likewise, Prefect Habyalimana was removed from office and killed after working to prevent genocide in Butare. As with the elimination of opposition leaders within Nyakizu, the prefect's removal resulted in greater participation in the genocide within Nyakizu. It also led to the beginning of genocide elsewhere in Butare, such as in the communes of Maraba and Gishamvu, where the genocide began immediately after Habyalimana's removal (African Rights 2003; McDoom 2005:4).

10. There was a high degree of participation in the communal labor program, though it is not known with precision exactly what percentage of the population participated. One study of perpetrators found that 87.5 percent reported performing *umuganda* (Straus 2004:191).

7 JEWS AND GENTILES IN EUROPE

1. The annexation of Vilna and of part of Vilna's province added 100,000 Jews to the Lithuanian population—75,000 from Vilna alone (Beinfeld 1997:28).

2. Accounts of this incident vary. Most agree that it occurred on June 27, though there may have been two such massacres, one of which may have occurred earlier (Beinfeld 1997:31; Eidintas 2003:191).

3. There is a discrepancy in the accounts as to which side was the "good" side and which the "bad." Here I have followed the majority of the sources in presenting the right as the "bad" side—where those who were to be killed the next day were sent.

4. In Poland, German occupiers also instigated genocide, usually with the assistance of local Poles (Strzembosz 2001). As in the case of Lithuania, these massacres are sometimes erroneously described as the result of "neighbors" turning on the Jews living alongside them. For example, historian Jan Gross (2001) says that in the summer of 1941 the Jews of Jedwabne were killed by the town's Poles without direction or aid from the Nazis. But the evidence suggests that Germans instigated, supervised, and conducted the killings. Only about two dozen local Poles were involved—and many of these were coerced—while others resisted or even aided their Jewish neighbors (Pogonowski 2002; Strzembosz 2001).

5. Social closeness also explains aid to Jews by other Jews. Because they made work assignments and distributed rations, the Jewish Council and the administration within the Kovno ghetto could intervene to save particular Jews or make their living conditions better. Such aid was disproportionately given to the ghetto elite and to their family, friends, and employees (Ginaite-Rubinson 2005:50; Gordon 1992:45). Those without connections, on the other hand, might be transferred to undesirable jobs so better positions could be given to friends of the administration, and they might have difficulty being excused from work even when suffering from severe injuries (Gordon 1992:86–94).

6. They did, however, help make arrangements for Jews to be taken in by Lithuanian families. Here social closeness was also important, as their priority was to find placements for children of the Jews who had joined with the partisans (Neshamit 1977:318).

7. Table 4 compares the features of the five cases of genocide addressed in these chapters, but we can analyze any genocide in the same way. Consider a case we have not discussed: the 1937 massacre of Haitians in the Dominican Republic. The Dominican Republic was a dictatorship under President Rafael Trujillo, who had come to power in a 1930 coup. Trujillo and his cabinet members advocated a nationalist version of modernization and sought to use and expand the state's power to bring about their goals (Turits 2002:603–4). The frontier areas particularly concerned them, and they considered the presence of Haitians near the border with Haiti a "pacific invasion" that threatened the Dominican nation. In the event of an invasion launched by exiles from Haiti, they feared that the border areas would allow for easy passage. They also thought of the Haitian-Dominican culture that flourished on the frontier as backward, uncivilized, and African. In particular they saw the unconventional religious practices of those on the border—such as their fanaticism and their practice of Voudou—as a threat to the project of modernization and homogenization (Turits 2002:599, 605). To deal with these grievances, hundreds of soldiers from the Dominican army, along with some civilian reserves, killed between 10,000 to 20,000 Haitians during a five-day period in October of 1937 (Roorda 1996; Turits 2002). Here conditions were conducive to genocide, and the killing was highly genocidal in many ways. Although Dominicans and Haitians in the frontier area were socially close—maintaining distinct identities but similar and intermingled enough that they shared a common culture (Turits 2002:594–98)—the state officials who formulated the grievances and planned the genocide and the Dominican soldiers who carried out the killings were extremely socially distant and superior outsiders. The worry about an invasion from Haiti also meant that they were unlikely to use expulsion as an option, so the situation was characterized by the high levels of inseparability, social distance, and inequality conducive to highly thorough and one-sided killing. The one-sidedness was especially extreme. The violence was not a response to previous violence, and as historian Richard Lee Turits notes, for the targets "the genocidal rampage appeared to come out of nowhere, like an act of madness" (2002:620). The scale was not extremely high, but because the organized aggressors were able to carry out a genocide over a fairly large territory and over a period of several days, it was not extremely low, either. The degree to which it was ethnically based, however, was low. The killers did not limit the killing to men or to elites, as is often the case, but they did limit it so that they attacked Haitians only in the northwestern frontier region—not those throughout

the rest of the country. The Haitians in other parts of the country were socially closer to the aggressors. They were migrant workers who worked on the sugar plantations and whose migration the government regulated for the benefit of the sugar companies. These workers, then, had interdependent relations with Dominicans in the interior and with the regime itself (Roorda 1996:304–6).

CONCLUSION

1. Bauman's work on genocide is mostly macrosociological. The modern bureaucratic state, he says, weakens presocietal moral drives and replaces moral responsibility with technical responsibility. The rationality of modern society can thus be directed toward immoral ends such as genocide rather than toward the moral ends assumed by the modern notion of progress (Bauman 1989:1–30). Here I focus on the microsociological element of his work, which seeks to explain how rational processes common to certain locations in modern societies enable individuals to kill.

2. In explaining how people overcome inhibitions to killing, Bauman's approach is similar to many other explanations of genocide (for example, Alvarez 2001:115–28; Kelman 1973; Kressel 2002; Lifton 1986; Waller 2002) as well as of violence more broadly (Collins 2008; Grossman 1996).

3. This is not an explanation either Bauman or Browning offers, however, since neither applies this approach to rescuing. Bauman even argues that rescuing results not from the kinds of situational factors he uses to explain killing, but from innate personality characteristics. Those who saved victims of the Holocaust, he says, did so when their dormant moral consciences became aroused. Such behavior was their "own personal attribute and possession—unlike immorality, which had to be socially produced" (Bauman 1989:168). Interestingly, Janine Natalya Clark, who unlike Bauman does address contradictory behavior by the same individuals, also speculates that altruistic behavior, unlike killing behavior, is not produced by the social situation: "Does a perpetrator's capacity to be both cruel and kind at the same time suggest that however strong the pull of circumstances, personality will ultimately but temporarily prevail, with the result that the former law-abiding citizen may emerge even as he violates the law?" Here the idea seems to be that situational factors might lead people to kill, while their personalities lead them to rescue. Apparently each behavior would require a different kind of explanation. But Clark goes on to speculate that perhaps, instead, killing and rescuing are both expressions of power, "a means for an individual to show that *he* can decide who lives and who dies" (2009:437). In this case both behaviors would result from the same situation, but this would not be able to explain who is killed and who is rescued.

4. It might also be argued that roles rather than situations determine killing and rescuing. Bauman, for example, speaks of the "easiness with which most people slip into the role requiring cruelty or at least moral blindness" (1989:168). He also uses the concept in briefly discussing the Stanford prison experiment, in which college men randomly assigned to be guards or prisoners ended up behaving in vastly different ways—with the guards authoritative and cruel and the prisoners submissive (Haney et al., 1973). Here, he says, roles rather than personalities produced the behaviors: "Were the subjects of the experiment assigned to the opposite roles, the overall result would not be different" (Bauman 1989:167). A similar approach could be applied to contra-

dictory behavior, with the idea that individuals act as killers or rescuers depending on the role they are playing. This might be a way of interpreting such behavior, but it would not explain it. As sociologist George C. Homans notes, interpreting behaviors in terms of roles associated with various social positions does nothing to explain the behaviors themselves (1967:11–13). And in any case people may engage in killing and rescuing while acting in the same roles—soldiers, militia group members, guards, or SS officers.

5. Similarly, in Markus Zusak's novel *The Book Thief,* the narrator tells of a boy who went from being a stealer to a giver of bread, and he says that this is "proof again of the contradictory human being. So much good, so much evil. Just add water" (Zusak 2007:164).

6. It is certainly much more common to think of genocide as a deviant behavior than to think of it as a form of social control—a response to the deviant behavior of others. After all, most genocide scholars identify with the targets of genocide and condemn their killers. But social science is "value-free" (Berger 1963:5–6; Black 2013; Campbell 2014a; Michalski 2008:529–31; Seubert 1991; Weber 1958). It cannot tell us whether the targets' or the killers' or our own values are correct, and in any case, such information would be sociologically useless—a distraction from the task of explanation. Understanding this difference—the difference between factual statements and value judgments—is especially important in the study of deviant behavior and social control, where we are otherwise in danger of completely misunderstanding our subject. In this case if we were to mistake our condemnation of genocide for a sociological classification, we might be tempted to think of genocide and the social control of genocide as behaviors completely unlike one another. But both are acts of social control, reactions to deviant behavior. Genocide involves moral judgments against the targets, and the condemnation and punishment of genocide involve moral judgments against the aggressors. They can be understood similarly.

7. Likewise underintimacy is more serious between intimates, overintimacy between strangers, understratification between unequals, and overstratification between equals (Black 2011:139).

8. But the possibility of intervention may increase the likelihood of genocide in some cases. Aggrieved members of subjugated ethnic groups may rebel against their governments—despite the likelihood of retaliatory genocide and despite the impossibility of military success—in the expectation that outside intervention in response to the genocide will enable them to achieve their goals (Kuperman 2005; 2009). Conceivably, then, increasing intervention, if it leads to more rebellions that provoke genocide, could lead to more genocide overall. This does not appear to be happening, though, and in the long term, if intervention becomes more certain and more effective, genocide is likely to decrease.

9. In some cases, though, increasing democratization may lead to genocide by giving political power to otherwise disadvantaged ethnic majorities who have grievances against economically successful ethnic minorities (Chua 2003:163–75; see also Mann 2005). To some extent this is what happened in Rwanda. But overall, democracies are less genocidal than other governments, and we can expect less genocide in the long term.

10. Media theorist Marshall McLuhan (1964) coined the term *global village* to

emphasize that modern technology had made instantaneous communication—something originally possible only face-to-face and at the village level—possible on a global scale. Donald Black (2011:148–51) points out that as the relationships between people throughout the world come to resemble those of villagers in their closeness, they also resemble them morally. People become more concerned about what happens to one another, and they behave more altruistically (see also Pinker 2011:292).

REFERENCES

Abed, Mohammed. 2006. "Clarifying the Concept of Genocide." *Metaphilosophy* 37(3–4): 308–30.
Adam, Heribert. 1996. "Anti-Semitism and Anti-Black Racism: Nazi Germany and Apartheid South Africa." *Telos* 108: 25–46.
Adorno, Theodor W., Else Frenkel-Brunswik, Daniel J. Levinson, and R. Nevitt Sanford. 1950. *The Authoritarian Personality.* New York: Harper.
African Rights. 1995. *Rwanda: Death, Despair, and Defiance.* London: African Rights.
———. 1999. *Damien Biniga: A Genocide without Borders.* London: African Rights.
———. 2003. *Rwanda: The History of the Genocide in Sector Gishamvu.* London: African Rights.
Akers, Ronald L., and Adam L. Silverman. 2004. "Toward a Social Learning Model of Violence and Terrorism." In *Violence: From Theory to Research*, edited by Margaret A. Zahn, Henry H. Brownstein, and Shelly L. Jackson, 19–35. Newark, N.J.: LexisNexis/Anderson Publishing.
Allen, Tim. 2011. "Is 'Genocide' Such a Good Idea?" *British Journal of Sociology* 62(1): 26–36.
Alvarez, Alex. 2001. *Governments, Citizens, and Genocide: A Comparative and Interdisciplinary Approach.* Bloomington: Indiana University Press.
Aly, Götz. 2000. "'Jewish Resettlement': Reflections on the Political Prehistory of the Holocaust." In *National Socialist Extermination Policies*, edited by Herbert Ulrich, 53–82. New York: Berghahn.
———. 2006. *Hitler's Beneficiaries: Plunder, Racial War, and the Nazi Welfare State.* New York: Metropolitan.
Arendt, Hannah. 1963. *Eichmann in Jerusalem: A Report on the Banality of Evil.* New York: Viking.
Aronson, Ronald. 1987. "Social Madness." In *Genocide and the Modern Age: Etiology and Case Studies of Mass Death*, edited by Isidor Wallimann and Michael N. Dobkowski, 125–44. New York: Greenwood.
Balakian, Peter. 2003. *The Burning Tigris: The Armenian Genocide and America's Response.* New York: HarperCollins.
Bancroft, Hubert Howe. 1963. *History of California, Vol. VII, 1860–1890. Volume XXIV of the Works of Hubert Howe Bancroft.* Santa Barbara: Wallace Hebberd.
Barlow, Angela M. 2013. *Sexualities and Conflicting Moralities at Work: An Empirical Test of Black's Theory of Moral Time.* Ph.D. dissertation, Department of Sociology, Virginia Polytechnic Institute and State University, Blacksburg, Virginia.

Barta, Tony. 1987. "Relations of Genocide: Land and Lives in the Colonization of Australia." In *Genocide and the Modern Age: Etiology and Case Studies of Mass Death*, edited by Isidor Wallimann and Michael N. Dobkowski, 237–51. New York: Greenwood.

Bartrop, Paul. 2002. "The Relationship between War and Genocide in the Twentieth Century: A Consideration." *Journal of Genocide Research* 4(4): 519–32.

Battiata, Mary. 1992. "A Town's Bloody 'Cleansing': Serbs Systematically Killed Muslim Elites, Exiled the Rest." *The Washington Post*, November 22.

Bauer, Yehuda. 1999. "Comparison of Genocides." In *Studies in Comparative Genocide*, edited by Levon Chorbajian and George Shirinian, 31–43. New York: St. Martin's.

Baum, Steven K. 2008. *The Psychology of Genocide: Perpetrators, Bystanders, and Rescuers*. New York: Cambridge University Press.

Bauman, Janina. 1986. *Winter in the Morning: A Young Girl's Life in the Warsaw Ghetto and Beyond, 1939–1945*. New York: Free Press.

Bauman, Zygmunt. 1989. *Modernity and the Holocaust*. Ithaca, N.Y.: Cornell University Press.

Baumgartner, M. P. 1988. *The Moral Order of a Suburb*. New York: Oxford University Press.

———. 1992a. "The Myth of Discretion." In *The Uses of Discretion*, edited by Keith Hawkins, 129–62. Oxford: Clarendon.

———. 1992b. "War and Peace in Early Childhood." In *Virginia Review of Sociology*, volume 1: *Law and Conflict Management*, edited by James Tucker, 1–38. Greenwich, Conn.: JAI.

———. 1993. "Violent Networks: The Origins and Management of Domestic Conflict." In *Aggression and Violence: Social Interactionist Perspectives*, edited by Richard B. Felson and James T. Tedeschi, 209–31. Washington, D.C.: American Psychological Association.

———. 1998. "Moral Life on the Cultural Frontier: Evidence from the Experience of Immigrants in Modern America." *Sociological Focus* 31: 155–79.

Becker, Howard S. 1963. *Outsiders: Studies in the Sociology of Deviance*. New York: Free Press.

Bedoukian, Kerop. 1978. *The Urchin: An Armenian's Escape*. London: John Murray.

Beeghley, Leonard. 2003. *Homicide: A Sociological Explanation*. Lanham, Md.: Rowman and Littlefield.

Beinfeld, Solon. 1997. "Life and Survival." In *Hidden History of the Kovno Ghetto*, edited by United States Holocaust Memorial Museum, 25–41. Boston: Bulfinch.

Bejski, Moshe. 1977. "The 'Righteous among the Nations' and Their Part in the Rescue of Jews." In *Rescue Attempts during the Holocaust*, edited by Yisrael Gutman and Efraim Zuroff, 627–47. Jerusalem: Yad Vashem.

Bell-Fialkoff, Andrew. 1996. *Ethnic Cleansing*. New York: St. Martin's.

Berger, Peter L. 1963. *Invitation to Sociology: A Humanistic Perspective*. New York: Anchor.

———. 2004. *Questions of Faith: A Skeptical Affirmation of Christianity*. Malden, Mass.: Blackwell.

Berkovits, Eliezer. 1973. *Faith after the Holocaust*. New York: Ktav.

Berkowitz, Leonard. 1962. *Aggression: A Social Psychological Analysis.* New York: McGraw-Hill.

Bjørnlund, Matthias. 2009. "'A Fate Worse than Dying': Sexual Violence during the Armenian Genocide." In *Brutality and Desire: War and Sexuality in Europe's Twentieth Century,* edited by Dagmar Herzog, 16–58. London: Palgrave Macmillan.

Black, Donald. 1976. *The Behavior of Law.* San Diego: Academic Press.

———. 1983. "Crime as Social Control." *American Sociological Review* 48: 34–45.

———. 1995. "The Epistemology of Pure Sociology." *Law and Social Inquiry* 20: 829–70.

———. 1998 [1993]. *The Social Structure of Right and Wrong,* revised edition. San Diego: Academic Press.

———. 2004a. "The Geometry of Terrorism." *Sociological Theory* 22(1): 14–25.

———. 2004b. "Violent Structures." In *Violence: From Theory to Research,* edited by Margaret A. Zahn, Henry H. Brownstein, and Shelly L. Jackson, 145–58. Newark, N.J.: Anderson.

———. 2011. *Moral Time.* New York: Oxford University Press.

———. 2013. "On the Almost Inconceivable Misunderstandings Concerning the Subject of Value-Free Social Science." *British Journal of Sociology* 64(4): 763–80.

Blau, Judith R., and Peter M. Blau. 1982. "The Cost of Inequality: Metropolitan Structure and Violent Crime." *American Sociological Review* 47: 114–29.

Block, Gay, and Malka Drucker. 1992. *Rescuers: Portraits of Moral Courage in the Holocaust.* New York: Holmes and Meier.

Bonacich, Edna. 1973. "A Theory of Middleman Minorities." *American Sociological Review* 38(5): 583–94.

Bonner, Raymond. 1994. "Nyakizu Journal: And the Church Refuge Became a Killing Field." *New York Times,* November 17.

Borg, Marian J. 1992. "Conflict Management in the Modern World-System." *Sociological Forum* 7(2): 261–82.

Botev, Nikolai. 1994. "Where East Meets West: Ethnic Intermarriage in the Former Yugoslavia, 1962 to 1989." *American Sociological Review* 59(3): 461–80.

Bourne, Charles H. 1860. "Deposition of Charles H. Bourne." In *Majority and Minority Reports* 1860, 20–21.

Brass, Paul R. 2003. *The Production of Hindu-Muslim Violence in Contemporary India.* Seattle: University of Washington Press.

———. 2004. "The Gujarat Pogrom of 2002." Social Science Research Council, Contemporary Conflicts website, March 26. http://conconflicts.ssrc.org/gujarat/brass.

Bringa, Tone. 1995. *Being Muslim the Bosnian Way: Identity and Community in a Central Bosnian Village.* Princeton, N.J.: Princeton University Press.

Browning, Christopher R. 1992. *The Path to Genocide.* New York: Cambridge University Press.

———. 1998. *Ordinary Men: Reserve Police Battalion 101 and the Final Solution in Poland.* New York: HarperPerennial.

———. 2004. "The Decision-Making Process." In *The Historiography of the Holocaust,* edited by Dan Stone, 173–96. New York: Palgrave MacMillan.

Brownmiller, Susan. 1975. *Against Our Will: Men, Women, and Rape.* New York: Simon and Schuster.

Brustein, William I. 2003. *Roots of Hate: Anti-Semitism in Europe before the Holocaust.* New York: Cambridge University Press.

Budreckis, Algirdas Martin. 1968. *The Lithuanian National Revolt of 1941.* Boston: Lithuanian Encyclopedia Press.

Bunsha, Dionne. 2006. "A Serial Kidnapper and His 'Mission.'" *Frontline,* December 16–19. www.hinduonnet.com/fline/fl2325/stories/20061229001810100.htm.

Burton, John W. 1991. "Development and Cultural Genocide in the Sudan." *The Journal of Modern African Studies* 29(3): 511–20.

California Legislature. 1860. "Majority Report." In *Majority and Minority Reports 1860,* 3–8.

Campbell, Bradley. 2009. "Genocide as Social Control." *Sociological Theory* 27(2): 150–72.

———. 2010. "Contradictory Behavior during Genocides." *Sociological Forum* 25(2): 296–314.

———. 2011. "Genocide as a Matter of Degree." *British Journal of Sociology* 62(4): 586–612.

———. 2013. "Genocide and Social Time." *Dilemas: Revista de Estudos de Conflito e Controle Social* 6(3): 465–88.

———. 2014a. "Anti-Minotaur: The Myth of a Sociological Morality." *Society* 51(5): 443–51.

———. 2014b. "Sociology, Morality, and Social Solidarity: On Christian Smith's *Sacred Project of American Sociology.*" *Atruism, Morality, and Social Solidarity Forum: Newsletter of the AMSS Section of the American Sociological Association* 5(4): 4–8.

Campbell, Bradley, and Jason Manning. 2014. "Microaggression and Moral Cultures." *Comparative Sociology* 13(6): 692–726.

Carranco, Lynwood, and Estle Beard. 1981. *Genocide and Vendetta: The Round Valley Wars of Northern California.* Norman: University of Oklahoma Press.

Casiro, Jessica. 2006. "Argentine Rescuers: A Study on the 'Banality of Good.'" *Journal of Genocide Research* 8(4): 437–54.

Chalk, Frank, and Kurt Jonassohn. 1990. *The History and Sociology of Genocide: Analyses and Case Studies.* New Haven, Conn.: Yale University Press.

Chang, Iris. 1997. *The Rape of Nanking: The Forgotten Holocaust of World War II.* New York: Basic Books.

Charny, Israel W. 1994. "Toward a Generic Definition of Genocide." In *Genocide: Conceptual and Historical Dimensions,* edited by George J. Andreopoulos, 64–94. Philadelphia: University of Pennsylvania Press.

———. 1999. "'Ordinary People' as Perpetrators of Genocide." In *Encyclopedia of Genocide,* edited by Israel W. Charny, 451–54. Santa Barbara, Calif.: ABC-CLIO.

Chenoy, Kamal Mitra, Vishnu Nagar, Prasenjit Bose, and Vijoo Krishnan. 2002. "Ethnic Cleansing in Ahmedabad: A Preliminary Report by the SAHMAT Fact-Finding Team to Ahmedabad, 10–11 March 2002." *Outlook,* March 22. www.outlookindia.com/article/Ethnic-Cleansing-In-Ahmedabad/214962.

Chenoy, Kamal Mitra, S. P. Shukla, K. S. Subramanian, and Achin Vanaik. 2002. *Gujarat Carnage 2002: A Report to the Nation.* http://www.sacw.net/Gujarat2002/GujCarnage.html.

Chua, Amy. 2003. *World on Fire: How Exporting Free Market Democracy Breeds Ethnic Hatred and Global Instability*. New York: Doubleday.

Cigar, Norman. 1995. *Genocide in Bosnia*. College Station: Texas A&M University Press.

Clark, Janine Natalya. 2009. "Genocide, War Crimes and the Conflict in Bosnia: Understanding the Perpetrators." *Journal of Genocide Research* 11(4): 421–45.

Cohn, Norman. 1969. *Warrant for Genocide: The Myth of the Jewish World-Conspiracy and the Protocols of the Elders of Zion*. New York: Harper & Row.

Collins, Randall. 2008. *Violence: A Micro-sociological Theory*. Princeton, N.J.: Princeton University Press.

———. 2012. "C-Escalation and D-Escalation: A Theory of the Time-Dynamics of Conflict." *American Sociological Review* 77(1): 1–20.

Coloroso, Barbara. 2007. *Extraordinary Evil: A Short Walk to Genocide*. New York: Nation.

Concerned Citizens Tribunal. 2002a. *Crime Against Humanity: An Inquiry into the Carnage in Gujarat*, Vol. 1: *List of Incidents and Evidence*. Mumbai: Citizens for Justice and Peace. http://www.sabrang.com/tribunal/tribunal1.pdf.

———. 2002b. *Crime Against Humanity: An Inquiry into the Carnage in Gujarat*, Vol. 2: *Findings and Recommendations*. Mumbai: Citizens for Justice and Peace. http://www.sabrang.com/tribunal/tribunal2.pdf.

Cooney, Mark. 1994. "Evidence as Partisanship." *Law and Society Review*. 28(4): 833–58.

———. 1997a. "From Warre to Tyranny: Lethal Conflict and the State." *American Sociological Review* 62: 316–38.

———. 1997b. "Hunting among Police and Predators: The Enforcement of Traffic Law." *Studies in Law, Politics, and Society* 16: 165–88.

———. 1998. *Warriors and Peacemakers: How Third Parties Shape Violence*. New York: New York University Press.

———. 2003. "The Privatization of Violence." *Criminology* 41(4): 1377–406.

———. 2006. "The Criminological Potential of Pure Sociology." *Crime, Law, and Social Change* 46: 51–63.

———. 2009a. "Ethnic Conflict without Ethnic Groups: A Study in Pure Sociology." *British Journal of Sociology* 60(3): 473–92.

———. 2009b. *Is Killing Wrong? A Study in Pure Sociology*. Charlottesville: University of Virginia Press.

———. 2014. "Death by Family: Honor Violence as Punishment." *Punishment and Society* 16(4): 406–27.

———. Forthcoming. "Family Honour and Social Time." In *Violence and Society: Toward a New Sociology*, edited by Jane Kilby and Larry Ray. Hoboken, N.J.: Wiley-Blackwell.

Cooney, Mark, and Scott Phillips. 2002. "Typologizing Violence: A Blackian Perspective." *International Journal of Sociology and Social Policy* 22(7/8): 75–108.

———. 2013. "With God on One's Side: The Social Geometry of Death Row Apologies." *Sociological Forum* 28(1): 159–78.

Cowen, Tyler. 2002. "The Fate of Culture." *The Wilson Quarterly* 26(4): 78–84.

Cushman, Thomas. 2003. "Is Genocide Preventable? Some Theoretical Considerations." *Journal of Genocide Research* 5(4): 523–42.

Dadrian, Vahakn N. 1975. "A Typology of Genocide." *International Review of Modern Sociology* 5: 201–12.
Dagli, Kinjal J. 2006. *The Gujarat Carnage of 2002: A Rhetorical Analysis*. M.A. thesis, Department of Communication, Villanova University, Villanova, Pennsylvania.
Daldry, Stephen (director). 2008. *The Reader*. United States: The Weinstein Company.
Danticat, Edwidge. 1999. *The Farming of Bones*. New York: Penguin.
Davis, Stephen T. 2005. "Genocide, Despair, and Religious Hope: An Essay on Human Nature." In *Genocide and Human Rights: A Philosophical Guide*, edited by John K. Roth, 35–45. New York: Palgrave Macmillan.
de Brouwer, Anne-Marie, and Sandra Ka Hon Chu. 2009. *The Men Who Killed Me: Rwandan Survivors of Sexual Violence*. Vancouver: Douglas & McIntyre.
Des Forges, Alison. 1995. "The Ideology of Genocide." *Issue: A Journal of Opinion* 23(2): 44–47.
———. 1999. *Leave None to Tell the Story: Genocide in Rwanda*. New York: Human Rights Watch.
Diamond, Jared. 1999. *Guns, Germs, and Steel: The Fates of Human Societies*. New York: W. W. Norton.
———. 2005. *Collapse: How Societies Choose to Fail or Succeed*. New York: Viking.
Dieckmann, Christoph. 2000. "The War and the Killing of the Lithuanian Jews." In *National Socialist Extermination Policies*, edited by Herbert Ulrich, 240–75. New York: Berghahn.
Dillon, Edward. 1860. "Deposition of Edward Dillon." In *Majority and Minority Reports* 1860, 56–60.
Dollard, John, Neal E. Miller, Leonard W. Doob, O. H. Mowrer, and Robert R. Sears. 1939. *Frustration and Aggression*. New Haven, Conn.: Yale University Press.
Doubt, Keith. 2000. *Sociology after Bosnia and Kosovo*. New York: Rowman and Littlefield.
Drechsler, Horst. 1980 [1966]. *Let Us Die Fighting: The Struggle of the Herero and Nama against German Imperialism (1884–1915)*, translation. London: Zed.
Durkheim, Emile. 1933. *The Division of Labor in Society*. New York: Free Press.
Eidintas, Alfonsas. 2003. *Jews, Lithuanians, and the Holocaust*. Vilnius, Lithuania: Versus Aureus.
Einwohner, Rachel L. 2003. "Opportunity, Honor, and Action in the Warsaw Ghetto Uprising of 1943." *American Journal of Sociology* 109(3): 650–75.
Elkes, Joel. 1999. *Dr. Elkhanan Elkes of the Kovno Ghetto: A Son's Holocaust Memoir*. Brewster, Mass.: Paraclete.
Engineer, Asghar Ali. 2003. "Introduction." In *The Gujarat Carnage*, edited by Asghar Ali Engineer, 1–24. New Delhi: Orient Longman.
Etzioni, Amitai. 2001. *The Monochrome Society*. Princeton, N.J.: Princeton University Press.
Evans, Gareth. 2008. *The Responsibility to Protect: Ending Mass Atrocity Crimes Once and For All*. Washington, D.C.: Brookings Institutions Press.
Fein, Helen. 1979. *Accounting for Genocide: National Responses and Jewish Victimization during the Holocaust*. New York: Free Press.
———. 1993a. "Accounting for Genocide after 1945: Theories and Some Findings." *International Journal on Group Rights* 1(2): 79–106.
———. 1993b. *Genocide: A Sociological Perspective*. London: Sage.

Felson, Richard B. 2002. *Violence and Gender Reexamined.* Washington, D.C.: American Psychological Association.

Flaschka, Monika J. 2010. "'Only Pretty Women Were Raped': The Effect of Sexual Violence on Gender Identities in Concentration Camps." In *Sexual Violence against Jewish Women during the Holocaust,* edited by Sonja M. Hedgepeth and Rochelle G. Saidel, 77–93. Waltham, Mass.: Brandeis University Press.

Flescher, Andrew Michael. 2003. *Heroes, Saints, and Ordinary Morality.* Washington, D.C.: Georgetown University Press.

Fletcher, Luke. 2007. "Turning *Interahamwe:* Individual and Community Choices in the Rwandan Genocide." *Journal of Genocide Research* 9(1): 25–48.

Fogelman, Eva. 1994. *Conscience and Courage: Rescuers of Jews during the Holocaust.* New York: Anchor.

Foster, George M. 1944. "A Summary of Yuki Culture." *University of California Anthropological Records* 5(3): 155–244.

Fox, Nicole. 2011. "'Oh, Did the Women Suffer, They Suffered so Much': Impacts of Gendered Based Violence on Kinship Networks in Rwanda." *International Journal of Sociology of the Family* 37(2): 279–305.

Freeman, Michael. 1991. "The Theory and Prevention of Genocide." *Holocaust and Genocide Studies* 6(2): 185–99.

———. 1995a. "Genocide, Civilization and Modernity." *The British Journal of Sociology* 46(2): 207–23.

———. 1995b. "Puritans and Pequots: The Question of Genocide." *New England Quarterly* 68: 278–93.

French, Sarah. 1998. "Healing Hands for the Children of War." *The Northern Echo,* December 5.

Friedländer, Saul. 1997. *Nazi Germany and the Jews,* vol. 1. New York: HarperCollins.

Friedman, Philip. 1980. *Roads to Extinction: Essays on the Holocaust.* New York: Jewish Publication Society of America.

Fujii, Lee Ann. 2004. "Transforming the Moral Landscape: The Diffusion of a Genocidal Norm in Rwanda." *Journal of Genocide Research* 6(1): 99–114.

———. 2009. *Killing Neighbors: Webs of Violence in Rwanda.* Ithaca, N.Y.: Cornell University Press.

———. 2011. "Rescuers and Killer-Rescuers During the Rwanda Genocide: Rethinking Standard Categories of Analysis." In *Resisting Genocide: The Multiple Forms of Rescue,* edited by Jacques Semelin, Claire Andrieu, and Sarah Gensburgers, 145–57. New York: Columbia University Press.

Gagnon, V. P. 1994–1995. "Ethnic Nationalism and International Conflict: The Case of Serbia." *International Security* 19(3): 130–66.

Garrett, Gary E. 1969. *The Destruction of the Indian in Mendocino County: 1856–1860.* M.A. thesis, Department of History, Sacramento State College, Sacramento, California.

Gellately, Robert. 2003. "The Third Reich, the Holocaust, and Visions of Serial Genocide." In *The Specter of Genocide: Mass Murder in Historical Perspective,* edited by Robert Gellately and Ben Kiernan, 241–63. New York: Cambridge University Press.

Gendercide Watch. 2002. "Case Study. The Srebrenica Massacre, July 1995." www.gendercide.org/case_srebrenica.html.

"Genocide—Gujarat 2002." 2002. Special issue of *Communalism Combat*, Year 8 (Nos. 76–77). http://www.sabrang.com/cc/archive/2002/marapril/index.html.

George, Terry (producer and director). 2004. *Hotel Rwanda*. Beverely Hills, Calif.: United Artists.

Ghassem-Fachandi, Parvis. 2006. "Sacrifice, Ahimsa, and Vegetarianism: Pogrom at the Deep End of Non-Violence." Ph.D. dissertation, Department of Anthropology, Cornell University, Ithaca, New York.

Ghista, Garda. 2006. *The Gujarat Genocide*. Bloomington, Ind.: AuthorHouse.

Gibbs, Jack P. 1989. "Conceptualization of Terrorism." *American Sociological Review* 54(3): 329–40.

Gibbs, Nancy, Clive Mutiso, Andrew Purvis, Thomas Sancton, and Ann M. Simmons. 1994. "Why? The Killing Fields of Rwanda." *Time*, May 16.

Gilbert, Martin. 1985. *The Holocaust: A History of the Jews of Europe during the Second World War*. New York: Holt, Rinehart, and Winston.

Ginaite-Rubinson, Sara. 2005. *Resistance and Survival: The Jewish Community in Kaunas, 1941–1944*. Oakville, Ont.: Mosaic.

Godard, Ellis. 2003. "Reel Life: The Social Geometry of Reality Shows." In *Survivor Lessons: Essays on Communication and Reality Television*, edited by Matthew J. Smith and Andrew F. Wood, 73–96. Jefferson, N.C.: McFarland and Company.

Goldhagen, Daniel Jonah. 1996. *Hitler's Willing Executioners: Ordinary Germans and the Holocaust*. New York: Vintage.

———. 2009. *Worse Than War: Genocide, Eliminationism, and the Ongoing Assault on Humanity*. New York: Public Affairs.

Goldstein-Golden, Lazar. 1985. *From Ghetto Kòvno to Dachau*. New York: Esther Goldstein.

Gordon, Harry. 1992. *The Shadow of Death: The Holocaust in Lithuania*. Lexington: The University Press of Kentucky.

Gourevitch, Philip. 1998. *We Wish to Inform You that Tomorrow We Will Be Killed with Our Families: Stories from Rwanda*. New York: Farrar, Straus, and Giroux.

Gregor, Thomas. 1990. "Male Dominance and Sexual Coercion." In *Cultural Psychology: Essays on Comparative Human Development*, edited by James W. Stigler, Richard A. Shweder, and Gilbert Herdt, 477–95. New York: Cambridge University Press.

Greve, Hanne Sophie. 1994. *The Prijedor Report. Final Report of the United Nations' Commission of Experts Established Pursuant to Security Council Resolution 780, 1992*. http://balkanwitness.glypx.com/un-annex5-prijedor.htm.

Gross, Jan T. 2001. *Neighbors: The Destruction of the Jewish Community in Jedwabne, Poland*. Princeton, N.J.: Princeton University Press.

———. 2006. *Fear: Anti-Semitism in Poland after Auschwitz*. New York: Random House.

Gross, Jan T., and Irena Grudzinska Gross. 2012. *Golden Harvest: Events at the Periphery of the Holocaust*. New York: Oxford University Press.

Grossman, Dave. 1996. *On Killing: The Psychological Cost of Learning to Kill in War and Society*. New York: Back Bay Books.

Gushee, David P. 2003. *Righteous Gentiles of the Holocaust*. St. Paul, Minn.: Paragon House.

Gutman, Roy. 1993. *A Witness to Genocide*. New York: Macmillan.

Guzder, Cyrus. 2002. "Is Secularism Good for Business?" Address on the occasion of the Confederation of Indian Industries Gujarat Annual Day, March 30. *Seminar* 13 (May). www.india-seminar.com/2002/513/513%20cyrus%20guzder.htm.

Hagan, John, and Joshua Kaiser. 2011a. "The Displaced and Dispossessed of Darfur: Explaining the Sources of a Continuing State-Led Genocide." *British Journal of Sociology* 62(1): 1–25.

———. 2011b. "Forms of Genocidal Destruction: A Response to Commentators." *British Journal of Sociology* 62(1): 62–68.

Hagan, John, Wenona Rymond-Richmond, and Patricia Parker. 2005. "The Criminology of Genocide: The Death and Rape of Darfur." *Criminology* 43(3): 525–61.

Haidt, Jonathan. 2012. *The Righteous Mind: Why Good People Are Divided by Politics and Religion.* New York: Pantheon.

Hall, H. L. 1860. "Deposition of H. L. Hall." In *Majority and Minority Reports* 1860, 41–44.

Haney, Craig, Curtis Banks, and Philip Zimbardo. 1973. "A Study of Prisoners and Guards in a Simulated Prison." *Naval Research Reviews* 30(9): 4–17.

Harff, Barbara. 2003. "No Lessons Learned from the Holocaust? Assessing Risks of Genocide and Political Mass Murder since 1955." *American Political Science Review* 97(1): 57–73.

Harff, Barbara, and Ted Robert Gurr. 1988. "Toward Empirical Theory of Genocides and Politicides: Identification and Measurement of Cases since 1945." *International Studies Quarterly* 32(3): 359–71.

Hatzfeld, Jean. 2005a. *Into the Quick of Life.* New York: Trans-Atlantic.

———. 2005b. *Machete Season.* New York: Farrar, Straus, and Giroux.

Hawdon, James. 2014. "On the Forms and Nature of Group Violence." In *The Causes and Consequences of Group Violence: From Bullies to Terrorism,* edited by James Hawdon, John Ryan, and Marc Lucht, 3–20. Lanham, Md.: Lexington.

Hawdon, James, and John Ryan. 2009. "Hiding in Plain Sight: Community Organization, Naïve Trust, and Terrorism." *Current Sociology* 57(3): 323–43.

Heinsohn, Gunnar. 2000. "What Makes the Holocaust a Uniquely Unique Genocide?" *Journal of Genocide Research* 2(3): 411–30.

Hempel, Carl G. 1952. "Fundamentals of Concept Formation in Empirical Science." *International Encyclopedia of Unified Science,* Vol. II, No. 7. Chicago: University of Chicago Press.

Henry, Frances. 1984. *Victims and Neighbors: A Small Town in Nazi Germany Remembered.* New York: Bergin and Garvey.

Herf, Jeffrey. 2005. "The 'Jewish War': Goebbels and the Antisemitic Campaigns of the Nazi Propaganda Ministry." *Holocaust and Genocide Studies* 19(1): 51–80.

Hildreth, William J. 1860. "Deposition of William J. Hildreth." In *Majority and Minority Reports* 1860, 31–33.

Hintjens, Helen M. 1999. "Explaining the 1994 Genocide in Rwanda." *The Journal of Modern African Studies* 37(2): 241–86.

Hinton, Alexander Laban. 2002. "The Dark Side of Modernity: Toward an Anthropology of Genocide." In *Annihilating Difference: The Anthropology of Genocide,* edited by Alexander Laban Hinton, 1–40. Berkeley: University of California Press.

Hoffmann, Heath C. 2006. "Criticism as Deviance and Social Control in Alcoholics Anonymous." *Journal of Contemporary Ethnography* 35(6): 669–95.

Hola, Barbara, Alette Smeulers, and Catrien Bijleveld. 2011. "International Sentencing Facts and Figures: Sentencing Practice at the ICTY and ICTR." *Journal of International Criminal Justice* 9(2): 411–39.

Homans, George C. 1967. *The Nature of Social Science.* New York: Harcourt, Brace & World.

Horowitz, Donald L. 2000 [1985]. *Ethnic Groups in Conflict,* 2nd edition. Berkeley: University of California Press.

———. 2001. *The Deadly Ethnic Riot.* Berkeley: University of California Press.

Horowitz, Irving Louis. 2002. *Taking Lives: Genocide and State Power,* 5th edition. New Brunswick, N.J.: Transaction.

Horwitz, Allan V. 1982. *The Social Control of Mental Illness.* New York: Academic Press.

Hovannisian, Richard G. 1992. "The Question of Altruism during the Armenian Genocide." In *Embracing the Other: Philosophical, Psychological, and Historical Perspectives on Altruism,* edited by Pearl M. Oliner, Samuel P. Oliner, Lawrence Baron, Lawrence A. Blum, Dennis L. Krebs, and M. Zuzanna Smolenska, 282–385. New York: New York University Press.

Howe, K. R. 1977. *Race Relations Australia and New Zealand: A Comparative Survey, 1770s–1970s.* Wellington, U.K.: Methuen.

Hukanovic, Rezak. 1996. *The Tenth Circle of Hell: A Memoir of Life in the Death Camps of Bosnia.* New York: Basic Books.

Human Rights Watch, Africa. 1994a. "Genocide in Rwanda: April-May 1994." *Human Rights Watch* 6(4).

———. 1994b. "Rwanda: A New Catastrophe?" *Human Rights Watch/Africa* 6(12). www.hrw.org/reports/pdfs/r/rwanda/rwanda94d.pdf.

———. 1997. "The Unindicted: Reaping the Rewards of 'Ethnic Cleansing.'" www.hrw.org/reports/1997/bosnia.

———. 1999. "Politics by Other Means: Attacks against Christians in India." *Human Rights Watch* 11(6). http://www.hrw.org/reports/1999/indiachr.

———. 2002. "'We Have No Orders to Save You': State Participation and Complicity in Communal Violence in Gujarat." *Human Rights Watch* 14(3). http://hrw.org/reports/2002/india/gujarat.pdf.

Hurtado, Albert L. 1988. *Indian Survival on the California Frontier.* New Haven, Conn.: Yale University Press.

Huttenbach, Henry R. 1988. "Locating the Holocaust on the Genocide Spectrum: Towards a Methodology of Definition and Categorization." *Holocaust and Genocide Studies* 3(3): 289–303.

Iacobelli, Teresa. 2009. "The 'Sum of Such Actions': Investigating Mass Rape in Bosnia-Herzegovina through a Case Study of Foca." In *Brutality and Desire: War and Sexuality in Europe's Twentieth Century,* edited by Dagmar Herzog, 261–83. London: Palgrave Macmillan.

ICTR (International Criminal Tribunal for Rwanda). 1996. "The Prosecutor against Ladislas Ntaganzwa." Case No. ICTR-96-9. Indictment.

ICTY (International Criminal Tribunal for the Former Yugoslavia). 1995. "The Prosecutor of the Tribunal against Dusko Tadic and Goran Borovnica." Case No. IT-94-1-I. Amended Indictment.

———. 1998. "The Prosecutor of the Tribunal against Milan Kovacevic." Case No. IT-97-24-I. Amended Indictment.

———. 2000. "The Prosecutor v. Miroslav Kvocka, Dragoljub Prcac, Milojica Kos, Mlado Radic, and Zoran Zigic." Amended Indictment.

———. 2001a. "The Prosecutor of the Tribunal against Dusko Sikirica, Damir Dosen, Dusan Fustar, Dragan Kolundzija, Nenad Banovic, Predrag Banovic, and Dusko Knezevic." Case No. IT-95-8-PT. Second Amended Indictment.

———. 2001b. "The Prosecutor of the Tribunal against Zeljko Meakic, Momcilo Gruban, and Dusko Knezevic." Case No. IT-95-4-I. Amended Indictment.

———. 2002. "The Prosecutor of the Tribunal against Milomir Stakic." Case No. IT-97-24-PT. Fourth Amended Indictment.

Ilibagiza, Immaculée. 2007. *Left to Tell: Discovering God amidst the Rwandan Holocaust.* Carlsbad, Calif.: Hay House.

Jacques, Scott, and Richard Wright. 2008. "The Relevance of Peace to Studies of Drug Market Violence." *Criminology* 46(1): 221–54.

———. 2010. "Right or Wrong? Toward a Theory of IRBs' (Dis)Approval of Research." *Journal of Criminal Justice Education* 21(1): 42–59.

Jaffrelot, Christophe. 2011. *Religion, Caste, and Politics in India.* New York: Columbia University Press.

Janzen, John M. 2000. "Historical Consciousness and a 'Prise de Conscience' in Genocidal Rwanda." *Journal of African Cultural Studies* 13(1): 153–68.

Jaret, Charles. 1995. *Contemporary Racial and Ethnic Relations.* New York: HarperCollins.

Jeffress, George W. 1860. "Deposition of George W. Jeffress." In *Majority and Minority* 1860, 63–65.

Jefremovas, Villia. 1995. "Acts of Human Kindness: Tutsi, Hutu and the Genocide." *Issue: A Journal of Opinion* 23(2): 28–31.

Jennings, Francis. 1975. *The Invasion of America: Indians, Colonialism, and the Cant of Conquest.* New York: W. W. Norton.

Johnson, Paul. 1987. *A History of the Jews.* New York: Harper and Row.

Jonassohn, Kurt, and Frank Chalk. 1987. "A Typology of Genocide and Some Implications for the Human Rights Agenda." In *Genocide and the Modern Age: Etiology and Case Studies of Mass Death,* edited by Isidor Wallimann and Michael N. Dobkowski, 3–20. New York: Greenwood.

Jones, Adam. 2004. "Gendercide and Genocide." In *Gendercide and Genocide,* edited by Adam Jones, 1–38. Nashville, Tenn.: Vanderbilt University Press.

———. 2006. *Genocide: A Comprehensive Introduction.* New York: Routledge.

Judah, Tim. 1997. *The Serbs: History, Myth, and the Destruction of Yugoslavia.* New Haven, Conn.: Yale University Press.

Kaplan, Robert D. 1993a. *Balkan Ghosts: A Journey through History.* New York: St. Martin's.

———. 1993b. "A Reader's Guide to the Balkans." *The New York Times,* April 18, www.nytimes.com/1993/04/18/books/a-reader-s-guide-to-the-balkans.html?pagewanted=print.

Katz, Jack. 1988. *Seductions of Crime: Moral and Sensual Attractions in Doing Evil.* New York: Basic Books.

Katz, Steven T. 1991. "The Pequot War Reconsidered." *New England Quarterly* 64: 206–24.
———. 1994. *The Holocaust in Historical Context*, vol. 1. New York: Oxford University Press.
———. 2001. "The Uniqueness of the Holocaust: The Historical Dimension." In *Is the Holocaust Unique?*, edited by Alan S. Rosenbaum, 49–68. Boulder: Westview.
Kelman, Herbert C. 1973. "Violence without Moral Restraint: Reflections on the Dehumanization of Victims and Victimizers." *Journal of Social Issues* 29(4): 25–61.
Klusemann, Stefan. 2010. "Micro-Situational Antecedents of Violent Atrocity." *Sociological Forum* 25(2): 272–95.
Kopel, David B., Paul Gallant, and Joanne D. Eisen. 2006. "Is Resisting Genocide a Human Right?" *Notre Dame Law Review* 81(4): 1275–346.
Krain, Matthew. 1997. "State-Sponsored Mass Murder: The Onset and Severity of Genocides and Politicides." *Journal of Conflict Resolution* 41(3): 331–60.
———. 2005. "International Intervention and the Severity of Genocides and Politicides." *International Studies Quarterly* 49: 363–87.
Kressel, Neil J. 2002. *Mass Hate: The Global Rise of Genocide and Terror*. Boulder, Colo.: Westview.
Kroeber, Theodora. 1961. *Ishi in Two Worlds: A Biography of the Last Wild Indian in North America*. Berkeley: University of California Press.
Kuper, Leo. 1981. *Genocide: Its Political Use in the Twentieth Century*. New Haven, Conn.: Yale University Press.
Kuperman, Alan J. 2005. "Suicidal Rebellions and the Moral Hazard of Humanitarian Intervention." *Ethnopolitics* 4(2): 149–73.
———. 2009. "Darfur: Strategic Victimhood Strikes Again?" *Genocide Studies and Prevention* 4(3): 281–303.
Kwiet, Konrad. 1998. "Rehearsing for Murder: The Beginning of the Final Solution in Lithuania in June 1941." *Holocaust and Genocide Studies* 12(1): 3–26.
Lawson, John. 1860. "Deposition of John Lawson." In *Majority and Minority Reports 1860*, 68–69.
Laycock, Dryden. 1860. "Deposition of Dryden Laycock." In *Majority and Minority 1860*, 48–51.
Lee, Sander. 2005. "Rights, Morality, and Faith in the Light of the Holocaust." In *Genocide and Human Rights: A Philosophic Guide*, edited by John K. Roth, 18–28. New York: Palgrave Macmillan.
Lemarchand, René. 2004. "The Rwandan Genocide." In *Century of Genocide: Critical Essays and Eyewitness Accounts*, edited by Samuel Totten, William S. Parsons, and Israel W. Charny, 395–412. New York: Routledge.
Lerner, Richard M. 1992. *Final Solutions: Biology, Prejudice, and Genocide*. University Park: The Pennsylvania State University Press.
Lifton, Robert Jay. 1986. *The Nazi Doctors: Medical Killing and the Psychology of Genocide*. New York: Basic Books.
Littman, Sol. 1983. *War Criminal on Trial: The Rauca Case*. Toronto: Lester and Orpen Dennys.
Longman, Timothy. 1995. "Genocide and Socio-Political Change: Massacres in Two Rwandan Villages." *Issue: A Journal of Opinion* 23(2): 18–21.
———. 2004. "Placing Genocide in Context: Research Priorities for the Rwandan Genocide." *Journal of Genocide Research* 6(1): 29–45.

Lundsgaarde, Henry P. 1977. *Murder in Space City: A Cultural Analysis of Houston Homicide Patterns.* New York: Oxford University Press.

Maass, Peter. 1996. *Love Thy Neighbor: A Story of War.* New York: Knopf.

MacQueen, Michael. 2004. "Lithuanian Collaboration in the 'Final Solution': Motivations and Case Studies." In *Lithuania and the Jews: The Holocaust Chapter,* edited by Center for Advanced Holocaust Studies, United States Holocaust Memorial Museum, 1–16. Washington, D.C.: United States Holocaust Memorial Museum.

Madley, Benjamin. 2004. "Patterns of Frontier Genocide 1803–1910: the Aboriginal Tasmanians, the Yuki of California, and the Herero of Namibia." *Journal of Genocide Research* 6(2): 167–92.

———. 2005. "From Africa to Auschwitz: How German South West Africa Incubated Ideas and Methods Adopted and Developed by the Nazis in Eastern Europe." *European History Quarterly* 35(3): 429–64.

Maier-Katkin, Daniel, Daniel P. Mears, and Thomas J. Bernard. 2009. "Towards a Criminology of Crimes against Humanity." *Theoretical Criminology* 13(2): 227–55.

Majority and Minority Reports of the Special Joint Committee on the Mendocino War. 1860. Appendix to the Journals of the Eleventh Session of the Legislature of the State of California. Sacramento: C. T. Botts, State Printer. Micropublished in "Western Americana: Frontier History of the Trans-Mississippi West, 1550–1900." New Haven, Conn.: Yale University Library and Newberry Library.

Malcolm, Noel. 1994. *Bosnia: A Short History.* New York: New York University Press.

Mamdani, Mahmood. 2001. *When Victims Become Killers: Colonialism, Nativism, and the Genocide in Rwanda.* Princeton, N.J.: Princeton University Press.

Mann, Michael. 2005. *The Dark Side of Democracy: Explaining Ethnic Cleansing.* New York: Cambridge University Press.

Manning, Jason. 2012. "Suicide as Social Control." *Sociological Forum* 27(1): 207–27.

———. 2014. "The Social Structure of Homicide-Suicide." *Homicide Studies.* August 21. doi: 10.1177/1088767914547819.

———. 2015. "Suicide and Social Time." *Dilemas: Revista de Estudos de Conflito e Controle Social* 8(1): 97–126.

———. Forthcoming. "Aggressive Suicide." *International Journal of Crime, Law and Justice.*

Markusen, Eric. 1987. "Genocide and Total War: A Preliminary Comparison." In *Genocide and the Modern Age: Etiology and Case Studies of Mass Death,* edited by Isidor Wallimann and Michael N. Dobkowski, 97–124. New York: Greenwood.

———. 1996. "Genocide and Warfare." In *Genocide, War, and Human Survival,* edited by Charles B. Strozier and Michael Flynn, 75–86. Lanham, Md.: Rowman & Littlefield.

Matthäus, Jürgen. 1997. "Assault and Destruction." In *Hidden History of the Kovno Ghetto,* edited by United States Holocaust Memorial Museum, 15–24. Boston: Bulfinch.

———. 2004. "Key Aspects of German Anti-Jewish Policy." In *Lithuania and the Jews: The Holocaust Chapter.* Washington, D.C.: United States Holocaust Memorial Museum, 17–32.

Matthews, Donald R., and James W. Prothro. 1966. *Negroes and the New Southern Politics.* New York: Harper.

Mazian, Florence. 1990. *Why Genocide? The Armenian and Jewish Experiences in Perspective.* Ames: Iowa State University Press.

McDoom, Omar. 2005. "The London School of Economics

McLuhan, Marshall. 1964. *Understanding Media: The Extensions of Man.* New York: New American Library.

Melson, Robert. 1992. *Revolution and Genocide: On the Origins of the Armenian Genocide and the Holocaust.* Chicago: University of Chicago Press.

Melvern, Linda. 2004. *Conspiracy to Murder: The Rwandan Genocide.* New York: Verso.

Messner, Steven F., and Richard Rosenfeld. 2007. *Crime and the American Dream.* Belmont: Thomson Wadsworth.

Michalski, Joseph H. 2003. "Financial Altruism or Unilateral Resource Exchanges?: Toward a Pure Sociology of Welfare." *Sociological Theory* 21(4): 341–58.

———. 2004. "Making Sociological Sense out of Trends in Intimate Partner Violence: The Social Structure of Violence against Women." *Violence against Women* 10(6): 652–75.

———. 2008. "Scientific Discovery in Deep Social Space: Sociology without Borders." *Canadian Journal of Sociology* 33(3): 521–53.

Midlarsky, Elizabeth, Stephanie Fagin Jones, and Robin P. Corley. 2005. "Personality Correlates of Heroic Rescue during the Holocaust." *Journal of Personality* 73(4): 907–34.

Midlarsky, Manus I. 2005. *The Killing Trap: Genocide in the Twentieth Century.* New York: Cambridge University Press.

Miles, William F. S. 2006. "Labeling 'Genocide' in Sudan: A Constructionist Analysis of Darfur." *Genocide Studies and Prevention* 1(3): 251–64.

Milgram, Stanley. 1969. *Obedience to Authority: An Experimental View.* New York: Harper & Row.

Miller, Donald E., and Lorna Touryan Miller. 1993. *Survivors: An Oral History of the Armenian Genocide.* Berkeley: University of California Press.

Miller, Virginia P. 1979. *Ukomno'm: The Yuki Indians of Northern California.* Socorro, New Mexico: Ballena.

Milton, Sybil. 1983. "The Righteous Who Helped Jews." In *Genocide: Critical Issues of the Holocaust,* edited by Alex Grobman and Daniel Landes, 282–87. Los Angeles: Simon Wiesenthal Center.

Mishell, William M. 1988. *Kaddish for Kovno: Life and Death in a Lithuanian Ghetto, 1941–1945.* Chicago: Chicago Review Press.

Modelski, George, and Gardner Perry III. 2002. "'Democratization in Long Perspective' Revisited." *Technological Forecasting and Social Change* 69: 359–76.

Moltmann, Jürgen. 1974. *The Crucified God.* New York: Harper & Row.

Monroe, Kristen R., Michael C. Barton, and Ute Klingemann. 1990. "Altruism and the Theory of Rational Action: Rescuers of Jews in Nazi Europe." *Ethics* 101: 103–22.

Moore, Bob. 2003. "The Rescue of Jews from Nazi Persecution: A Western European Perspective." *Journal of Genocide Research* 5(2): 293–308.

———. 2010. *Survivors: Jewish Self-Help and Rescue in Nazi-Occupied Western Europe.* New York: Oxford University Press.

Morrill, Calvin. 1989. "The Management of Managers: Disputing in an Executive Hierarchy." *Sociological Forum* 4(3): 387–407.

———. 1995. *The Executive Way: Conflict Management in Corporations.* Chicago: University of Chicago Press.

Moses, A. Dirk. 2000. "An Antipodean Genocide? The Origins of the Genocidal Moment in the Colonization of Australia." *Journal of Genocide Research* 2(1): 89–106.

———. 2002. "Conceptual Blockages and Definitional Dilemmas in the 'Racial Century': Genocides of Indigenous Peoples and the Holocaust." *Patterns of Prejudice* 36(4): 7–36.

———. 2004. "Genocide and Settler Society in Australian History." In *Genocide and Settler Society: Frontier Violence and Stolen Indigenous Children in Australian History*, edited by A. Dirk Moses, 3–48. New York: Berghahn.

Mullins, Christopher W. 2009a. "'He Would Kill Me with His Penis': Genocidal Rape in Rwanda as a State Crime." *Critical Criminology* 17(1): 15–33.

———. 2009b. "'We Are Going To Rape You and Taste Tutsi Women': Rape During the 1994 Rwandan Genocide." *British Journal of Criminology* 49(6): 719–35.

Mullis, Jeffrey. 1995. "Medical Malpractice, Social Structure, and Social Control." *Sociological Forum* 10: 135–63.

Naimark, Norman M. 2001. *Fires of Hatred: Ethnic Cleansing in Twentieth-Century Europe.* Cambridge, Mass.: Harvard University Press.

———. 2010. *Stalin's Genocides.* Princeton, N.J.: Princeton University Press.

Nandy, Ashis. 2002. "Obituary of a Culture." *Seminar* 13 (May). www.india-seminar.com/2002/513/513%20ashis%20nandy.htm.

Nash, Gary B. 2000 [1974]. *Red, White, and Black: The Peoples of Early North America*, 4th edition. Upper Saddle River, N.J.: Prentice Hall.

Neshamit, Sarah. 1977. "Rescue in Lithuania during the Nazi Occupation." In *Rescue Attempts during the Holocaust*, edited by Yisrael Gutman and Efraim Zuroff, 289–330. Jerusalem: Yad Vashem.

Newbury, Catherine. 1998. "Ethnicity and the Politics of History in Rwanda." *Africa Today* 45(1): 18–25.

Nieminen, Tommi. 2007a. "On the Trail of a Genocide." *Helsingin Sanomat International Edition—Foreign*, April 17.

———. 2007b. "Plenty of Questions Remain Unanswered." *Helsingin Sanomat International Edition—Foreign*, April 17.

———. 2007c. "The Witnesses of Nyantanga." *Helsingin Sanomat International Edition—Foreign*, May 22.

Nowrojee, Binaifer. 1996. *Shattered Lives: Sexual Violence During the Rwandan Genocide and Its Aftermath.* Human Rights Watch. www.hrw.org/legacy/reports/1996/Rwanda.htm.

Nussbaum, Martha C. 2007. "Fears for Democracy in India." *The Chronicle of Higher Education*, May 18.

Nyseth Brehm, Hollie. 2013. "The Crime of Genocide." In *Crime and the Punished*, edited by Douglas Hartmann and Christopher Uggen, 124–37. New York: W. W. Norton.

Oberschall, Anthony. 2000. "The Manipulation of Ethnicity: From Ethnic Cooperation to Violence and War in Yugoslavia." *Ethnic and Racial Studies* 23(6): 982–1001.

———. 2001. "From Ethnic Cooperation to Violence and War in Yugoslavia." In *Ethnopolitical Warfare: Causes, Consequences, and Possible Solutions*, edited by

Daniel Chirot and Martin E. P. Seligman, 119–50. Washington, D.C.: American Psychological Association.

Oliner, Samuel P. 1982. "The Need to Recognize the Heroes of the Nazi Era." *Reconstructionist* 48(4): 7–14.

Oliner, Samuel P., and Pearl M. Oliner. 1988. *The Altruistic Personality: Rescuers of Jews in Nazi Europe*. New York: Free Press.

Olusanya, Olaoluwa. 2013. "A Macro-Micro Integrated Theoretical Model of Mass Participation in Genocide." *British Journal of Criminology* 53: 843–63.

Opdyke, Irene Gut, and Jennifer Armstrong. 1999. *In My Hands: Memories of a Holocaust Rescuer*. New York: Knopf.

Oshry, Ephraim. 1995. *The Annihilation of Lithuanian Jewry*. New York: Judaica Press.

Paldiel, Mordecai. 1986. "*Hesed* and the Holocaust." *Journal of Ecumenical Studies* 23(1): 90–106.

Palmer, Alison. 2000. *Colonial Genocide*. London: Crawford House.

Pandit, Rajat. 2002. "Centre Delayed Deployment of Paramilitary Forces." *The Times of India*, March 13. http://timesofindia.indiatimes.com/india/Centre-delayed-deployment-of-paramilitary-forces/articleshow/2504513.cms.

Parekh, Bhikhu. 2002. "Making Sense of Gujarat." *Seminar* 13 (May). www.india-seminar.com/2002/513/513%20bhikhu%20parekh.htm.

Payne, James L. 2004. *A History of Force: Exploring the Worldwide Movement against Habits of Coercion, Bloodshed, and Mayhem*. Sandpoint, Idaho: Lytton.

People's Union for Democratic Rights. 2002. *Maaro! Kaapo! Baalo!: State, Society, and Communalism in Gujarat*. Delhi: People's Union for Democratic Rights. www.onlinevolunteers.org/gujarat/reports/pudr/pdf/full_report.pdf.

Pervanic, Kemal. 1999. *The Killing Days*. London: Blake.

Phillips, Scott. 2003. "The Social Structure of Vengeance: A Test of Black's Model." *Criminology* 41(3): 673–708.

Phillips, Scott, and Mark Cooney. 2005. "Aiding Peace, Abetting Violence: Third Parties and the Management of Conflict." *American Sociological Review* 70(2): 334–54.

Pinker, Steven. 2011. *The Better Angels of Our Nature: Why Violence Has Declined*. New York: Viking.

Piotrowski, Tadeusz. 1998. *Poland's Holocaust*. Jefferson, NC: McFarland & Company.

Podolsky, Anatoly. 2010. "The Tragic Fate of Ukrainian Jewish Women Under Nazi Occupation, 1941–1944." In *Sexual Violence against Jewish Women during the Holocaust*, edited by Sonja M. Hedgepeth and Rochelle G. Saidel, 94–107. Waltham, Mass.: Brandeis University Press.

Pogonowski, Iwo Cyprian. 2002. "Jedwabne: The Politics of Apology and Contrition, Defamation: The Price of Poland's Heroism." Presented at the annual meeting of the Polish Institute of Arts and Sciences in America, Georgetown University, Washington, D.C., June 8. http://www.pacwashmetrodiv.org/events/jedwabne/pogonowski.text.htm.

Pohl, Dieter. 2000. "The Murder of Jews in the General Government." In *National Socialist Extermination Policies*, edited by Herbert Ulrich, 83–103. New York: Berghahn.

Polanski, Roman. 2002. *The Pianist*. France: R. P. Productions.

Porat, Dina. 1996. "The Holocaust in Lithuania: Some Unique Aspects." In *The Final

Solution: Origins and Implementation, edited by David Cesarani, 159–74. New York: Routledge.

Porter, Jack Nusan. 1982. "Introduction: What is Genocide? Notes Toward a Definition." In *Genocide and Human Rights: A Global Anthology*, edited by Jack Nusan Porter, 2–32. Lanham, Md.: University Press of America.

Power, Samantha. 2002. *"A Problem from Hell": America and the Age of Genocide*. New York: Basic Books.

Prunier, Gérard. 1995. *The Rwanda Crisis, 1959–1994: History of a Genocide*. London: Hurst.

———. 2001. "Genocide in Rwanda." In *Ethnopolitical Warfare: Causes, Consequences, and Possible Solutions*, edited by Daniel Chirot and Martin E. P. Seligman, 109–16. Washington, D.C.: American Psychological Association.

Punwani, Jyoti. 2002. "Gujarat Revisited." *The Hindu*, April 15. www.thehindu.com/2002/04/15/stories/2002041500161000.htm.

Rawls, James J. 1984. *Indians of California: The Changing Image*. Norman: University of Oklahoma Press.

Reed, John Shelton. 2001. "Why Has There Been No Race War in the American South?" In *Ethnopolitical Warfare: Causes, Consequences, and Possible Solutions*, edited by Daniel Chirot and Martin E. P. Seligman, 275–85. Washington, D.C.: American Psychological Association.

Reuters. 2012. "French Probe Exonerates Rwanda Leader in Genocide." January 10. www.reuters.com/article/2012/01/10/us-rwanda-genocide-report-idUSTRE80924720120110.

Reynolds, Henry. 1990. *With the White People*. Melbourne: Penguin.

———. 2006. *The Other Side of the Frontier*. Sydney: University of New South Wales Press.

Ringelheim, Joan. 1990. "Thoughts about Women and the Holocaust." In *Thinking the Unthinkable: Meanings of the Holocaust*, edited by Roger S. Gottlieb, 141–49. New York: Paulist Press.

———. 1993. "Women and the Holocaust: A Reconsideration of Research." In *Different Voices: Women and the Holocaust*, edited by Carol Rittner and John K. Roth, 374–405. St. Paul, Minn.: Paragon House.

Rittner, Carol. 2002. "Using Rape as a Weapon of Genocide. In *Will Genocide Ever End?*, edited by Carol Rittner, John K. Roth, and James M. Smith, 91–97. St. Paul, Minn.: Paragon House.

Ron, James. 2000. "Boundaries and Violence: Repertoires of State Action along the Bosnia/Yugoslavia Divide." *Theory and Society* 29(5): 609–49.

Roorda, Eric Paul. 1996. "Genocide Next Door: The Good Neighbor Policy, the Trujillo Regime, and the Haitian Massacre of 1937." *Diplomatic History* 20(3): 301–19.

Rosenberg, Alan. 1987. "Was the Holocaust Unique?: A Peculiar Question?" In *Genocide and the Modern Age: Etiology and Case Studies of Mass Death*, edited by Isidor Wallimann and Michael N. Dobkowski, 145–61. New York: Greenwood.

Rubenstein, Richard L. 1983. *The Age of Triage: Fear and Hope in an Overcrowded World*. Boston: Beacon.

———. 2001. "Religion and the Uniqueness of the Holocaust." In *Is the Holocaust Unique?*, edited by Alan S. Rosenbaum, 33–40. Boulder: Westview.

Rummel, R. J. 1994. *Death by Government*. New Brunswick, N.J.: Transaction.

———. 1995. "Democracy, Power, Genocide, and Mass Murder." *Journal of Conflict Resolution* 39(1):3–26.

———. 1997. *Statistics of Democide: Genocide and Mass Murder since 1900.* Charlottesville: Center for National Security Law, University of Virginia School of Law.

Sanders, Jon. 2005. "Activist: Exterminate White People." *Carolina Journal Online,* October 21. http://carolinajournal.com/exclusives/display_exclusive.html?id=2869.

Savelsberg, Joachim J. 2010. *Crime and Human Rights.* Los Angeles: Sage.

Scheff, Thomas J. 1984 [1966]. *Being Mentally Ill: A Sociological Theory,* 2nd ed. New York: Aldine.

Scherrer, Christian P. 2002. *Genocide and Crisis in Central Africa: Conflict Roots, Mass Violence, and Regional War.* Westport, Conn.: Praeger.

Schoenburg, Nancy, and Stuart Schoenburg. 1991. *Lithuanian Jewish Communities.* New York: Garland.

Sciolino, Elaine. 1994. "For West, Rwanda Is Not Worth the Political Candle." *New York Times,* April 15. www.nytimes.com/1994/04/15/world/for-west-rwanda-is-not-worth-the-political-candle.html?pagewanted=print.

Scott, William T. 1860. "Deposition of William T. Scott." In *Majority and Minority* 1860, 21–24.

Sells, Michael. A. 1996. *The Bridge Betrayed: Religion and Genocide in Bosnia.* Berkeley: University of California Press.

Senechal de la Roche, Roberta. 1996. "Collective Violence as Social Control." *Sociological Forum* 11(1): 97–128.

———. 1997. "The Sociogenesis of Lynching." In *Under Sentence of Death: Lynching in the American South,* edited by W. Fitzhugh Brundage, 48–76. Chapel Hill: University of North Carolina Press.

———. 2001. "Why Is Collective Violence Collective?" *Sociological Theory* 19(2): 126–44.

———. 2004. "Toward a Scientific Theory of Terrorism." *Sociological Theory* 22(1): 1–4.

Sethi, Harsh. 2002. "The Problem." *Seminar* 13 (May). www.india-seminar.com/2002/513/513%20the%20problem.htm.

Seubert, Virginia. 1991. "Sociology and Value Neutrality: Limiting Sociology to the Empirical Level." *The American Sociologist* 22(3–4): 210–20.

Shafak, Elif. 2008. *The Bastard of Istanbul.* New York: Penguin.

Shani, Ornit. 2007. *Communalism, Caste, and Hindu Nationalism: The Violence in Gujarat.* New York: Cambridge University Press.

Shanon, Isaac W. 1860. "Deposition of Isaac W. Shanon." In *Majority and Minority Reports* 1860, 72–73.

Sharma, Radha, and Sanjay Pandey. 2002. "Mob Burns to Death 65 at Naroda-Patia." *Times of India,* March 2. http://timesofindia.indiatimes.com/india/Mob-burns-to-death-65-at-Naroda-Patia/articleshow/2473565.cms.

Sharma, Rakesh, producer and director. 2004. *Final Solution* (documentary). India.

Shaw, Martin. 2011. "Darfur: Counter-Insurgency, Forced Displacement and Genocide." *British Journal of Sociology* 62(1): 56–61.

Shik, Na'ama. 2009. "Sexual Abuse of Jewish Women in Auschwitz-Birkenau." In *Brutality and Desire: War and Sexuality in Europe's Twentieth Century,* edited by Dagmar Herzog, 221–46. London: Palgrave Macmillan.

Shochat, Azriel. 1974. "Jews, Lithuanians, and Russians: 1939–1941." In *Jews and*

Non-Jews in Eastern Europe: 1918–1945, edited by Bela Vago and George L. Mosse, 301–14. New York: John Wiley and Sons.

Silberman, Matthew. 1985. *The Civil Justice Process: A Sequential Model of the Mobilization of Law.* Orlando, Fla.: Academic Press.

Sinnreich, Helene J. 2010. "The Rape of Jewish Women during the Holocaust." In *Sexual Violence against Jewish Women during the Holocaust,* edited by Sonja M. Hedgepeth and Rochelle G. Saidel, 108–23. Waltham, Mass.: Brandeis University Press.

Smith, Robert C., and Richard Seltzer. 2000. *Contemporary Controversies and the American Racial Divide.* Lanham, Md.: Rowman & Littlefield.

Smith, Roger W. 1987. "Human Destructiveness and Politics: The Twentieth Century as an Age of Genocide." In *Genocide and the Modern Age: Etiology and Case Studies of Mass Death,* edited by Isidor Wallimann and Michael N. Dobkowski, 21–40. New York: Greenwood.

Snyder, Justin. 2014. "'Blood, Guts, and Gore Galore': Bodies, Moral Pollution, and Combat Trauma." *Symbolic Interaction* 37(4): 524–40.

Snyder, Timothy. 2010. *Bloodlands: Europe between Hitler and Stalin.* New York: Basic Books.

Solzhenitsyn, Aleksandr I. 1985. *The Gulag Archipelago.* New York: Perennial Classics.

Sontag, Frederick. 2005. "How Should Genocide Affect Philosophy?" In *Genocide and Human Rights: A Philosophic Guide,* edited by John K. Roth, 29–34. New York: Palgrave Macmillan.

Sousa, Ashley Riley. 2004. "'They Will Be Hunted Down Like Wild Beasts and Destroyed': A Comparative Study of Genocide in California and Tasmania." *Journal of Genocide Research* 6(2): 193–209.

Stannard, David E. 1992. *American Holocaust: Columbus and the Conquest of the New World.* New York: Oxford University Press.

Staub, Ervin. 1989. *The Roots of Evil: The Origins of Genocide and Other Forms of Group Violence.* New York: Cambridge University Press.

———. 1993. "The Psychology of Bystanders, Perpetrators, and Heroic Helpers." *International Journal of Intercultural Relations* 17: 315–41.

Steiner, John M. 1980. "The SS Yesterday and Today: A Sociopsychological View." In *Survivors, Victims, and Perpetrators: Essays on the Nazi Holocaust,* edited by Joel E. Dimsdale, 405–56. Washington, D.C.: Hemisphere.

Stiglmayer, Alexandra. 1994. "The Rapes in Bosnia-Herzegovina." In *Mass Rape: The War against Women in Bosnia-Herzegovina,* edited by Alexandra Stiglmayer, 82–169. Lincoln: University of Nebraska Press.

Stoltzfus, Nathan. 1996. *Resistance of the Heart: Intermarriage and the Rosenstrasse Protest in Nazi Germany.* New York: W. W. Norton.

Storms, S. P. 1860. "Deposition of S. P. Storms." In *Majority and Minority Reports 1860,* 36–38.

Straus, Scott. 2004. *The Order of Genocide: Race, Power, and War in Rwanda.* Ph.D. dissertation, Department of Political Science, University of California, Berkeley.

———. 2006. *The Order of Genocide: Race, Power, and War in Rwanda.* Ithaca, N.Y.: Cornell University Press.

Strzembosz, Tomasz. 2001. "Jedwabne 1941." Translated by Mariusz Wesolowski.

Footscray, Victoria, Australia: Strzelecki Holding Ply. Ltd.www.antyk.org.pl/ojc zyzna/jedwabne/strzembosz.htm.
Tatz, Colin. 2003. *With Intent to Destroy: Reflecting on Genocide.* New York: Verso.
Taylor, Christopher C. 2002. "The Cultural Face of Terror in the Rwandan Genocide of 1994." In *Annihilating Difference: The Anthropology of Genocide,* edited by Alexander Laban Hinton, 137–78. Berkeley: University of California Press.
Tec, Nechama. 1986. *When Light Pierced the Darkness: Christian Rescue of Jews in Nazi-Occupied Poland.* New York: Oxford University Press.
———. 2011. "Who Dared to Rescue Jews, and Why?" In *Resisting Genocide: The Multiple Forms of Rescue,* edited by Jacques Semelin, Claire Andrieu, and Sarah Gensburger, 101–12. New York: Columbia University Press.
Tevosyan, Hasmik. 2011. "Rescue Practices during the Armenian Genocide." In *Resisting Genocide: The Multiple Forms of Rescue,* edited by Jacques Semelin, Claire Andrieu, and Sarah Gensburger, 163–82. New York: Columbia University Press.
Thomas, Dorothy Q., and Regan E. Ralph. 1999. "Rape in War: The Case of Bosnia." In *Gender Politics in the Western Balkans,* edited by Sabrina P. Ramet and Branka Magas, 203–18. University Park: Pennsylvania State University Press.
Thompson, Hunter S. 1996. *Hell's Angels: A Strange and Terrible Saga.* New York: Ballantine.
Thornton, Russell. 1986. "History, Structure, and Survival: A Comparison of the Yuki (*Ukomno'm*) and Tolowa (*Hush*) Indians of Northern California." *Ethnology* 25: 119–30.
———. 1987. *American Indian Holocaust and Survival: A Population History Since 1492.* Norman: University of Oklahoma Press.
Tobin, James. 1860. "Deposition of James Tobin." In *Majority and Minority Reports 1860,* 54–55.
Tory, Avraham. 1990. *Surviving the Holocaust: The Kovno Ghetto Diary.* Cambridge, Mass.: Harvard University Press.
Trafzer, Clifford E., and Joel R. Hyer. 1999. *"Exterminate Them": Written Accounts of the Murder, Rape, and Slavery of Native Americans during the California Gold Rush, 1848–1868.* East Lansing: Michigan State University Press.
Traverso, Enzo. 2003. *The Origins of Nazi Violence.* New York: The New Press.
Tucker, James. 1989. "Employee Theft as Social Control." *Deviant Behavior* 10: 319–34.
———. 1999. *The Therapeutic Corporation.* New York: Oxford University Press.
Tucker, James, and Susan Ross. 2005. "Corporal Punishment and Black's Theory of Social Control." In *Corporal Punishment of Children in Theoretical Perspective,* edited by Michael Donnelly and Murray A. Straus, 277–86. New Haven, Conn.: Yale University Press.
Turits, Richard Lee. 2002. "A World Destroyed, A Nation Imposed: The 1937 Haitian Massacre in the Dominican Republic." *Hispanic American Historical Review* 82(3): 589–635.
Üngör, Ugur Ümit. 2011. "Conversion and Rescue: Survival Strategies in the Armenian Genocide." In *Resisting Genocide: The Multiple Forms of Rescue,* edited by Jacques Semelin, Claire Andrieu, and Sarah Gensburgers, 201–17. New York: Columbia University Press.
United Nations. 1948. *Convention on the Prevention and Punishment of the Crime of Genocide.*

———. 1999. *Report of the Independent Inquiry into the Actions of the United Nations during the 1994 Genocide in Rwanda.*

United States Holocaust Memorial Museum. 2007. "Kovno." *Holocaust Encyclopedia.* www.ushmm.org/wlc/article.php?lang=en&ModuleId=10005174; http://www.us hmm.org/wlc/en/.

Uvin, Peter. 2001. "Reading the Rwandan Genocide." *International Studies Review* 3(3): 75–79.

Valentino, Benjamin A. 2004. *Final Solutions: Mass Killing and Genocide in the Twentieth Century.* Ithaca: Cornell University Press.

van den Berghe, Pierre. 1981. *The Ethnic Phenomenon.* New York: Elsevier.

Varshney, Ashutosh. 2002. *Ethnic Conflict and Civic Life: Hindus and Muslims in India.* New Haven, Conn.: Yale University Press.

———. 2004. "Understanding Gujarat Violence." Social Science Research Council, Contemporary Conflicts website, March 26. http://conconflicts.ssrc.org/gujarat/varshney.

Volf, Miroslav. 2006. *Free of Charge: Giving and Forgiving in a Culture Stripped of Grace.* Grand Rapids, Mich.: Zondervan.

Vulliamy, Ed. 1994. *Seasons in Hell: Understanding Bosnia's War.* New York: St. Martin's.

———. 1998. "Bosnia: The Crime of Appeasement." *Foreign Affairs* 74(1): 73–91.

Wagner, Michele D. 1998. "All the 'Bourgmestre's' Men: Making Sense of Genocide in Rwanda." *Africa Today* 45(1): 12–37.

Waller, James. 2002. *Becoming Evil: How Ordinary People Commit Genocide and Mass Killing.* New York: Oxford University Press.

Weber, Max. 1958. "Science as a Vocation." In *From Max Weber: Essays in Sociology,* edited by H. H. Gerth and C. Wright Mills, 129–56. New York: Oxford University Press.

———. 1978. *Economy and Society: An Outline of Interpretive Sociology.* Berkeley: University of California Press.

Weiss, Gordon. 1997. "In the Land of the War Criminals." *Salon,* January 6.

Weitz, Eric D. 2003. *A Century of Genocide: Utopias of Race and Nation.* Princeton, N.J.: Princeton University Press.

Wesselingh, Isabelle, and Arnaud Vaulerin. 2005. *Raw Memory: Prijedor, Laboratory of Ethnic Cleansing.* London: Saqi.

Wolfe, Patrick. 2006. "Settler Colonialism and the Elimination of the Native." *Journal of Genocide Research* 8(4): 387–409.

Wolfgang, Marvin E., and Franco Ferracuti. 1967. *The Subculture of Violence.* London: Social Science Paperbacks.

Woodruff, Paul B., and Harry A. Wilmer, eds. 2001. *Facing Evil: Confronting the Dreadful Power behind Genocide, Terrorism, and Cruelty.* Chicago: Open Court.

Wright, Richard T., and Scott H. Decker. 1997. *Armed Robbers in Action: Stickups and Street Culture.* Boston: Northeastern University Press.

Wright, Robert. 2000. *Nonzero: The Logic of Human Destiny.* New York: Pantheon.

———. 2009. *The Evolution of God.* New York: Back Bay Books.

Wringe, Bill. 2006. "Collective Action and the Peculiar Evil of Genocide." *Metaphilosophy* 37(3–4): 376–92.

Zenner, Walter P. 1987. "Middleman Minorities and Genocide." In *Genocide and the*

Modern Age: Etiology and Case Studies of Mass Death, edited by Isidor Wallimann and Michael N. Dobkowski, 253–81. New York: Greenwood.

Zusak, Markus. 2007. *The Book Thief.* New York: Knopf.

Zwick, Edward, director. 2008. *Defiance.* Hollywood, Calif.: Paramount Vantage.

INDEX

Aborigines, Australian: characteristics of, 19, 208n16, 209n20; genocide of, 3, 5, 12, 19, 23–24, 32–33, 66, 67, 93, 122, 208n16, 209n20, 210n21, 212–13n7, 213n9; grievances against, 12, 32
Advani, L. K., 91
African Americans, 26–28, 85
Ahmedabad, 72–96
Albanians, 99, 119
Alexander the Great, 211n9
Allah, 82. *See also* God
Allen, Tim, 206n5
altruism, 5, 30, 62–63, 89–90, 98, 117–18, 123, 142, 174–76, 181, 184–86, 188–97, 215–16nn13–14, 219nn5–6, 220–21nn3–4, 222n10. *See also* genocide: contradictory behavior during
Aly, Götz, 37
American Indians, 3, 5, 12, 16–20, 22–23, 24, 32–33, 35, 39–40, 42, 49–71, 73, 85, 89, 112, 124, 184, 209n17, 212nn2–3, 212nn5–6. *See also specific peoples*
Anderson, Robert, 57, 62
apartheid, 17. *See also* South Africa
Arendt, Hannah, 1
Argentina, 212n1, 215–16n14
Aristotle, 211n9
Armenian genocide, 3, 4, 5, 15, 35, 191–92, 193, 198, 206n3, 211n6, 211–12n1, 215n14
Arusha Accords, 13, 131, 137
Asbill, Frank and Pierce, 52, 53, 58
Auschwitz, 47, 166, 211n7

Australia. *See* Aborigines, Australian
Ayodhya, 74

Babri mosque, 74, 76, 214n10
Bagriansky, Lida, 176
Bajrangi, Babu, 213–14n3
Banja Luka, 116, 117, 118
Bano, Kauser, 82
Bastard of Istanbul, The (Shafak), 6
Bauman, Janina, 195–96
Bauman, Zygmunt, 1, 186–89, 220nn1–4
Bazaramba, Francois, 132, 136
BD (Bajrang Dal), 73, 84
Becoming Evil (Waller), 6
Behavior of Law, The (Black), 8, 9
Beinfeld, Solon, 170
Bejski, Moshe, 215n13
Belgians, 127–29
Belgrade, 99, 104, 119, 120
Berger, Peter, 196
Berkeley, William, 39
Bhavanagar, 91
Bibi, Rosam, 80
Biniga, Damien, 134–35
Birenbaum, Halina, 47
Biscani, 108
BJP (Bharatiya Janata Party), 73, 75, 76, 91, 94
Black, Donald, xi–xii, 7–9, 12, 64, 94, 112, 145, 183, 200, 207n9, 210n2, 211n4, 220n10; *The Behavior of Law*, 8, 9; *Moral Time*, 9
Black Thursday Massacre, 161
Bland, John, 61, 66

Bobelis, Jurgen, 157, 174
Book Thief, The (Zusak), 6, 221n5
Bosnia-Herzegovina: history of, 98–100; secession of, 98, 101–2, 113, 199. *See also* Bosnian genocide
Bosnian genocide, 3, 42–43, 97–124, 178, 185, 216–17nn1–8
Botev, Nikolai, 114–15, 216n5
Brass, Paul, 213n2
Browning, Christopher, 2, 186–89, 212n1, 220n3
Brownmiller, Susan, 46
Bulgaria, 21, 98
Burnett, Peter, 50
Burundi: exiles from, 129; genocide in, 3, 132, 143, 147; history of, 139; presidential assassination in, 13, 132, 147, 217n5; refugees from, 126, 132–33, 135, 136, 137–38, 140–41, 148, 217–18nn5–6
Butare (city), 135, 136, 189, 192
Butare prefecture, 126, 131, 137, 139, 140, 141, 143, 144, 148, 217n4, 218n9
Byumba prefecture, 144

California, 3, 5, 12, 16–20, 22–23, 28, 32–33, 39, 42, 49–71, 73, 85, 89, 92, 93, 112, 122, 124, 145, 178, 209n17, 212nn2–3, 212nn5–6
Cambodia, 212n1
Carakovo, 108
Casiro, Jessica, 216n14
Catholics, 98–99, 103, 170, 175, 189, 192
Catholic Church, 128, 175, 177. *See also* Cyahinda Catholic Church
Central America, 39–40
Cesic, Ranko, 118
Chalk, Frank, 206nn4–5
Cherokee, 22, 35
Chetniks, 100
Cheyenne, 41
Children's Action, 166, 176
Chopin, Frédéric, 201
Christians, 4, 20, 21, 85, 98–99, 156, 168, 215n13; Catholic, 98–99, 103, 170, 175, 189, 192; Orthodox, 98–99; Protestant, 26–27

Churchill, Winston, 199
CIA (Central Intelligence Agency), 26, 216n6
Clark, Janine Natalya, 185, 220n3
collective liability, 93, 208n12, 212n2, 213n8
collective violence, 68, 207n9, 208n12
Collins, Randall, 96
colonialism, 12, 14, 16–20, 31, 32–34, 42, 55, 58, 67, 126–28, 139–40, 202, 209n16
Coloroso, Barbara, *Extraordinary Evil*, 6
communism, 15, 154, 156, 157, 158
communists, 15, 100, 101, 114, 151, 154–55, 158, 169, 172, 175, 179
Convention on the Prevention and Punishment of the Crime of Genocide, 199
Cooney, Mark, xii, 30, 210n1
Copernicus, Nicolaus, 201
Creeks, 22
Croatia, 98–103; secession of, 101–2, 113
Croats, 97–108, 113, 114–15, 121, 124, 216nn1–2
Curie, Marie and Pierre, 201
Cushman, Thomas, 202
Cyahinda Catholic Church, 125, 133, 134–36, 137, 139, 141, 142, 145
Cyangugu prefecture, 138
Cyanwa, 134, 141

Dachau, 167
Danticat, Edwidge, *The Farming of Bones*, 6
Darfur genocide, 3, 202, 206n5, 212n4
Decker, Scott, 210n2
Defiance, 193
democracy, 26, 156, 201, 203, 209n19, 221–22n9
deportation. *See* ethnic cleansing
Des Forges, Alison, 217n2
deviant behavior, 6, 8, 9–10, 28, 29, 31, 198–201, 207n6, 210n3, 221n6; continuity of, 68, 120, 177
Devil, the, ix, 156
Dijk, Ans van, 194
Dominican Republic, 3, 219–20n7
Dosen, Damir, 117

Dubsingh, Meghsingh, 79
Dvorak, Antonin, 201

Eastern Orthodoxy, 98–99
Eel River Rangers, 54–55, 56, 61, 66, 68–69
Eichmann, Adolf, 1, 198
Einsatzgruppen, 155, 167, 169, 171. *See also* SS (Schutzstaffel)
Einstein, Albert, 201
Elkes, Elkhanan, 164
Elstein, Leah, 176
Estonia, 152, 166
Estonian Action, 166
Ethiopia, 130
ethnic cleansing, 4, 20, 22–23, 35, 43, 58, 72–73, 85–86, 93, 101, 102, 107, 108, 111, 116, 117, 121–22, 123, 128, 138, 148, 153, 168–69, 180, 181, 191–92, 199, 206n3, 206n5, 211n6, 216n6, 219n7
ethnicity: in Bosnia, 98–99, 114, 123–24, 217n8; conceptualization of, 11–12, 205n2, 210n22; killing on the basis of, 4, 15, 24, 25, 69, 71, 92, 93, 121, 122, 177, 181, 208n12, 210n22, 212n2, 213n8; in Rwanda, 126–28, 139–40, 217n3
evil, ix, x, 1, 6, 15, 29, 30, 95–96, 188, 190, 195, 196–97, 198, 200, 207n7, 221n6
expulsion. *See* ethnic cleansing
Extraordinary Evil (Coloroso), 6

Facing Evil (Woodruff and Wilmer), 6
false accusations, 10, 14–15, 26, 74–75, 76, 104, 109, 156–57, 160, 168, 208n11
Farming of Bones, The (Danticat), 6
Feingold, Michael, 210n23
Fein, Helen, 209n19
feuding, 207n9
Foster, George, 52
Fujii, Lee Ann, 127

Gagnon, V. P., 217n8
Gandhi, Indira, 73

Garsden, 155
Gasasa hill, 136, 139, 142
Gasingwa, Jean-Marie Vianney, 145
Geist, Edwin, 176
genocide: absence of, 25–28; in ancient and classical civilizations, 38, 198, 200; contradictory behavior during, 61–62, 90, 117–18, 123, 142, 175–76, 181, 184–97, 220nn3–5; decline of, 202; definitions of, 4, 199, 205–7nn1–5, 212n2; denial of, 199; future of, 201–3, 221–22nn8–10; as matter of degree, 23–25, 66–71, 92–95, 97–98, 120–22, 145–48, 177–81, 209–10nn21–22, 219–20n7; morality of, x–xi, 4, 6–7, 48, 196–97, 207nn7–8, 221n6; other explanations of, ix–x, 6, 183, 185–89, 211–12n1, 220–21nn1–4; prevention of, 202–3; significance of, 4–6; social control of, 5, 184, 197–203, 221–22nn6–10. *See also* Aborigines, Australian: genocide of; Armenian genocide; Bosnian genocide; Burundi: genocide in; Darfur genocide; Gujarat genocide; Haitians, genocide of; Hereros, genocide of; Holocaust; Round Valley genocide
Gens, Jacob, 195
Germans, 1–2, 12, 20–21, 23, 32, 33–34, 36–38, 40–41, 46–47, 99, 127, 139, 150–81, 190–91, 193, 194, 211n7, 212n1, 218n4. *See also* Germany; Holocaust
Germany, 14, 15, 20–21, 23, 36–38, 46–47, 150–81, 194, 200, 209n18, 212n1. *See also* Germans; Holocaust
Ghassem-Fachandi, Parvis, 77, 92
Gikongoro prefecture, 131, 133, 134, 135, 141
Ginaite-Rubinson, Sara, 170
Gishamvu commune, 131, 218n9
Gitarama prefecture, 140, 143, 189
Giti commune, 144
global village, 202, 222n10
Glogowski, Icek, 194
God, 6, 32, 51, 52, 191
Godhra, 76, 85, 88, 214n11

Goebbels, Joseph, 15
Goecke, Wilhelm, 166, 176
Gold Action, 162–63
Goldberg, Jacob, 174
Golden Rule, the, 48
Goldhagen, Daniel Jonah, 14, 30, 46
Gold Rush, 18, 19
Gomtipur and Sundaramnagar, 83–84, 86, 89, 214n8
Good, Hiram, 57, 62
Gordon, Harry, 150, 154
Göring, Hermann, 36
gossip, 197, 207n9
Great Action, 164–65, 176, 218n3
Greece, 21
Gross, Jan, 212n1, 218n4
Gujarat genocide, 3, 72–96, 112, 120, 178, 213–15nn2–13, 216n15
Gulberg Society, 78–81, 86, 89, 214n6, 215n12
guns, targets' possession of, 18, 63, 77, 135, 208n11, 212n4, 213n9, 216n6
Gurr, Ted, 205n2
Gushee, David P., 184
Gut, Irene. *See* Opdyke, Irene Gut
Gypsies, 3, 100

Habyalimana, Jean-Baptiste, 131, 135, 140, 143, 144, 218n9
Habyarimana, Agathe, 146
Habyarimana, Juvénal, 13–14, 130, 131, 134, 140, 144, 147, 218n9
Hagan, John, 206n5
Haitians, genocide of, 3, 219–20n7
Hall, H. L., 49, 54, 58, 67, 68
Hambarine, 106, 107, 116
Harff, Barbara, 205n2, 209n19
Hastings, Serranus, 68–69
Hatzfeld, Jean, 217n3
Hells Angels, 41
Henley, Thomas, 53, 59, 64, 68
Hereros, genocide of, 3, 12, 32, 206n3. *See also* South-West Africa
Hildreth, W. J., 54
Hindus, 3, 72–96, 112, 124, 213–16nn2–13, 216n15. *See also* Gujarat genocide

Hindutva movement, 73–77, 81, 83, 85–86, 88, 94, 95, 213–14nn3–4
Hitler, Adolf, 15, 151, 158, 200
Holocaust, 1–2, 3, 4–5, 6, 14–15, 16, 20–21, 23, 24, 25, 33–34, 36–38, 40–41, 46–47, 66, 71, 90, 145, 150–82, 184, 186–88, 190–91, 193, 194–96, 198, 200, 206n5, 209n18, 210n5, 211nn7–8, 211–12n1, 215nn13–14, 218–19nn1–6, 220–21nn3–4
Homans, George C., 221n4
homicide, 10, 29, 57, 61, 65–66, 67, 207n9
honor killings, 207n9
Horowitz, Donald, 213n1
Hôtel des Mille Collines, 190, 193
Hotel Rwanda, 6, 190
Hovannisian, Richard G., 215n14
Howe, H. R., 208n16
Hukanovic, Rezak, 117–18
hunter-gatherers, xi, 19, 32, 33, 51, 63, 208n16
Huss, Jan, 201
Hussain, Mohammed, 82
Hutu Manifesto, 128
Hutu Revolution, 13, 128–30, 148
Hutus. *See* Burundi; Rwandan genocide
hypergenocide, 24–25, 66, 122, 145, 177–81. *See also* genocide: as matter of degree

ICTR (International Criminal Tribunal for Rwanda), 199, 217n1
ICTY (Internationl Criminal Tribunal for the Former Yugoslavia), 117, 199
Ilibagiza, Immaculée, 189, 208n11
Incas, 39
India, 3, 72–96, 124, 213–16nn1–15
Indians, American. *See* American Indians
inequality. *See* social inequality
inseparability, 21–25, 50, 58–59, 67, 71, 85–86, 95, 113, 122, 123, 138–39, 146, 148, 168–69, 178, 180, 219n7
Intellectuals Action, 162, 173
interethnic marriage, 21, 42, 45–46, 114–15, 126, 140, 142, 148, 211n8, 216n5, 217n4

Islam, 4, 98, 103, 215n14. *See also* Muslims
Israel, 198, 200
Italy, 20–21, 209n18

Jafri, Ehsan, 78–81
Jarboe, Walter S., 54–56, 61, 66
Jasenovac, 100
Jedwabne, 212n1, 218n4
Jeffress, George W., 56
Jelisic, Goran, 118
Jesus, 103, 156; crucifixion of, 85, 156, 168
Jewish Councils, 41, 46, 162, 163, 164, 167, 173, 176, 194–95, 219n5
Jewish Police, 163, 167, 194–96
Jews, 1–2, 3, 4–5, 14–15, 16, 20–21, 23, 34, 36–38, 40–41, 46–47, 71, 85, 90, 100, 150–81, 186–88, 190–91, 193, 194–96, 200–201, 208n14, 209n18, 211n5, 211nn7–8, 212n1, 215n13, 218–19nn1–6. *See also* Holocaust; Israel; Jewish Councils; Jewish Police; Judaism
JNA (Yugoslav Army), 115
Johnson, Theodore T., 18
Jonassohn, Kurt, xii, 206nn4–5
Jones, Adam, ix
Jordan, Fritz, 163. *See also* "Jordan passes"
"Jordan passes," 163, 164, 173
Joseph, Bernard, 194
Józefów, 1
Judah, Tim, 119
Judaism, 170. *See also* Israel; Jews

Kaiser, Joshua, 206n5
Kalajic, Dragos, 103
Kambanda, Jean, 133
Kambon, Kamau, 26, 210n23
Kant, Immanuel, 48
Kaplan, Robert, 123
Karama parish, 139
Katz, Jack, 29–30
Katz, Steven T., 206n5
Kaunas. *See* Kovno
Kelman, Herbert C., 207n8

Kelsey, Samuel, 52
Keraterm Camp, 108, 110–11, 117, 121
Kevljani, 104, 216n6
Kibuye prefecture, 138
Kigali, 189, 190
Klimaitis, Algirdas, 172
Kolundzija, Dragan, 117
Kosovo, 100, 101, 119, 216n5
Kovno, 150, 151, 153, 154, 157, 158, 159–77, 178, 218n3. *See also* Kovno Ghetto
Kovno Ghetto, 152, 161–67, 190, 194–95, 218n3, 219n5
Kozarac, 104, 106–7, 109, 110, 116, 118, 121
Kozlowski Action, 163
Krajina, Serb Republic of, 101, 105
Kristallnacht riots, 46, 211n5
Kroeber, Theodora, 62
kubohoza, 132
kulaks, 210n22
Kuper, Leo, 208n13
Kurds, 3, 5, 191–92
Kutch, 91

LAF (Lithuanian Activist Front), 179
land theft, 30, 31–34, 38, 47
Latvia, 152
law, xi, 8, 28, 29, 46, 47, 153, 183, 197, 199, 207n9, 214n4, 220n3
Lawson, John, 54
Lazar of Serbia, 103
lebensraum. *See* living space
Lemkin, Raphael, 199, 200, 205n3
Libya, 199
Lietukis garage, massacre at, 159–60, 172, 218n2
Lipman, Chaim, 175–76
Lithuania, 5, 41, 46, 150–82, 195, 218–19nn1–6; history of, 152–53; Nazi invasion of, 154–55; Soviet invasion of, 154
Lithuanian partisans, 154–55, 157, 160–61, 169, 171–72, 174–75, 180
Litvaks, 169–70
living space, 33–35
Ljubija, 104

250 Index

Lohse, Hinrich, 172–73
looting, 30, 31, 35–38, 47, 75, 82, 83, 107, 108, 134, 141, 160, 162–63, 165–66, 180, 195, 211n5
lynching, 27, 28, 181, 197, 207n9, 210n22

Maass, Peter, 217n8
MacKenzie, Lewis, 216–17n7
Macedonians, 99
Madagascar, 23
Maidu, 42, 62
Malcolm, Noel, 115
Mamdani, Mahmood, 126, 184
Mann, Michael, 138
Mansoori, Mehboob, 72, 80
Mantel, William, 65
Maoris, 33, 208–9n16
Maraba commune, 131, 218n9
Markovic, Ante, 216n3
Marsh, John, 18
Matthews, Donald, 26, 28
Mazian, Florence, 211n1
McLuhan, Marshall, 222n10
MDR-Power, 132
Mehinaku, 41
Melson, Robert, 211n1
Mendocino County, 50
Midianites, 198, 200
Midlarsky, Manus, 6
Milgram, Stanley, 187
Miller, Virginia, 59
Milosevic, Slobodan, 101
Mishell, William, 158, 174
Mochi, Dayarum, 79, 89, 215n12
Modasa, 87
Modi, Narendra, 75, 77, 79, 84, 91, 96
Molotov-Ribbentrop Pact, 154
Montenegro, 101, 115
moralism, 29–33, 40, 41, 44–45, 47, 48, 58, 95, 183, 210n1, 211nn4–5. *See also* social control
Moral Time (Black), 9
Morioris, 33
Morocco, 208n14
Moses, 198
MRND (National Republican Movement for Democracy and Development), 132, 144, 217n1
Munyeshyaka, Wenceslas, 190, 193
Muslims: in Bosnia, 42–43, 97–124, 184, 216–17nn1–8; in India, 3, 72–96, 112, 123, 213–15nn2–13, 216n15; in Morocco, 208n14. *See also* Bosnian genocide; Gujarat genocide; Turks
mutilation, 2–3, 43–44, 78, 79–80, 82, 95, 97, 109, 150

Naimark, Norman, 210n22
Nama, 32
Namibia. *See* South-West Africa
Nandy, Ashis, 91
Nanjing, Rape of, 3, 43
Naroda Gaon and Naroda Patiya, 81–83, 86, 89, 90, 213n3, 214n7
Natchez, 17–18
Native Americans. *See* American Indians
Native Police, 24, 209n20, 212–13n7
Ndadaye, Melchior, 147
negotiation, 207n9, 210–11n4
Nephus, Jim, 52, 59
New England, 16, 39
New Zealand, 33, 208–9n16
Nikolic, Dragon, 118
Ninth Fort, 163, 164, 165, 166, 176
Nkakwa sector, 133, 134, 135
Nome Cult Indian Farm. *See* Round Valley Reservation
Nome Lackee Indian Reservation, 57
Ntaganzwa, Ladislas, 125, 131–37, 141, 144–45, 217n1
Nyakizu commune, 125, 126, 131–48, 218n9
Nyakizu Hill, 136
Nzimbirinda, Albert, 133

Oliner, Pearl M. and Samuel P., 215n13
Omarska Camp, 108–10, 111, 117–18, 121, 216n4
Opdyke, Irene Gut, 5, 196
"ordinary men," 186–89
overdiversity, 10–11, 13, 14, 16, 17, 21, 50, 58, 85, 112–13, 183, 200. *See also* social time

overintimacy, 10, 221n7. *See also* social time
overstratification, 10, 221n7. *See also* social time

Pakistan, 72, 74, 75, 76, 86, 87
Paldiel, Mordecai, 215n13
Parekh, Bhikhu, 94
partisanship, 11, 28, 63–64, 68–69, 91–92, 94–95, 120–21, 145, 177, 178, 179, 207n10, 212nn5–6, 216n15, 218n9
Pasha, Talaat, 198
Pequots, 16–17, 39
Phillips, Scott, 210n1
philosophy, 6, 47–48
Pianist, The, 6
Pinker, Steven, 196, 198
Plato, 201
pogroms, 73, 92, 147, 153, 155, 159–60, 169, 171–72, 211n5, 218n4
Poland, 1, 2, 5, 20, 23, 36, 37–38, 40–41, 47, 153, 154, 177, 195, 212n1, 218n4
Police Battalion, 101, 186–88, 212n1
politicide, 4, 205n2, 210n23
Prajapati, Chunilal, 79
predation, 29–48, 52, 58, 68, 80, 112, 210–11nn1–8; definition of, 29–30; explanation of, 30–31, 47–48, 180. *See also* land theft; looting; rape; robbery; slavery; taxation
Prijedor (district), 97, 103, 104–24, 216nn3–4
Prijedor (town), 107, 116
Prothro, James, 26, 28
protogenocide, 24–25, 66, 71, 122, 178. *See also* genocide: as matter of degree
Prunier, Gérard, 34, 35
psychology, ix, 6, 7, 183, 187–88
Punjab, the, 72
Puskar, Abdullah, 118
Punwani, Jyoti, 214n11
pure sociology, x, xi, 7–9, 183, 184, 186, 196–97, 207n9, 208n12

Rajput, Jagrup Singh, 79
Ram, 74, 82, 84; temple of, 73–74, 76, 85
rape, 3, 8–9, 10, 30, 31, 35, 41–47, 52,
66, 72, 75, 78, 80, 82, 83, 94, 95, 102, 104, 108, 109, 111, 137, 142, 160, 162, 180, 211nn6–8, 212n4, 216n4
Rath, Ernst vom, 37, 211n5
Ratzel, Friedrich, 33–34
Rawls, James, 67
Rauca, Helmut, 164, 176
Reader, The, 6
Reed, John Shelton, 26
Republika Srpska, 102, 104
rescuing. *See* altruism; genocide: contradictory behavior during
responsibility to protect, 199
rioting, 27–28, 46, 72–73, 86, 87–88, 92, 213nn1–2, 214nn10–11
robbery, 29, 30, 41, 80, 117, 210nn1–2
Roman Catholic Church. *See* Catholic Church
Ron, James, 116
Roots of Evil, The (Staub), 6, 212n1
Round Valley genocide, 5, 12, 49–71, 89, 95, 112, 184, 212nn2–3, 212nn5–6. *See also* Round Valley Reservation; Yuki
Round Valley Reservation, 49, 53, 54, 56, 57, 58–59, 60–61, 63, 64, 65–66, 67, 69. *See also* Round Valley genocide; Yuki
RPF (Rwandan Patriotic Front), 13–14, 131, 133, 137, 144, 147, 148, 208n11, 217n4
RSS (Rashtriya Swayamsevak Sangh), 73
Ruhengeri prefecture, 217n4
Rumania, 21
Rumkowski, Mordecai Chaim, 4, 195
Rummel, R. J., 209n19
Rusesabagina, Paul, 190
Rutobwe sector, 134
Rwandan genocide, 2, 4, 5–6, 12–14, 23, 34, 35–36, 44–46, 125–149, 178, 184, 189–90, 192–93, 194, 196, 208n11, 217–18nn1–10, 222n9

SA (Sturmabteilung), 166, 174
Sabarmati Express, 74, 75–76, 85, 95
Sacramento Valley, 53, 65
Sana River, left bank of, 107–8, 117

Sandzak region, 116
Sangh Parivar. *See* Hindutva movement
Sarajevo, 115, 123, 216n7
Sciolino, Elaine, 126
SDA (Party of Democratic Action), 105
SDS (Serb Democratic Party), 105, 216n3
Senechal de la Roche, Roberta, xi, 68, 208n12
Serbia, 42–43, 98–103, 105, 115–17, 120–21, 124, 217n8
Serbian Memorandum, 100–101
Serbs, 42–43, 97–124, 216–17nn2–8. *See also* Bosnian genocide
Seventh Fort, 160–61, 169, 174–75
Shafak, Elif, *The Bastard of Istanbul*, 6
Shanon, Isaac, 61–62
Sharma, Rahul, 91
Shaw, Martin, 206n5
Sheik, Shafi Mohammed Munawar, 80
Sherman, William T., ix
Sherwood Valley, 65
Shostakovich, Dmitri, 201
Sikhs, 72–73
Sindikubwabo, Théodore, 131, 136
Škirpa, Kazys, 179
slavery, 17–18, 30, 31, 38–41, 45–46, 47, 85, 165, 167, 172–74, 180, 195, 210n3
Slobodka, 150, 159, 161, 172
Slovenia, 101, 113
Small Ghetto Action, 163–64
Smelser, Neil, 211n1
social control, 6–7, 8, 9, 29–30, 40, 128, 183–84, 197–98, 200, 207n9, 208n12, 210–11nn3–4, 221n8. *See also* genocide: social control of; moralism
social distance, 8–9, 16–21, 26–28, 31, 38, 50, 60–63, 64, 68–69, 71, 73, 86–90, 92, 93–95, 98, 113–19, 123, 126, 139–42, 148, 169–76, 178, 180–81, 183, 192–93, 196, 201, 208nn12–14, 209nn17–18, 209n20, 214–16nn10–14, 217–18nn3–7, 218–20nn4–7, 222n10
social geometry, 8, 9, 16, 21, 30, 66, 123, 125, 138, 186, 197, 210n23, 211n4. *See also* social distance; social inequality; social space; social time

social inequality, 11, 16–21, 26–28, 31, 50, 63–66, 68–69, 71, 73, 88, 90–92, 93–95, 98, 119–20, 122, 123, 143–45, 147–48, 176–77, 178, 180, 183, 201, 203, 208–9nn15–17, 209n19, 210n4, 212n4, 213n9, 218nn8–9, 219n7
social science, ix, 6, 7, 211–12n1, 221n6. *See also* pure sociology
social space, 8–9, 16–21, 25, 60, 114, 176, 183, 186, 197. *See also* social distance; social geometry; social inequality
social time, 8, 9–15, 16, 17, 21, 25, 58, 60, 71, 73, 85, 86, 95, 98, 112–13, 123, 137–38, 148, 159, 168, 183, 197, 200, 202. *See also* overdiversity; overintimacy; overstratification; social geometry; underdiversity; underintimacy; understratification
sociology. *See* pure sociology; social science
Socrates, 201
Solzhenitsyn, Aleksandr, 197
South Africa, 17
South America, 39–40
South-West Africa, 3, 12, 32–33, 34, 206n3
Soviet Union, 15, 20, 21, 23, 41, 151, 153–55, 159, 168, 169, 180, 210n22
Spinoza, Baruch, 201
Srebrenica, 102
Srivsatava, Vivek, 91
SS (Schutzstaffel), 102, 155, 166, 167, 173–74, 221n4
Stahlecker, Franz, 171–73
Stalingrad Action, 165
Stalin, Josef, 158
Stannard, David, 39
Stanford Prison Experiment, 220–21n5
Staub, Ervin, *The Roots of Evil*, 6, 212n1
Stone, John, 16
Storms, Simmon P., 53, 56, 59, 64, 65
Straus, Scott, 143, 212n1, 218n6, 218n8
suicide, 44, 176, 197, 207n9
Sundaramnagar. *See* Gomtipur and Sundaramnagar

Surat, 88
Syria, 206n3
Szapira, Dana, 191

Tasmania, 19
Tassin, A. G., 65
Tatz, Colin, 17
taxation, 37, 125, 210n3, 211n5
Tec, Nechama, 190, 215n13
Tehlirian, Soghomon, 198
terrorism, 75, 76, 207n9
theology, ix, 6, 47–48
therapy, 31, 207n9
Thornton, Russell, 50
Tolstoy, Leo, 201
Tornbaum, Alfred, 176
torture, 97, 108–9, 110, 111, 166, 215n14, 217n5
Trail of Tears, 35
Treblinka, 38, 41
Trnopolje Camp, 108, 111–12, 121
Trujillo, Rafael, 219n7
Turits, Richard Lee, 219n7
Turks, 3, 35, 102, 191–92, 193, 198, 215n14. *See also* Armenian genocide
Tutsis. *See* Burundi; Rwandan genocide

Uhlmann, Emil and Henny, 37
Ukomno'm. *See* Yuki
Ukraine, 46, 153
Ukrainians, 191
umuganda, 146, 218n10
underdiversity, 10, 200. *See also* social time
underintimacy, 10, 221n7. *See also* social time
understratification, 10, 11–15, 16, 50, 58, 73, 85, 112–13, 183, 221n7. *See also* social time
United Nations, 120, 199, 200, 205n3, 206n5
United States of America, xi, 15, 26, 29, 199, 200
USSR. *See* Soviet Union
Ustashas, 102
Uwilingiyimana, Agathe, 218n9

Vadodara, 78, 88
Valentino, Benjamin, 212n1
Vajpayee, Atal Bihari, 76, 77, 96
Valančius, Motiejus, 171
Valuables Action. *See* Gold Action
Varshney, Ashutosh, 87
Vatwa, 84–85, 86
VHP (Viswa Hindu Parishad), 73, 214n11
Vilijampole. *See* Slobodka
Vilna, 153, 154, 218n1
Vilna Ghetto, 41, 195
Vilnius. *See* Vilna
Virginia, 39
Vojvodina, 100, 101, 216n5
Voldemarists, 180
Vora, Noor Mohammed Rasool Bhai, 90
Vytautas the Great, 157

Wagner, Michelle, 144
Wailaki, 51
Walker, Frederick, 213n7
Waller, James, 196; *Becoming Evil,* 6
warfare, ix, 4, 15, 19, 22, 33, 36, 41, 52, 64, 101, 126, 128, 139, 147, 151, 178, 181, 202, 203, 205n1, 208–9n16, 209–10n21, 216n6
Warsaw Ghetto, 5, 46, 195
Watts, Samuel, 65
Weinreb, Friedrich, 194
White Eagles, 116
Wilmer, Harry A., *Facing Evil,* 6
Wolfe, Patrick, 32
Woodruff, Paul B., *Facing Evil,* 6
Woods, Bill, 42
World War I, 14, 15, 99, 152, 156, 168
World War II, 15, 20–21, 100, 102, 112, 128, 150, 153, 202
Wright, Richard, 210n2
Wright, Robert, 211n9
Yahi, 3, 58, 62, 70. *See also* Yana
Yamasee, 22
Yana, 56–58, 62–63, 70, 71
Yugoslavia, 21, 97–124, 199, 216–17nn1–8. *See also* Bosnia-Herzegovina;

Yugoslavia (*continued*)
  Bosnian genocide; Croatia; Serbia;
  Slovenia; Montenegro
Yuki, 5, 12, 32, 49–71, 212n2. *See also*
  Round Valley genocide; Round Valley
  Reservation

Zaire, 138–39
Zionism, 158, 170
Zusak, Markus, *The Book Thief,* 6,
  221n5

STUDIES IN PURE SOCIOLOGY

Mark Cooney
Is Killing Wrong? A Study in Pure Sociology

Bradley Campbell
The Geometry of Genocide: A Study in Pure Sociology